Waking Up In Cuba

Printed in the United Kingdom by Butler & Tanner Ltd, Somerset

Published by Sanctuary Publishing Limited, Sanctuary House, 45-53 Sinclair Road, London W14 0NS, United Kingdom

www.sanctuarypublishing.com

Copyright: Stephen Foehr, 2001

Photographs: courtesy of the author
Front cover photograph: © Getty Images, London

ISBN: 1-86074-364-3

Waking Up In Cuba

Stephen Foehr

Acknowledgements

Jose Antonio Fernández was indispensable as my friend, assistant, and gifted translator for this book. Jose is a musician, in that the melodies of Spanish went in his ears, he heard the notes in English, and then gave them voice in a simultaneous translation. He is remarkably gifted. Thanks also and appreciation to Ramiro de la Cuesta for his trust in taking me into his religion and into his heart. Nefertit Telleria deserves special recognition for her research into the types of Cuban music and their historical context. Richard Haight read the text before anyone else and corrected my gaffes. Again, Richard, my eternal gratitude.

Thanks also to all of the Cuban musicians who generously gave of their time for interviews. Thank you for sharing your knowledge and for welcoming me with unreserved friendship. And thanks, too, to the Cuban people. It was great. What can I say? Let's do it again soon.

About The Author

 Stephen Foehr has made a career out of being curious. He has spent years traveling around the world asking, Why? Why not? What? Who did what? How come? Is that true? and writing about the answers. He has been a teacher in Ethiopia, a crewmember on a sailboat in the Mediterranean, a construction worker in Sweden, a movie extra in Japan, a copywriter in Hong Kong, a witness in Vietnam, a smuggler in India, a layabout in Malaysia, and a police reporter and journalist in the United States. He is the author of four books and numerous articles for national and international publications.

Foehr grew up in the small farm town of Carthage, Illinois, and while he was supposed to be studying Latin in the high-school library he secretly read the books of Richard Halliburton, whose adventures fired his ambition to explore the world. He attended Regis College (now University) in Denver, Colorado, and got his first taste of foreign travel while a student at Loyola University of Rome. After earning a college degree and serving in the Peace Corp, he became a travel writer to support his curiosity habit. He has lived and worked in 88 counties and now lives in Boulder, Colorado, with his 13-year-old son, Lucian.

Contents

"Musical innovation is full of danger to the State, for, when modes of music change, the laws of the State always change with them."
        Plato (BC 428-347)

1 Lennon In Havana

John Lennon sits on a bench in the park a block from my place in Havana. I'd walk to the park nearly every evening to chat with John, the only other native-English-speaker in my neighborhood, or just to watch the Cubans relate to him. The life-sized bronze statue appears uncannily alive, its right leg casually resting on its left knee. His left arm is draped over the back of deep green, cast-iron bench as an invitation to join him. The look on John's face says, Welcome, friend. Sit down and let's share a laugh.

Entire families come to visit. Mothers place their babies on Lennon's lap, as if he is a talisman to bring luck or a blessing. Children sit next to him, as if snuggling with a favorite uncle. Young women pose for pictures curled against his chest, as if wanting to make out. Men don't pose with Lennon but keep their distance, arms crossed. They remind me of veterans visiting a war memorial, or, in this case, a peace memorial. People stand close, then back away for a long perspective, then approach again, as if in a silent call-and-response dialog. They get within inches of his face to peer through the empty eyeglass frames, as if looking for a magical life force that gives the statue its vitality. Actually, they're checking out the glasses, which have been stolen twice.

A 24-hour custodian and an around-the-clock cop guard John Lennon's glasses, which are firmly welded to the bridge of the statue's nose. The custodian is very solicitous of his charge. He flicks dirt off Lennon's shirt. He sweeps away leaves. If there had been pigeons (I never saw a pigeon in Cuba), I'm sure he would wipe Lennon clean and shoo away the disrespectful birds. If anyone is too attentive, perhaps crowding John a bit too much, the custodian hovers, but he does not prevent touching. When a crowd gathers, which is often, the policeman posts himself officiously at John's side.

I suggested to the custodian that a statue of Groucho Marx should be placed on the other end of John's bench. "That way, Marx and Lennon would be together in a socialist country." That was just too juicy to pass up, even if of questionable taste. The guard looked at me uncomprehendingly, and then the lightbulb popped on. He laughed.

I adopted the statue as my mascot. I'd sit on the bench and say, "Well, John. Guess who I talked with today?" And I'd tell him about that day's interview with the Cuban jazz musician, or the Afro-Cuban rock bandleader, or the fusion-guitar player.

After I'd been in Havana for a while, I told John, "You know, John, all is not as I've been led to believe about this place. There's a lot more going on musically than Buena Vista Social Club. And another thing: propaganda has it that these people live under a repressive communist government run by a dictator. I expected to find fearful, dark shadows, but that's not the case. These people are not cowed. They're not afraid to speak their minds. This is not some backwater burg where people don't look beyond their provincial noses. The other day, I heard an elderly man and a young boy discussing Plato as they walked down the street."

At this point, a shiny new car drove past with New York rap booming from the speakers.

"There are misunderstandings about this place, John. And, frankly, I'm surprised to find you here. You're not sitting in Strawberry Fields in New York's Central Park, or standing fossilized, with guitar in hand, in a Liverpool square. How did you end up in Havana?"

Lennon sits in the park because Cubans have a special affinity with The Beatles. Cuban music was very popular worldwide when the United States' economic blockade against Cuba went in effect in 1962. The music became less accessible as a result of the blockade. Record companies, not wanting to lose a profit-leader, sought a replacement with a similar sound. The bossa nova was being created in Brazil, so the record companies latched onto it, and there was a brief bossa nova boom. Rock 'n' roll was also emerging, with The

Beatles at the head of the parade. European rock 'n' roll in the 1960s had a lot of Latin influence, especially in the drumming, according to Joaquin Gilberto Valdés Zequirez, a 73-year-old Cuban drummer.

"How do I know that?" Gilberto said during one of our talks. "I was living in Paris at the time and was one of the Cuban drummers who taught European rock drummers the Cuban style and patterns. Those patterns can be heard in the drumming. Cubans recognized their own music in The Beatles' music."

During the 1960s and '70s, The Beatles' music, and rock 'n' roll in general, was not encouraged in Cuba. "It was forbidden by narrow-minded people responsible for culture in Cuba," the esteemed musicologist Helio Orovio told me, "but in the 1980s the official attitude toward rock 'n' roll changed, following the impact of our Nueva Trova movement on Cuban music and the society as a whole, and The Beatles did not exist as a group anymore. They were not fashionable in music. But they were recognized as an important reference in the world's music history. Things changed again in the 1990s, when Abel Prieto became the Minister of Culture."

The Minister of Culture is still a big fan of The Beatles and, especially, of John Lennon. He listened to The Beatles while a high-school student, as did many other Cubans. As a university student, he wore long hair and granny glasses similar to Lennon's. He and other members of the Cuban *intelligentsia* – the artists and writers and musicians – believed that homage should be paid to The Beatles as a message to generations of future Cubans. They wanted to acknowledge the mistakes of the past, according to Helio, and to honor Lennon as a great creator.

"Lennon was of great interest to Cuban writers and poets because of his rich life," Helio told me. "John Lennon was chosen because of his songs and the sensational way in which he was killed. The other Beatles are still alive. They can come to Cuba to play concerts and walk the streets. They have not become history the way John Lennon has."

The statue was created by José Villa, the president of the Cuban Sculpture Society, and was dedicated by Fidel Castro. Dago, a young rock 'n' roll electric-guitar player, and one of the more talented producers in Cuba, was at the unveiling ceremony. "When Castro approached the draped sculpture, I cringed," Dago recalled when I asked about that day. "I, and the other young musicians present, feared that a fiasco was in the making." With military music thumping in the background, Castro, in his crisp green army uniform, was about to unveil a monument of a rock 'n' roll musician whose message was love and peace. With the fanfare of horns and drums, Castro reached over and lifted the sheet. He looked at the bronze Lennon, very nonmilitary in his relaxed pose, and said, "He was a good man."

Castro admitted that it had been a mistake to ban The Beatles' music, according to Dago. He had believed that, back then, the Revolution was too vulnerable to outside influences. "We over-reacted," he said in his speech before Lennon. It was time to embrace the music. Castro, however, declined to pose for photos with Lennon.

At the base of the statue is written, in brass script, "People call me dreamer, but I'm not the only one." Perhaps that's why Cuban people are John Lennon fans – they recognize one of their own.

John Lennon and The Beatles were musical revolutionaries. I came to Cuba to discover what was happening musically in the world's longest-sustained revolution (42 years and counting). On a Monday night, I told John, "Tomorrow, I'm going to meet some people you'd probably like. I'll tell you all about it later."

On Tuesday afternoons, rappers meet at Pablo Herrera's place in Santos Suarez, a working-class section of Havana. He lives in a large room on the second floor of a corner house. I always identified the house by looking for a bush of red-and-purple flowers, because the streets in Santos Suarez, as in many older areas of Havana, are not well marked, if at all. To find your way, you sense the lay of the land, which is how many things work in Cuba. Pablo's room has a gray cement floor. The kitchen sink fills one wall. A lavish altar to Chango, the Santeria orisha (spirit or saint) of thunder and lightning and the patron of drummers, takes up a third of another wall from floor to ceiling. It's not an altar in the Catholic sense but rather a shrine, ablaze with cloth of bright colors, flowers, figurines, and a place to make an offering. Whenever I entered the room, I knelt – as does everyone – before this shrine and rang the handbell to announce myself and to get Chango's attention. Then I'd make an offering – a piece of fruit, or a dollar bill, or a flower. Chango is one of the most powerful and fearsome spirits in the Santeria pantheon and must always be treated with respect.

Pablo's room is always full of light, because windows form two of the walls. The door, which is falling out of its frame, is also a pane of glass. The room is sparsely furnished, which gives it the atmosphere of a monk's cell. Two couches of foam pads double as beds. The only chair is before a small table. On the table is Pablo's computer. On another table, within arm's reach, is a small mixing board and a stack of CDs and tapes.

When I arrived, Pablo was perched on the arm of the chair so that he could work the keyboard and mixing board simultaneously. He was fussing over a new backing track. "Hip-hop artists are the avant-garde thinkers in Cuba," he said over his shoulder to where I was sitting on a couch. I was about to argue that the Cuban painters would question the universal certitude of his statement when in walked Alexey and Magia, a couple who are the professional rap group Obsesión. They have been singing together since 1995. I decided not to quibble with Pablo. Besides, Pablo – linguist, poet, and Cuba's only full-time hip-hop producer – was speaking within a musical context, a context in which hip-hop and rap are interchangeable.

"Youth and hip-hop are the spearhead of the Revolution," Pablo claims. "Hip-hop artists are a major challenge to the social and cultural structures, so as to make them better." He gestured to Alexey and Magia as living examples. At 34, Pablo is a handsome man, articulate and thoughtful in the manner of an academic. He has a nervous habit of twisting his nappy hair when he's on an intellectual probe. As we spoke, he twisted his hair into little tufts all over his head. "What they are implementing is the evolution of the 1959 Revolution. It's almost the same ideological agenda as Castro's Revolution, but the next step. The agenda has changed, forms and content have changed, but it's coming from the same source. We need to protect ourselves. We need to fight. We need to resist.

Pablo Herrera, the only full-time rap producer in Cuba, on his balcony in the Santos Suarez neighborhood of Havana

"Now, for the first time, we can hear a voice coming from a different angle that is still part of the whole tradition of the Revolution. This voice of youth and hip-hop is speaking from another perspective. This voice is not trying to stop the Revolution but is talking along with it. A new way of speaking, conveyed through the style of music, is being created. The hip-hop avant garde is not an alternative. It's like looking into a mirror and saying, 'Yeah, I need to fix myself a bit. I'm looking a little scruffy. There are a few things I need to rearrange for myself [to] make it better.'"

Magia interrupted, "In my case, I will not speak of politics, because, if I talk about politics, I will have to study politics. I don't want to make a theme about politics without knowing the whys and hows and what is going on." She wears a silver ring in her left nostril. Her face is pretty and her hair in short dreads. She emanates a sense of grounded, solid purpose and natural, unaffected warmth. I could easily imagine her as a mother, which she is not, even at the age of 28. She is a female pioneer of Cuban hip-hop. She has paved the way for groups like Instinto, a female rap trio that, with Obsesión, is considered to be one of the best rap groups in Cuba.

"I have no limits," Alexey joined in. "If I have to talk about politics, I talk about politics. What I don't know I don't talk about, but there is no area I deliberately stay out of." He is slender and dark, with curly black hair. His smile has the voltage of a marquee announcing a hit show. He doesn't wear gold chains or stylin' clothes or a poseur's attitude; he's polite and sweet. You wouldn't know that he's a rapper until you heard his music.

He and Magia launched into an intense discussion on what boundaries, if any, separate culture and politics. Magia mentioned their song about the man and the woman, where she decides to end the relationship and he tries to forbid her, but she stands her ground. That's not about politics, Magia said in support of her position. It's bold for the woman to do that, to claim her independence in this society that is so male dominated. It's a song about the roles in the society.

But only since women were given more individual economic power – which is since the Revolution – have they been able to declare their independence, Alexey rejoined. That makes it a political song.

No, it's a cultural song because, in a larger sense, it's about the rap world in Cuba, Magia countered. There aren't many other women rappers. There are a lot of men rappers but few women rappers. I want people to know that there are a number of women rappers equal to men rappers. We, the women, have many important things to say.

Is our song about the negro, with his macho strut, his *guapo*, his chest-out attitude, his showy way of dressing – is that cultural or political?, Alexey asked. The song speaks against the stereotypical image, the old image, which the negro conjured up to give him an identity. But that's not an authentic image. I think it's a very political song about a cultural image. Jimi Hendrix had the right *guapo*, that which comes from an internal sense of worth. Jimi Hendrix was a cultural man acting politically.

This discussion, which is part of a larger chorus, accompanied the

Cuban dance of which comes first, culture or politics?, a dance that has a prominent place on the country's cultural program. The government and artists have had to learn the complexities of the dance as they go. The Castro government, and its school of dance, spent years trying to figure out the rock 'n' roll moves. Commercial music for the tourist economy and cultural music for the soul of the nation are on the dancefloor trying to decide who should lead. Religious music and secular music are waltzing together, after stepping on each other's toes before finding a complementary glide.

Alexey and Magia agreed that anything of interest to them was a legitimate subject for a song and music. "If we can give encouragement to improve things, we do it. There are no barriers. We never say that we can't go there," Alexey says.

"That means coming from a perspective of openly addressing things that deserve criticism and trying to find ways to get solutions to the problems," said Pablo, swiveling off the arm of the chair and into the conversation. "What's important about hip-hop, and what is delicate at the same time, is to use hip-hop as a vehicle to create an awareness and consciousness about how we are. Here I'm talking about black youth as a social group, to create a space where we as black youth can participate constructively and positively in the development of our society and our nation, 'positively' and 'constructively' meaning that, if the Revolution is in place and has given us proof that it's valid and worthwhile, then we should devote ourselves to making it better, to making it greater. Not to make it die, but to make it flourish. Not that the mainstream discourse doesn't have that talk; it's just that mainstream is the officials, the State.

"What happens in Cuba is that the State is very protective of its people. It's almost patronizing, almost condescending. I'm not saying it's offensively condescending; it's just that the officials are so worried about what could happen to us, the people. They don't leave space for us to act as individuals and to create together with them. It's more like things are done *for* the people rather than the people doing, although the people are definitely working; that's part of the machinery of the Revolution. But a lot of decisions are taken for us, and then we say, 'Yes, we're going to do this because we're in agreement.'

"Once again, the voice of the people is saying, 'Yes, we can do this, we want to be part of this, and there are things we haven't touched on.' The State is striving to cover everything, and that's impossible. There are too many things, too many people, lots of different subcultures and spheres of interest in Cuba. The State needs the assistance of the people in their own realms. Right now, that voice is coming mostly from the youth through hip-hop, and the strongest voice is from the black youth. It's important to understand that black youth and people of color in Cuba are still suffering [from] prejudices."

Cuban socialism has been forced to adopt new methods and systems in order to survive, especially since the collapse of the Soviet Union, which, until 1992, was the one and only economic benefactor of Cuba. A chief component of the developing mixed economy is tourism. The government is directing resources into building new resorts, developing a service industry, and training the personnel. This has economic and social consequences that, in the opinion of some Cubans, compromise the ideals of the Revolution. Money and building materials that could go into fixing up homes and neighborhoods, like the poorer ones in which Pablo lives, is diverted into the construction of resort hotels for rich white folk. Cubans who work in the tourist industry, and who tend to be "white," have access to dollars, a big economic advantage in Cuba. Cubans without access to the dollar economy can't shop in "dollar stores," which sell imported food and goods. You can't buy a television without dollars, or a stereo, or a CD player, or almost any consumer goods imported into Cuba. A schism is developing in the Cuban society between the dollar haves and the peso have-nots.

"We, the hip-hop people – that is, mainly black youth – are more targeted by the systems of control," Pablo said. "It's very difficult for a black person to get a job in the tourist economy, which means we can't get dollars, which means we are at a disadvantage. We're coming and saying, 'Hey, this is not completely right. We want to work as part of the whole system. That's cool. But if the system has certain parts that are malfunctioning, as to who we are and how we are taken within the society, then we need to come forth and say, 'This cannot happen.'"

I mulled over the supposition that hip-hop musicians are the spearhead of the Revolution. That depends on the hip-hop. There is slick, syncopated Cuban hip-hop, whose only ideological thrust is to make 13-year-old girls squeal, and then there is Cuban rap, which is virtually indistinguishable from the United States' gangsta rap in its rhythms, gestures, and posturing. It's a bit absurd to hear Cuban rappers going on about bank robberies (which never happen in Cuba) and crack houses (which don't exist in Cuba), and yet it's understandable. Cuban hip-hop is a derivate of the North American rap style. 'Rapper's Delight' was perhaps the first hip-hop record to reach Cuba, when Pablo's aunt sent him a copy from Spain in 1979. And Pablo, who produces backing tracks for Cuban hip-hop groups, borrows from the United States rappers because they are his primary source.

"Hip-hop has always been an imported culture," Pablo explained. "It always will be looked at that way. But at this point, it's definitely embedded in the Cuban culture, in the sense that there are a lot of kids out there who have the mentality of the '90s, which are the values of the youth in the world. The pieces and fragments of cultures that have been sold to the world as commodities have affected this world youth culture. Hip-hop is one of these phenomena.

"We in Cuba are affected, since we have been going through the process of our people trying to insert themselves within the world structure and the world economy. That has affected us socially, this new implementation of economics and culture and social process. This has affected how the youth sees itself and how the youth wants to express itself and claim its independence."

Cubans had an ear for rap before there was rap. Spontaneous rhyming is in the Spanish tradition of *decima*, a ten-line rhyming scheme that is one of the foundations of Cuban country music dating back nearly 300 years. The Cuban poet Luis Carbonel recited his poems with a rhythm reminiscent of the staccato of rap, while the Cuban singer Harry Lewis used the spoken style in his songs. The improvisation in rap is a hallmark of Cuban music, especially *son*, a fundamental root source of Cuban music. The flow of hip-hop delivery has antecedents in the rhythm patterns of rumba, a *sui generis* Cuban music. These were not precursors to rap, but the musical concept was already ringing in Cubans' heads when hip-hop/rap – born from the Jamaican sound system on the streets of Brooklyn – shoved itself into the music market.

Pablo is experimenting to give the Cuban hip-hop sound less North American guttural aggression and more melodic fusion, a distinctive mark of Cuban music. The Cuban flavor heard in the music of the rap groups Obsesión and Instinto gives them a uniqueness when compared with rap's stereotypical sound. North American rap has been called urban blues with a chisel's hard steel edge. In their version of the song 'Siguaraya,' Obsesión gave rapper's blues the harmonic irony heard in Billy Holiday's 'Strange Fruit.' Both songs, in both their message and delivery, are the velvet gloves that hold the chisel.

A siguaraya is a sacred tree in the African-based Santeria religion. Permission must be asked from the orishas (the spirits) to cut down the tree. The song 'Siguaraya,' made popular by Benny Moré in the 1950s and then by Celia Cruz, is a lament to a lost culture and at the same time a defiant declaration of the values of that culture. In Obsesión's version, Magia slyly hides the underlying anger in a lilting, seductive voice, which, as in Holiday's 'Strange Fruit,' makes the song an even stronger lethal injection. The song appears on Obsesión's first album, *Un Montón De Cosas*, produced by jazz pianist Roberto Fonseca.

Obsesión's rap has a melodic, even gentle nature, as opposed to the driving aggression of North American rap. "There are people who live in a rough way and people who live in a peaceful way," explained Magia. "If you live in a peaceful way, that is what you reflect. In the United States, you live a busy active life, but in Cuba, that is not so. In the beginning, Cuban hip-hop groups were aggressive because they imitated the American groups they saw in the videos. But that aggression is disappearing as we find our own voice. We realized that we don't live in [such a] busy, active, aggressive society. We live very differently from the people in the United States or any other part of the world. There are aggressive-sounding rap groups in Cuba, but that's because we are working with American

Magia Lopez and Alexey Rodriguez, the rap duo Obsesión, are pioneers in creating Cuban rap with its own distinct sound

background tracks. If you have aggressive background music, the lyrics have to be aggressive. We have to use those American tracks because we don't have any of our own."

The most successful Cuban rap group, Orishas, uses the vocal style of North American rap and yet maintains a distinct Cuban instrumental sound. Now based in Paris, the group has had songs on the hit-lists of 18 countries. Pablo finds a warning in Orishas' experience of leaving the country to make music of the country: "The motherland's culture can be produced in places other than the motherland, but I don't think it will be as authentic and legitimate to what we Cubans are trying to say. You have to be on the street every day, hear what people are saying, complaining about, joking about, to really produce authentic music from the place. Orishas use Cuban rhythms and older Cuban musical traditions in their rap, so you can say that it's Cuban, but it's being led and implemented because of what the CEOs of record companies want to sell, rather than coming from the spirit of the place and of the music."

Pablo is moving toward creating tracks with live instruments, from the bata drums to full percussion sets to guitars and bass. On his current project, he dubs bass lines and percussions over machine sounds, which gives a richer complexity and more freedom to shift into melodies and rhythms.

"In Cuba, there are several DJs who work with techno equipment, turntables, and mixers," Pablo told me as he doodled at his mix, "but Cuba has never been about electronics. Cuba has always been about the live instrument, the musician, the band. It's been more about being an instrumentalist than going out and buying a piece of equipment and making music out of a machine. Basically, because of the economic blockade on Cuba for the past 42 years, we can't buy such equipment, anyway. This has been, in a good sense, a miracle. We've been able to keep our traditional means of expressing ourselves. But it's also been a miracle because we have a lot of different issues and problems that have created uniquely Cuban dynamics."

Cuban rappers don't want to be co-opted, even if that means forgoing commercial success, according to Pablo. "We see ourselves as resisters, as survivors, and we don't want to be weakened by compromising for money. That would weaken our view of ourselves as people in the resistance, as a people still struggling for our ideals. It's ugly to see yourself co-opted. We don't want to see ourselves playing ourselves, like a black man in blackface. Hip-hop doesn't want to see itself playing itself.

"Ultimately, hip-hop is trying to keep in our hands the value of being winners – not just resisters and survivors but winners, meaning that we are warriors who won the war against the biggest empire, the United States. Ultimately, that's what we, as rappers, are trying to do. It's real subtle and mellow how we say that. We're doing our thing. But the fact that the Revolution is in place after 42 years is a way of saying that we're winning. We're doing our thing. Hip-hop should be the voice that keeps it as simple as saying, 'No matter what happens, we're still going to do our thing.' It's beyond being a warrior; it's just you. As people, we want to implement ourselves, no matter what somebody says that we should do or how we should do it. Hip-hop should be that voice, the voice that could keep our society from co-opting itself, from deviating from our original path that we've been walking on."

Being co-opted means being lured from the purity of socialistic goals for the betterment of the whole community, according to Pablo and many other Cuban musicians. The group Orishas has been co-opted because "what they do is not how we from the island would talk about ourselves. Cuban groups that look and sound like Ricky Martin – that is co-optation. They are a distraction from the real needs and values of the society. The commercial hip-hop, the kind that appeals to 13-year-old girls, stalls the society from getting where it needs to go. You are submerged in a bubble of nothingness with the consciousness of that music. That type of commercial hip-hop, the empty-bubble kind, is creating and perpetuating patterns of slavery and patterns of colonization and patterns of exploitation of yourself. That's what capitalism does – it co-opts cultures. Once the corporate state of mind takes over and makes money on something a community produces, that becomes a problem for the community. Capitalism is exploitative in its very nature.

"Hip-hop wants socialism, at least in Cuba. Ultimately, what hip-hoppers across the world want is not capitalism or socialism; they just want the best for their people. Hip-hoppers are defenders of their peoples. They are protesting against the bad things in society. The best hip-hoppers come from the people with the heart of the people. What hip-hop really wants to see implemented are societies that work in the best way for their people as communities, for people living the best lives possible, not exploiting each other, not killing each other, not doing crack, not pimping ourselves. This is where hip-hop artists are avant-garde thinkers.

"Hip-hop is·the force that can definitely bring awareness and consciousness to the whole society. It is the vehicle to express what are the mistakes and how to work with those mistakes, how to address those mistakes and make them better. The hip-hop generation could be the second wave of the Revolution that was started rolling by the Nueva Trova movement in the early 1970s. I would love to have that role. I wish I could define myself as part of the Revolution in the same way that Fidel and his generation defined themselves.

"We do have a mission. We do have a role. Our mission right now is to maintain the strong hold that has been created by the ideals of the Revolution. It's an exciting thing to do. This is an important historical moment. Fidel's generation is leaving us with a legacy that needs to be kept and maintained."

That night, in the park, I reported all of this to John. It was probably a trick of the shadows, but I thought I saw him nod, although he didn't offer a definitive opinion. I told him that I'd find out more and report back.

2 Revolution Rap

Is Pablo's vision just a rapper's ideological delusion of grandeur? The hippies in the '60s had the same fervor to save society, and they created music to carry the message, but has anything basically changed, except the tunes? Poets eat redemptifying visions like cotton-candy, and cynics claim that this is really all that the visions are, insubstantial wisps that evaporate when the heat of reality is applied.

Alden Knight, an actor by profession, has been an astute observer/commentator on the Cuban music and social scenes for 30 years. One day, when he came to the house for coffee, I asked him, "How real are the hip-hop artists' aspirations of a better Revolution?"

"They are right," he answered in his resonant baritone. His voice is like a vibrator – it simultaneously soothes and stimulates. "The artists should criticize everything that is bad in every society. But not only rap does that; the new Cuban songs are a way to criticize everything known to be bad in the Revolution. It's a way of using music against what is known inside and outside the Revolution. It is to struggle, to become a dissident. But the best rap in the world is the Cuban Revolution. It's a constant rap, an energetic rap through which people express their protest. Cuba is a protest. Cuba is a social project that protests against all that has existed before. Who is going to protest against that? Protesting against what has been made in Cuba would be silly, because it would be a protest against the protest."

"What? Are you saying, Alden, that to protest against the Revolution would be...what? Redundant? Disloyal? Silly – isn't that what you said? Like a rap singer protesting against rap?"

"What happens is that some young musicians feel that, if they are dissidents and if they protest, they will be recognized more than others. I think that to join a stream of fair protest is better than to invent an unfair and unjust protest. I think that, conceptually, it is a mistake. I personally don't think that rap will be a music that will last a long time. I think it is the moment, an angry moment for the society in which it started. I think that rap appears as a need of the black and the poor man in the United States."

I thanked Alden and told him that I needed some time to appreciate his insights.

Pablo had invited me to a rap concert that night at the stadium in Alamar, a "scruffy" (Pablo's word) housing estate 15 kilometers east of Havana. Edesio Alejandro, the acknowledged father of Cuban rap, lives in Alamar. I decided to visit him before the concert, only I didn't know exactly where he lived. I figured that I'd just go out there and ask. Cubans keep close tabs on their artists, so someone should be able to direct me to his house.

I stood on the curb of Linea, a major avenue in Havana, wondering how to get to Alamar, which is on the other side of Havana Bay. A Czech Lada, a real junker, slid to a halt and the passenger, a thin young man with plastered-down hair, asked, "Where you go?" The car wasn't a taxi, but people in Havana pick up people looking for a ride in order a make a few dollars on the side.

"Alamar."

He spoke rapid-fire to the driver, a twitchy, angular peroxide blonde who looked anorexic. She hunched over the steering wheel and didn't reply. He used his hands to draw a map in the air, all right angles and curves. She leaned back in the seat, her arms straight on the wheel, as if to brace herself. He reached back and opened the rear door. As I settled on the seat, he turned with a big smile. "My sister. Isn't she pretty?" He caressed her cheek, lingering on her chin. She gave me a big smile, as if in invitation, but I couldn't figure out to what. She abruptly turned back to the steering wheel, put the car in gear, revved the engine, and cautiously edged into the traffic.

"You want to buy CDs cheap?" the brother asked. "Only four dollars. I burn them myself."

A CD cost $15US in the record shops, out of reach for most Cubans. That's given rise to a flourishing black market in CDs. I declined.

"My sister is pretty, yes?"

Not sure what kind of ride I was being offered, I indifferently agreed. "You *do* know how to get to Alamar?"

"Yes," the brother assured me.

We took the Malecón, the broad boulevard that serves as Havana's shoreline to the Atlantic Ocean. In high winds, waves dramatically spray over the Malecón's seawall, hosing down the traffic. In the summer months, the Malecón serves as Havana's front porch as thousands of people seek to escape the scorching heat of the inner city. You want to talk to someone, be talked to, find a deal of sin or pleasure? Take a stroll down the Malecón at any time of the day or night.

The sister drove erratically, too fast, too slow, starting to pass and then hesitating so that the car straddled lanes. Her brother gave running instructions, which made her more nervous. It was a driving lesson, I realized. He was teaching her how to drive.

A tunnel submerges under the narrow neck of Havana Bay that separates the city from the eastern suburbs, where Alamar is located. That day, the tunnel was closed to general traffic while leaks in the ceiling were being repaired. The sister looked at the brother. "Just follow the water around the bay," he said. But the streets didn't follow the water; they twisted around the dock area and veered inland. The sister stopped frequently so that the brother could ask directions. Sometimes he asked directions from other drivers while both cars were on the move. This required a good deal of shouting and hand gesturing, which he then translated into instructions for his confused sister. We missed a turn. She stopped in the middle of the road and attempted a U-turn, but the street was too narrow for the maneuver, so she jockeyed the car around, blocking both lanes of traffic, which made her even more nervous, so she stalled the engine, which caused the brother to smack his forehead with his palm, which made her even more nervous. Horns blared. People gathered to watch, hoping for a crash or a lively discussion.

We eventually got around the bay to Regla, its air thick with the sweet stench from the oil refineries. Regla, along with Matanzas (another port city), is the birthplace of rumba, Cuba's only indigenous music and dance. Regla is also home to the secret, all-male Abakuá society, whose chants have found their way into Cuban music and Latin jazz. Chano Pozo (born José Luciano Pozo) was an Abakuá member and, during the 1940s, played in Dizzy Gillespie's band in New York. Pozo taught Gillespie some Abakuá phrases, which Gillespie then sang on recordings. The partnership between Pozo and Gillespie is said to have given birth to Latin jazz.

Pozo, one of Cuba's cultural heroes, came to a sad end. He moved to New York and became a star...and a drug addict. He was a swaggering, self-assured, macho Latino who liked to boast of that latter image. One day, while sitting in a bar with a ladyfriend, his dealer approached and demanded payment for drugs. Pozo loudly proclaimed that he would not pay. He didn't have to pay. He was a star. The dealer said, "Fine," and left, only to return with a gun. He walked up to Pozo and, without a word, shot him dead. This was in 1948.

By this time we were at least on the same side of the bay as Alamar, further down the coast. The car was low on gasoline. The brother, out of his familiar territory, peered anxiously around for a gas station. Kilometer after kilometer, he kept one eye on the dropping gas gauge and the other out for road signs to Alamar. He feared his sister would miss yet another turn and waste more precious gas. "Do you know a gas station in Alamar?" he asked.

"Never been there before," I replied.

"Perhaps your friend can direct us to a gas station."

"I don't know where he lives."

That was when they lost heart. When the apartment slabs of Alamar came into sight, the brother announced, "We're here." The sister stopped the car. Maybe, just maybe, they could make it back to Havana, if they promptly turned around.

The flourishes of the baroque and rococo Spanish-colonial architecture give Havana the fussy fullness of an unpruned bush. The high-rise apartment blocks of Alamar, in contrast, resemble two-by-four planks. This is Soviet architecture at its most uninspired. Cubans built the buildings and the workers then owned their apartments. That scheme ended when the building supplies ran out. Chilean refugees who fled to Cuba to escape the Pinochet dictatorship were resettled in Alamar. Some Chileans still live there. Russian advisers and technicians also lived in Alamar during their heydays in Cuba, until the pull-out of Soviet Union aid in 1992. They lived in the single-story, cement-block houses with prefab, humped, cement roofs that I saw scattered among the apartment blocks.

An elderly man rode down the road on a bicycle. "Do you know where Edesio Alejandro lives?" I called out.

"Yes, yes," replied the man. "Follow me." Three blocks later, he pointed to one of the cement Quonset houses and waved goodbye.

It was a modest house for the man who has written 44 soundtracks for Cuban films; has won numerous awards; is one of Cuba's most prolific composers, creating music for symphony orchestras, television soap operas, and theater; and has composed and performed pop music. His CD *Black Angel* sold 600,000 copies in Europe. His arrangement of 'Blen-Blen,' a Chano Pozo song written in the 1940s, was a hit in Cuba. Edesio's singing voice and style would be reminiscent of Lou Reed, if Lou Reed were Cuban.

I knocked on the door. A tall woman with long, flowing black hair and stunning natural beauty answered. I recognized her from the 'Blen-Blen' video. "Is Edesio here?"

"Yes," she smiled. "Come in. I'm his wife, Idolka."

She led me to a small spare bedroom that had been converted into a studio. Edesio sat there before a computer and a mixing board. He has a long, blond ponytail, very white skin, blue eyes, a sharp Spanish nose, and a portly belly. "I was the first person to introduce rap in Cuban music, so I suppose that I can be considered the father of Cuban rap," he confirmed. "I began to rap with my son and thought it an interesting way to express feelings, but I don't like to rap only. I try to make something different in my music. I don't make salsa, or timba, or son, or rock, or rumba. I mingle everything together and then it goes out. I was the first to use rap this way in Cuba. Now rap bores me. I think it's my age." Edesio is 42.

Edesio Alejandro, credited as being the father of Cuban rap, with his wife, Idolka

"About rap, I'm going to give you my opinion as a musician, not as a critic. This is only my opinion. I made a little sociological study of what are the contact points between rap and Cuban music. Rap is black, it's from the streets, and the promises of the streets are told in it. The only original Cuban music, the rumba, is black, it's from the streets, and the promises of the streets are told in it. The difference is that in rap the story is spoken and in Cuban music the story is sung, so I mixed the rumba with the rap. That opened me to a wider context.

"Rap is a very strong culture. Many people thought that it would pass in a few years. I always thought it would last, because it was born as a manifestation of the people. Most Cuban rap is still in a period of imitation. Many Cuban rappers think they live in the Bronx, and in their songs they talk of American issues that we don't have here. Cuban rap doesn't have a gut aggression found in American rap. Cuban rappers sing the words but don't have the heat in the music. The reason is that rap is American in origin. In lyrics, you have to assume your problems and talk about your problems, not about the problems of another place.

"I think that Cuban rap is now on the verge [of] consciously [putting] Cuban cultural elements into the music. In the beginning, Cuban rappers were trying to imitate American gangsters, but it doesn't work, because they are not gangsters. You can see that from the way they move. They move Cuban. But the more they explore the music, the more they are making it Cuban. The Cuban is always smiling and laughing. He buries his brother. He cries in the moment. After that, he drinks a bottle of rum and is still laughing. Cubans are happy, no matter what is happening, socially or politically. I think this attitude is what will make Cuban rap different from other rap."

At that point, Idolka brought in two cups of coffee and quickly left. Edesio never took his eyes off her. "I have been a musician for 30 years and I have not made much of a living off this." He spoke as if picking up a thread left hanging from an unfinished discussion. "It has been difficult for a person like me, because I make a different music. All that I'm doing is Cuban. My music is the seal of my culture.

"I think that, when one finds – in a personal way – a vehicle to express the culture's environment, then you can become international and different at the same time. Music is very mixed in, all over the world. It uses this and that. Me, too, but I give it the context of my own culture. This can make it universal. No matter that you make commercial music, no matter that it be light or less light; if you make it different, if you make it consciously of your own culture, people will like it. Every artist continues this searching."

He finished his coffee with a quick toss of his head. "You know the moment I really started searching? In the Special Period, the worst moment in my life." The Special Period began in 1992 when the Soviet Union, which had been giving Cuba billions in subsidies, stopped the support literally overnight. As a consequence, the Cuban people underwent severe economic difficulties. Eight or nine years later, the country's economy is now showing signs of recovery. "I was eating the peelings of the bananas in order that my wife and little son could eat the banana. With the fish, I made a soup with the head so my family could eat the flesh. In order to drink that soup, I had to add sugar and anise so as not to vomit it up. In that moment, I found myself.

"I was always saying, 'I'm going to do this, to do that. I'm going to make Cuban music that is different.' At that time, all my instruments were broken. During a concert, it rained and they got quite wet. I was without instruments. With the chaotic situation in the country, I didn't have money even to eat. It was the same for everyone.

"I called a friend in Canada and told him to send me an invitation letter. I needed to go to Canada and knock on doors. I asked another friend for the money to buy the ticket. I went to Canada and began knocking on doors. At the same time, I began to wash dishes in order to earn my living. I bought two instruments and a little computer. I can make concert music, rock, pop, symphonic, hip-hop, dance. I had stopped writing symphonic and classical music to make money by doing pop. Producers listened to my music and said, 'Yes, that's good. I like the music. But it must be more personal, more Cuban, more individual.'

"That sent me into the direction of [putting] my culture in my music. But after all the sacrifices, of going in debt for the plane ticket, of washing dishes to make money, in the end I didn't sign a contract in Canada. I returned to Cuba and vowed that I wouldn't make popular music. I said, 'I will do what I know to do.' The symphonic music, concert music, music for films – that's what I will do. When I was studying music, I didn't explore jazz because I knew, once started, it would take me away from classical music.

"Then I became depressed. For a week I laid in bed without writing, without reading, without watching television. I was talking with myself. One of my neighbors, Adriano Rodriguez, was always singing, and I could hear him through the wall. Usually, he'd sing concert music, but one day he sang rumba. I listened to him and began to put together in my head hip-hop rhythms with the rumba. Incredible. This opened the way to do what I'm doing now."

Edesio later made a record with Adriano called *Corazón De Son* ("*Heart Of Cuba*"). At the time, Adriano was 73 and had never made a record. After that, Edesio made a CD with Adriano and two other old-time Cuban musicians and singers, Natalia Herrera and Alfonsin Quintana. This was before the old-time musicians were recorded on *Buena Vista Social Club*.

Edesio Alejandro working in his studio

It had grown dark outside, and I suddenly remembered the hip-hop concert. I asked Edesio if he wanted to come. "No," he said with a smile and waved at his computer. "I have to finish this soundtrack." I asked directions to the stadium, which proved to be a 20-minute walk from Edesio's house.

I went to the stadium with expectations of seeing a couple of thousand Cuban punk hip-hoppers all tricked out in rapper Revolutionary fatigues. I had seen men in Havana with purple hair in six-inch spikes tipped with red, so I expected some 'dos with Latin flair, maybe swirls or three-story pompadours. Tattoos, yes – I had seen young men and women with tattoos – so maybe Cuban skin art. What would that look like? Parrots riding in a 1950s Buick? And I expected Cuban rapper attitude, whatever that might be. I hadn't seen any real attitude on Havana's streets, except friendly curiosity and some soft hustles. I had seen nose rings and ear studs and pierced lips, so perhaps at the concert I might see a tongue stud in the shape of Che Guevara's famous profile.

Expectations are skilled boxers – they lead you with a right-hand promise and then knock your props out with a left jab. I've been bruised by that sucker-punch time and time again. I heard that left hand whistling toward me as I approached the "stadium."

The stadium was an outdoor movie theater. Cement slabs for seats stretched down the slope of the amphitheater to a stage backed with a cement screen decorated with graffiti. The stage was bare except for two modest speaker towers. There were no banks of stage lights, no smoke machines, no strobes, no accoutrements of a Stateside concert.

I spotted Pablo Herrera tuning up the soundboard. He was bundled in a jacket against the surprisingly cold wind blowing off the ocean a couple of blocks away. I was shivering in my short sleeves. "Glad to see you here, or I'd think I'd made a mistake," I said. "Wrong night or wrong event." The first act was supposed to have been on stage 30 minutes ago.

"Have you talked to Ariel Diaz?" he countered.

"Who?"

"He's a journalist who writes on the hip-hop scene. He has the only hip-hop radio show on the island, *The Rap Corner*. He can tell you a lot about the hip-hop scene here. Him. There." Pablo pointed to a slender man dressed from head to foot in white. "I told him about you."

I went over, introduced myself, and automatically reached out to shake his hand. He kept his hand out of reach and offered to bump forearms instead. "I'm being initiated into Santeria, and there are rather strict rules about purity to follow for the first year," he explained, "such as wearing only white, not contaminating the hands, about having sex, about drinking out of a pure cup."

About 200 people had drifted into the theater, hardly the crowd size I'd expected. For the most part, they were dressed like anyone from south-central LA or Detroit or the Bronx. Some wore clean, crisp bandannas as headwraps, but the dominant headgear was American baseball caps worn bill backwards. There were a few *faux* black leather jackets, but the preference was jerseys from United States baseball or basketball teams. The Mets, the Yankees, and the Bulls were the most popular. No teams from Florida, such as the

Marlins or the Dolphins, were represented. Their absence was a political statement.

"I thought Cuban rappers might have devised their own dress style," I said to Ariel.

"We are still in the first stage of evolution," he replied. "When hip-hop was still new here and people wanted to know how to do it, how to dress, how it is, the only choice was to learn the American style from the videos from TV. Now I can say that hip-hop has completely changed. In the beginning, people wanted to dress in Nike. Now they like to dress in Che T-shirts. They try to find an identity so, when you see them, you know that is Cuba. They're talking something different from the United States. They sound different than the US hip-hop. Cuban groups are finding their identity. Now they want to be Cubans. They want to sound like Cubans. They want their songs to be Cuban. They want to be different than the United States, you know?"

Ariel has been active in Cuban hip-hop as a promoter, DJ, and amanuensis of the music for twelve years. As a boy, growing up in the ghetto, he wanted to be a hip-hop singer. He couldn't sing very well, so he became a breakdancer. Then, back in the early 1980s, Cuban youths heard their hip-hop from American AM and FM stations being beamed in from Miami, New Orleans, even Boston and New York. "We put antennas up on top of the houses to get the radio shows and record them and make a party with the tapes," Ariel said. Television shows like *Soul Train* were illegally taped and avidly studied for rap fashions and dance moves. When sportsmen, artists, and musicians had a chance to travel outside Cuba, they came back with tapes and cassettes.

"It was like a family," Ariel said. "Anyone who had the material would make copies to give it to everyone else. That was one reason why the people who worked in the culture in Cuba, the officials, didn't like the rap. Because, you know, we had so many disappointments with the United States, especially political. Sometimes you try to separate the politics from the culture, but sometimes you cannot separate them. In Cuba, for so many reasons, the culture is together with the politics. I think it's not a bad thing. I think that the Cuban government and the Cuban people have to protest all the things from the United States. So many things the United States wants to do it can do through the power of its culture, and music has the power to influence a culture. In the beginning of the Revolution, our government was afraid what would happen with influence from the United States, so the government's first move was to close the door."

Hip-hop is seen as a second wave of the Nueva Trova movement, which had a profound social and cultural impact in Cuba during the 1970s, Ariel said. "The musicians like Silvio Rodriguez, Pablo Milanés, Pablo Menéndez, the founders of Nueva Trova, they showed the direction for how to make revolution with the music. Revolution of the sounds. Revolution in the lyrics. Revolution in the way to dress. In the beginning, Nueva Trova was very controversial. Those musicians explored how, as a revolutionary, you talk about the things that are bad within the Revolution. You can be a revolutionary in so many ways. If you are talking about what is bad, about how this bad can be made better, that's good. That's what hip-hop is doing now. We're talking about so many things that are wrong, so many things that are happening that are not right. But we're not saying to fuck the Revolution; we're talking about these things that are happening and how we influence the change to the better. Hip-hop is talking about all the contradictions in this society. The musicians are talking about how to change and when to change."

Specific issues raised by the hip-hoppers concern the negative consequences for the local people in the government's support of the tourist economy, such as prostitution, increased use of marijuana by Cuban youth, and schisms within the society caused by the dollar economy. The hip-hoppers bluntly address racism within the Cuban society, police harassment of youth (especially black youth), and why women do not have equality, despite the official policies. The rappers address basic democratic issues, such as why some Cubans are allowed to travel abroad, a permission denied to others, and why Cubans are banned from hotels reserved for tourists.

"Maybe, when you hear songs from Cuban hip-hop about these

issues, you can say this is against the Revolution," Ariel said, "but it's not. You have to interpret the song, the lyrics, the form. If you study the lyrics, you understand that hip-hop is part of a revolution to make the society better, to make better your life. I think that there is nobody else talking about this phase of the Revolution, so hip-hop is the voice of the ghetto, of the committee of the young people, you know?

"Every country needs that kind of voice to know what exactly is happening in the society. If you are living outside of Cuba, the only things you know about Cuba are that it is a beautiful country, beautiful weather, beautiful women, the music, but the music you hear about is the traditional, like Compay Segundo, or Los Van Van, or Chucho Valdés. This is important music, but it doesn't show the real Cuba, you know? When you hear Compay Segundo, you hear about Chan-Chan. In Los Van Van, you hear about the religion. When you hear Chucho Valdés, you hear about all kinds of songs of the Cuban music. But when you hear hip-hop, you know exactly what is happening in Cuba."

By this time, the duo Anonimo Consejo had taken to the stage. The audience – perhaps 300 strong, now – gathered at the front, near the speakers. Anonimo Consejo is a favorite with the noncommercial hip-hop crowd. The duo wore baggy jeans with the right cuffs rolled halfway to the knee. A statement, I supposed, akin to members of United States gangs who wear bandannas tied around one bicep. The duo described all of the gang gestures: fingers in cryptic and undecipherable positions; arms sweeping indolently in a dismissive downstroke; fists aggressively jabbing at the audience as if to incite them, the way cheerleaders thrust pompoms into the air to stir a football crowd. The audience obediently pumped their fists into the night air and shouted the choruses to the songs. This is the avant garde? These 20-somethings are the spear-carriers of the Revolution?

"I think hip-hop is having a real effect, but I think it's real slow," Ariel said. "The music talks about real things that have to be done so we can have a better life, and I don't mean just a better economic life. The rappers know how things are. If you hear a salsa band, the music says, 'I feel OK. I feel all right. Move your ass with a girl. Feel happy.' Right now, the young, and many others, prefer hip-hop over salsa music. Typically, salsa music doesn't say anything. The salsa artists bring to the society an image, a kind of life of rich people that many Cubans don't feel OK with. The salsa artists are traveling all the time, are on TV all the time, are talking about love, Cuba, religion, women, but they are not talking about how to be better, or about what happens in the street, or the problems. But when you know some critical areas in the society are not all right, not OK, you need to pay attention. That's what hip-hop does. Hip-hoppers know that they have to do something. In this way begins so many things. The change can come late or soon."

"Ariel, I have a problem believing that this—" I gestured toward the stage, "—has, or will have, any real force on the Revolutionary Cuban society. More people go to eat ice cream at Coppelia in one night than are here. This music is not available in the stores. It's never played on the radio, except for 45 minutes a week on your program."

"Hip-hop comes from the grass roots," Ariel responded. "It's still underground, because the revolution of hip-hop is still coming. In ten years, hip-hop will move as fast as other types of music that came before. More fast than rock 'n' roll. More fast than jazz. Every kind of music that came from the United States felt the frustration of emerging. The jazz music was so many years in the underground before the Cuban government accepted it. Rock 'n' roll was years underground before the government accepted it. I can say that hip-hop has moved, in ten years, faster than these musics. People have to understand that. Me, the rappers, everybody who lives inside Cuba knows that hip-hop has moved fast, but it will have to wait even more.

"Right now is the time of explosion of hip-hop inside Cuba. Now rappers are ready, and before they were not. Now people are ready, because they have their own identity, have their songs, have the support of the government, have the interest of the worldwide hip-hop community. Hip-hop music is the new kind of music that has the power of the young. The young are the power and the future of the society, you know?"

Rapper Josmel Savvias Klandesting of the duo Anóimo
Consejo, a popular underground rap group

In June 1999, Pablo Herrera and hip-hop artists met with the
Minister of Culture. According to Herrera, the Minister said that it
was time for the State to understand that Cuban hip-hop has to be
part of Cuban culture and embraced.

"It's good that the State knows that we are talking about things
in our country that only we can change," Ariel said. "The Ministry
of Culture needs to hear a voice about what is happening, you know?
A voice to hear how they can change bad things in Cuba and make

them better. That's hip-hop. You cannot go against this voice. You have to hear what this says and put that into your system, your culture, into everything, you know? I think it's positive for them. It's positive for us. Things begin to change. Now the government knows what is happening with hip-hop. It knows the force, the voice. It knows it has to support the movement of this music."

When Cuba's most famous hip-hop group, Orishas, came from France in December 1999 to perform in Havana, Castro threw a big party for them. He wanted to show the Cuban people that he had embraced hip-hop. Concerts were organized around the country featuring many kinds of music, including hip-hop. Castro had a meeting with all of the musicians, including the rappers. "He told us that he knows about rap," Ariel said. "He knows that maybe the government was wrong in the beginning about rock 'n' roll and about hip-hop. That really opened the door. [Now] we can say [that] hip-hop was born in Cuba on January 5, 2001, when Fidel made that statement. Now all the rap music can count on the support of the government. We can count on the support of the Ministry of Culture. That is the reality of hip-hop now."

Every year since 1991, an international hip-hop festival has been held in Havana. That's an encouraging sign, but hip-hop remains a small blip on the government's radar screen, especially the more outspoken hip-hop. Ariel agreed that the government hasn't shown any real interest in promoting hip-hop. He claimed that the hip-hoppers accept this and even welcome it, to some degree. They understand that the Revolution and its social ideals still need protection from forces against Cuba. Those forces – North American capitalism and its Miami-Cuban cheerleaders – can use the hip-hop criticism and twist it against the Revolution.

"The enemy can use the information that we say against the Revolution," Ariel said. "Capitalists can come into the ghetto and bring hip-hop T-shirts and CDs to the young to influence the youth. That kind of commercial pressure is against the young. When you are young, you don't know exactly what you want in life. You don't have exactly what you want to think. If you don't have strong youth, people can come in and sway their minds with material things. The music has power, so you can use music to sway the young.

"If you love hip-hop, you can support the government. You can bring something to help the government. You cannot put the movement against the Revolution. There are a few people in Miami who are trying to get Cuba put down. That cannot happen. The Revolution has to be protected. I think everything that we can change – political, cultural – we have to change ourselves."

To have a revolution, you need resources, and the rappers don't have many resources. There are 200 hip-hop groups in Havana, according to Ariel, and only one producer, Pablo Herrera. Rappers have difficulty getting studio time. "It's very hard to find a studio to make a demo, you know?" Ariel lamented. "The studios are all the time busy with salsa music, with country music, with trova music. All the studios in Cuba you have to pay in dollars, man. Every studio. EGREM (the Enterprise of Recordings and Musical Editions) is a government studio, but if you don't have dollars to pay for the materials, you don't go in. That's real. To make a record, you have to find somebody with the money to pay. Cuban record companies don't have interest in hip-hop, you know?"

Ariel takes great pleasure from the fact that the group Orishas was well known in Cuba but no record company got behind them. A French record company came and said, "You have talent. Come out." Orishas is a success that could have come from a Cuban record company. Now a Cuban record company, Bis Music, has to pay a licensing fee to the French company to release Orishas' records in Cuba. Ariel loves to make that point.

It is to the advantage of Cuban hip-hop to stay underground at the moment, according to Ariel. The music can be commercial, but it must be underground. "Those are two different things," Ariel said. "Every record is commercial. Every album, every CD, is commercial. When you record an album, you want to sell as many as you can. You want your CD to go to all the CD players. The point is, how do you want this to happen? With what kind of music? You can make music that will be easy to get access to promotion, and all that, or hip-hop, that is difficult to get the access. The majority of the Cuban hip-hop bands want to stay in the sounds that cannot be commercial. The record companies want a commercial sound. They think [that], to sell hip-hop to the majority of the Cuban people, it has to sound commercial, you know? The hip-hop artists think that the most important thing is the lyrics. They want to tell what is really happening in the streets. They want to record albums and sell copies, but they are still underground. In this way, so many groups are working to stay underground, to stay noncommercial.

"So many young people feel more into the hip-hop because, when they hear hip-hop, they say, 'That's my story. That's what is happening with me right now. That's what I see every day. That's what I live every day. I support that artist because he has the same problems [as] me. It's like he lives next door to me.'

"We are still controversial, you know? It's hard, because the hip-hop people love this country. They want to stay here. They want to sound like Cuba. They want to be Cuba. They want to change some things. But it's hard to change, you know? Because that's life. To win, you have to lose. To get some things, you have to sacrifice. Some things the hip-hop is talking about in the songs are the sacrifice for the Revolution, still. That's what's happening.

"The economic situation right now is a sacrifice. The government and the people don't want tourism in Cuba. We don't want prostitution. We don't want drugs coming in. All that is for the dollar, to get money. We are against that system, but to survive we have to support the capitalist people, so it's controversial.

"We are not against the Revolution; we are with the Revolution, but we want to change the wrong things of the Revolution. Every revolution, every system, every government [makes] mistakes. We want to repair the mistakes."

3 Nueva Trova

The first time I met Pablo Menéndez, he was unloading speakers from a van in front of the Teatro Municipal Playa in a "wrong-side-of-the-hill" neighborhood of Havana, where the light of prosperity had not shone in a long time. (I later learned that this is exactly the type of place in which Pablo and his band, Mezcla, make an effort to play.) Admission to the concert, featuring six bands, was 25¢. Pablo is committed to bringing music to the people at a price that they can afford.

Pablo Menéndez is considered to be a godfather of Cuban rock 'n' roll. Cuban rockers such as Carlos Varela, Gerardo Alfonso, and Santiago Feliú acknowledge their debt to Pablo and the song 'Cuba Va!,' on which he laid down electric-guitar riffs never heard before in Cuba. He was also an important contributor to the Nueva Trova movement that transformed Cuban music in the 1970s, a movement whose repercussions continue.

"Those musicians and that movement still overshadow us in the sense that they started a social/cultural movement within Cuban society," Pablo Herrera acknowledged. "The hip-hop generation could be the second wave of that movement."

On the night we met, Pablo wore his trademark long ponytail and farmer's overalls. He spoke perfect American English, which is not surprising, since he was born in Oakland, California, in 1953. His mother is the blues singer Barbara Dane. As a boy, Pablo toured the jazz/folk/blues clubs as part of his mother's act, playing guitar, harmonica, and washtub bass. When he graduated from junior high, at the age of 14, he traveled on his own to study music in Cuba, where he has lived ever since. When he was 15, he married Adria Santana, now a well-known Cuban actress. Pablo and Mezcla play a full card of gigs around Havana, and he also tours with them in the United States and Europe, records CDs, and makes music videos. Pablo is also a professor of Electric Guitar at his *alma mater*, Escuela Nacional de Arte (the National School of the Arts).

"Welcome to Cuba," he said when I introduced myself. "Sure, I'll be glad to talk about Nueva Trova and all the ins and outs of the Cuban music scene. Come over to the house for coffee."

Nueva Trova ("New Ballad") began as a very alternative, almost outlawed, movement of young singer/songwriters. They openly criticized the government and the failings within the society. They did not advocate the overthrow of Castro, for they believed in the ideals of the Revolution, but instead saw their role as a spur to jab the government to do better.

This was at a time when the Cuban government did not welcome rock 'n' roll, in the late 1960s and through the 1970s. The music was perceived as a bad influence, a diversion from the goals of the Revolution, and a force that could potentially mislead the Cuban youth. But rock 'n' roll was the music that influenced Nueva Trova. The young musicians studied The Mothers Of Invention and Frank Zappa; Crosby, Stills And Nash; Jimi Hendrix; The Beatles; King Crimson; and Blood, Sweat And Tears. They studied the jazz of Don Ellis, McCoy Tyner, Herbie Hancock, John Coltrane, Miles Davis, and all the greats. They knew as much about the Brazilian Tropicalia movement and the music of Chico Buarque, Caetano Veloso, and Gilberto Gil as they did about the English bands.

Cuban singer/songwriters such as Silvio Rodriguez, Pablo Milanés (the two best known of their generation), Noel Nicola, Eduardo Ramos, Sara Gonzales, and Emiliano Salvador formed the core of the Nueva Trova social movement, which was driven by music. Their mentor was Leo Brouwer, a professor of Music at the Escuela Nacional de Arte, a world-leading composer of classical works for the guitar, and a regular guest conductor of symphony orchestras around the world. Brouwer trained young musicians in a thinktank environment that he and like-minded music teachers set up at the ICAIC (the Cuban Institute of Art and Cinema Industry). These music professors had the unorthodox idea that the old-time music-school model bogged down students for years in academic studies at a time when the students' creativity was at its peak. Brouwer and the other teachers put their students on a fast track to read and write music, make their own arrangements, and learn other technical tools of the music trade, and then put them to work. The film-institute collective was to work with the film industry born basically with the Cuban Revolution.

"At the end of 1969, a musical thinktank called the Experimental Sound Collective of the Cuban Institute of Cinematographic Arts and Industries [Grupo de Experimentacion Sonora de ICAIC] was established," Pablo explained as we sat in the living of his second-floor duplex two blocks from the sea. Earlier that morning, he had worked out at a gym, and his dark-honey-colored hair was still wet from the shower. On the previous night he had played at a jazz club until 4am, but he was full of fresh energy. "We liked the fact that it had this really noncommercial name. At that point, we were happy to go against the grain of what we saw in the world, in a certain sense, as a dictatorship of...a straightjacket of record companies putting music into little boxes. We were happy to have been grouped together with people of different influences but with a basic rebellious spirit that wanted to make some new roads [and] open up new doors in music."

The film institute, with its own recording studio, was the perfect setting. Under Brouwer and the other teachers, the students were given projects to create soundtracks for real and imaginary films. The director of the film institute told the musicians that, if they didn't like a project, they had no obligation to work with the director. In fact, it was the obligation of the director to make the musicians fall in love with the project and be motivated by it. That was all that the young musicians had to hear. There was a predictable explosion of creativity.

"We wrote, recorded, and played all sorts of music," Pablo remembered, "from experimental electronic, so-called serious music, jazz, rock 'n' roll, Cuban fusion. One of the landmark songs to come

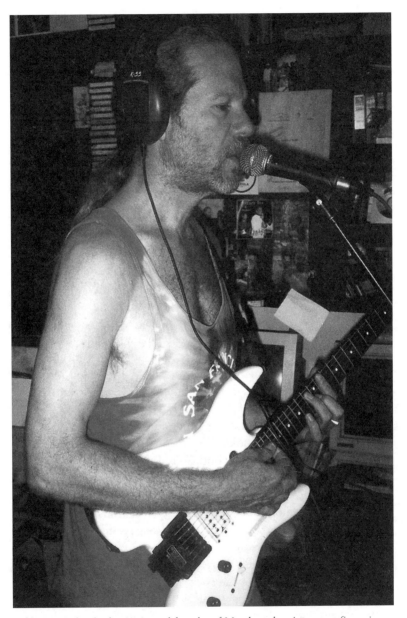

Pablo Menéndez, lead guitarist and founder of Mezcla and an important figure in the 1970s' Nueva Trova movement

out of this was 'Cuba Va!' It was collaboration between three singer/songwriters: Pablo Milanés, Noel Nicola, and Silvio Rodriguez. Each wrote a verse, [with] me – with a very rock 'n' roll-sounding electric guitar – being the glue between the verses. One reason that song had a big impact was that there was practically no Cuban music being made with this rock 'n' roll guitar sound. That was very much like a siren, an alarm, for young people in Cuba. It's a song today still used at the beginnings or endings of political rallies. It has been an inspiration now for generations of Cubans."

Pablo's wife, Adria Santana, set down two cups of sweet, dark coffee on the table. She divides her time between New York and Havana, performing experimental theater and the plays of Lorca, but she prefers Havana. Recently, she turned down an offer to spend six months acting in New York. That was too much time away. Her life is in Havana, where she and Pablo raised their son and where she is in constant demand in the theater. She is small, with dark hair and, at the moment of serving us coffee, a quiet disposition. She was so unobtrusive that I had mistaken her for the maid, until Pablo made the introductions. As she set the coffee before me, I glanced back and forth from her to a poster of her on the wall with her arm outstretched, rising dramatically from a stagefloor. Anguish literally screamed from the poster. How did this pleasant, soft-spoken woman now slipping out of the room transform herself into a person flinging bolts of raw emotion? Life must be interesting in the Menéndez/Santana household.

In the late 1960s, Cuban youth found it increasingly difficult to relate to the traditional dance music. They wanted to hear rock 'n' roll, not the old-time Cuban stuff, even though people like Juan Formell and Chucho Valdés with Irakere were transforming Cuban popular music and jazz. Covers of US songs sung in Spanish by different groups from Spain or Mexico were popular. In Cuba, only the Nueva Trova musicians were producing Cuban music with the North American and European rock 'n' roll flavor.

"It was all very exciting for me," Pablo said, taking a sip of coffee. "I produced all the albums we made at the National record company. I had the know-how and the energy to ramrod the projects

Orlando Sanches, tenor saxophonist with Mezcla

David Pimienta, drummer with Mezcla

L-r: Mezcla's Jose Hermida (bass guitar) and Julian Gutierrez (piano and vocals)

through. The actual leadership of the record company didn't know this was happening. I'd present them with the projects, produce them, and go out and sell them."

The Nueva Trova movement had a social impact because it mirrored and gave voice to the concerns of the youth. The 1959 Revolution was the idealist quest of a previous generation. Following on from that, the younger generation wanted to exercise its own idealism, not at the expense of the Revolution but as a further development of the Revolution.

"There was a lot of suspicion about Nueva Trova," Pablo said. "We had a big meeting at the Casa de las Americas, a social institution of singer/songwriters from around the world: Africa, Australia, England, Italy, the Americas, Asia – including South Vietnam – and the United States. The event was called Protest Song. There were simple-minded people in Cuba who said, 'In Cuba, you don't have anything to protest about. We have [the] Revolution. The things you have to protest about are already solved.' But we, the young people, didn't have that understanding.

"In our songs, we protested things that were wrong with Cuban society. We talked about things that were transforming Cuban society because of the Revolution. We sang about the changing relations between human beings. Our love songs didn't say, 'If you leave me, I'll die, or I'll kill you'; our love songs were about totally different relations, based on a new independence and respect for women. A lot of our songs talked about the transformation of Cuban youth. It was extremely appealing for the youth to hear songs written from a totally different viewpoint. The musical doors that were opened were very transcendental for Cuban music. It influenced a lot of bands that were starting at the time. The more experimental sounds and steps forward that have made monster contributions to the Cuban music of today – such as Juan Formell and Los Van Van and Chucho Valdés with Irakere – were influenced, if not directly, by the bands coming out of the film institute's thinktank. Some of the leading musicians of those bands jammed with us. There was a lot of collaboration and not much sense of competition with each other. The sense was [of] being part of this whole movement."

Adria, who had left the house, at this point reappeared carrying two new pillows. Pablo looked up as she passed through the living room. "You found some," he called out.

"Yes," she replied proudly. "They were there and I grabbed them."

"We have been looking for some time for new pillows," he explained. "The ones we have are just pieces of foam in a case and very lumpy. Adria finally found some solid foam ones." At the time, I did not realize the import of this shopping tidbit, but I was soon to find out.

The bands at the film institute, Pablo continued, had the mentality of conscious eclecticism. "We thought that we were at the avant garde of the world's struggle against the straightjacket dictatorship of the music industry telling us that we had to follow the latest thing that was selling. That thinking had, in the past, pigeonholed Cuban music into chachacha, or mambo, or one of the other commercial forms, like salsa nowadays. The attitude of Nueva Trova was that, the more different you could be from the hit bands, the more likely you were to draw the attention of the youth, who wanted to hear new and fresh and exciting sounds."

In the beginning, Nueva Trova was, like rap, an underground movement. The singer/songwriters and fans gathered in people's living rooms because there were practically no other places to play the music. Occasionally they played at parties sponsored by labor unions, but those older workers were bewildered by the music. They wanted to drink beer and dance, so what was this stuff? The musicians insisted on a clause in their contracts that banned the sale of alcohol and prohibited dancing during the performance. The Nueva Trova musicians were on a social mission to change how people listened to music. "We were out to change the whole structure of music experience in Cuba," Pablo explained. "Here people had the knee-jerk reaction [of], 'Oh, music. Let's get drunk, dance, vomit, [then] drink more beer and rum until we forget our bleak misery.' We wanted people to come listen to the lyrics of our songs."

Gradually, the movement gained a following. Cultural institutions such as the Casa de las Americas began to hold Nueva Trova concerts. The Young Communist Movement decided to back the movement, because they saw that it appealed to the youth, and invested in de luxe discos with the latest sound equipment, smoke machines, confetti blasters, and fancy light shows. Soon, Nueva Trova musicians were headline acts, with the Young Communist Movement helping to organize Nueva Trova festivals around the country.

"We went from playing in people's living rooms to playing in museums to doing free concerts to performing at Havana's Plaza de la Revolution for 500,000 people. In a city of two million people, that represents a quarter of the population. And this was without the backing of beer companies or tobacco companies or any commercial investment," Pablo pointed out with pride.

The government didn't have a determining position on cultural music. There was no Ministry of Culture in the nascent days of Nueva Trova. (It wasn't established until the late 1970s.) Each different cultural institution or area of culture had its own cultural line and logic. The radio and television, and each program director, had their own ideas about culture. One radio station might play a song and another station would ban it. The film institute backed the Nueva Trova musicians, naturally, but different cultural institutions thought that they were a threat, a negative force. It was a period of conflict, to say the least, and in that conflict the musicians found opportunity.

There was no official party line except the words of Fidel Castro, who in 1961 said, "Inside the Revolution, everything; against it, nothing." Pablo's eyes lit up when he recalled that. "The Revolutionary artists said, 'OK, that means anything goes. If we feel that we're part of this huge transformation of Cuban life then we're going to use this as a license to go out there and do what we want to do.'

"Our band at the film institute was following the lead of our national hero, Jose Martí, who had the idea that our culture should maintain its national roots but we should be able to splice onto that the best of world culture," Pablo said. "So that's what we were doing. We were reacting as a people living in a country where the mass media was nationalized, where the TV and radio and record distribution was all nationalized. We were the nation, so it was in our hands, from our perspective. We were free to transform our musical culture. We could define it ourselves. In other countries – namely those based in Anglo-Saxon culture and American culture – musicians and the public were fighting against the dictatorship of the record monopolies. The monopolies told the people, 'OK, the latest musical thing in the United States is what we're going to produce. We're going to put it up on the Internet. It's going to invade your home. You're going to be able to hear it every time you come out of your house, and that's what we're going to sell you and that's what you've got to buy.' But in Cuba and other places in the world, people were – and are – fighting to have their own national music be heard, not some corporate-dictated music.

"Since the Revolution, national music in Cuba was on the mass media. We didn't have to fight for this ultra-nationalism. We could base ourselves on national roots and have eclectic influences from the rest of the world. We, as musicians, were free to process it and have it come out in our own way. So when you hear timba bands with rap influences, or jazz influences, or rock 'n' roll influences, they are playing stuff based on *clave Cubana*, the Cuban clave, and the Cuban dance-music traditions. But it does have this attitude of 'I'm going to use whatever I want to use from whatever I hear in the world culture.' I think this is very much part of the legacy of what we did with bands like Experimentación Sonora.

"With nationalism, we the artists had control, not the State. This is how you can relate to life in general, no matter which country you're in or what the political system. If you think of yourself as someone who has a revolutionary attitude toward life then you know that you have a responsibility to take things in your own hands. Whatever risks are implied, you have to take those risks and fight for what you believe in. In Cuba, our cultural world was [such] that we had this very free and wide definition: 'Inside the Revolution, everything; against it, nothing.' Imagine what an incredibly wide definition that is, to say that within the Revolution anything goes and the Revolution is transforming culture and life. That meant that we had to define these things. We recognize that the United States, being the most powerful country in the world, is at war against the

Cuban Revolution, so the Cuban Revolution has to take some measures to defend itself. That's legitimate."

The late Carlos Pueblat wrote a song emblematic of the Revolution's values. The subject was equality. He used Varadero – once an exclusive beach resort three hours' drive from Havana – as the message. In pre-Revolution times, American millionaires (DuPont and Firestone), American mobsters (Al Capone), and the Cuban wealthy and powerful (Batista) had vacation homes at Varadero. When Castro overthrew Batista, he declared the resort a "people's beach." During the 1960s and '70s, workers were given free vacations at the hotels. The resorts were open to everyone at prices they could afford. But in the mid 1980s, when priority was placed on developing the tourist economy, the needs and comforts of rich tourists were given precedence. It became much more difficult for the ordinary Cuban to rent a cottage or stay in a hotel at the beach. This became a sore spot for Cubans who took to heart their government's preaching about social equality. Pueblat took the government to task in his song.

"This was at a time of a government campaign to abolish those privileges, erase them, and bring them out into the public eye and denounce anyone trying to have privileges instead of social equality and distribution of wealth in Cuba," Pablo told me. "The song was talking about these inequalities. In the real world, your 'rights' are often about money, but the Cuban Revolution made Cubans forget about the real world, and money, and social differences. People really believed that we were equal. Then, if you were some scheming bureaucrat who had written himself a permit for a free vacation in Varadero, you didn't want a song about social equality."

The song became a national hit but made at least one radio-program director nervous. Maybe if he played it he'd lose his job. After all, the song blatantly accused government officials of violating the principles of the Revolution. So that program director edited out a key phrase in the song, the phrase that drove the barb into the heart of this petty corruption. When Pablo heard the Bowdlerized version on the air, he exploded with indignation.

Pablo had butted heads with such "narrow-minded bureaucrats" on several occasions. If necessary, he would go to officials in the Cultural Ministry or the Cultural department of the Communist Party. "I'd say that I was an expert in Nueva Trova and [ask] what were the credentials of the person who thought a song should be recorded in a different way. If they wanted to discuss with me, then let's have a discussion, but if they are not world-known specialists like me, then who are they to censor us? The officials on the national level always back me."

Pablo directly confronted the offending program manager. The song might get Pablo in trouble, the program director quibbled. I'm trying to protect you by taking out the offending words. Pablo countered that those phrases were there precisely to irritate those types of people. We don't think they have any rights to privileges. That is the line of the party and of the Revolution. Are you going back to privilege and corruption?, Pablo challenged. Then he removed the edited tape from the files and inserted the original version, which the station played.

"Freedom is being able to do what you believe in," Pablo said. "That is something you have to struggle for every day, no matter where you live or what type of government you live under. People with that attitude are attracted toward each other, no matter where they live in the world. We know all the difficulties you come up against when you decide that's the way you're going to think about life.

"In Cuba, I've never seen anyone dragged off to jail or tortured or thrown in a dungeon for having this attitude in music. If you write a song [called] 'Down With Fidel,' well, you won't get the song played on the radio or TV. The songwriter is not going to be promoted by the Cultural Ministry to travel. They're not going to allow him to have access to major venues in Cuba. But if that's what he believes in, he should find alternative venues in which to sing 'Down With Fidel,' especially since he's not going to get his hands cut off or anything like that.

"That very wide definition of 'inside the Revolution, everything; against it, nothing' is part of the legitimate defense of a country that is a very small, very poor country that has a very small, poor government fighting against the policies of the United States, the most powerful nation in the world. Cuba has the right to defend itself, but that right doesn't mean that it's OK to break the hands of the artists or throw them in jail. If that did happen, I'd write a song about it. I'd say, 'What do you mean? You say we're living in a free country and you're throwing an intellectual in jail?' I believe that it is essential to my own sense of being free to express my disagreement, no matter what the risk.

"Cuban artists are able to travel around the world and can live anyplace they want. One of the reasons I live in Cuba – and this can be said of any artist here – is that we have the freedom to create as we wish. Cuban artists receive a salary from the State, so we can make a living from our music without having to constantly make concessions to what is going to sell or what the boss wants to hear. This is part of what makes it really interesting to make music in Cuba.

"Of course, you always have ass-kissing in any society and in any country and people who don't have the courage to stand up for what they believe."

4 Say What, Pedro?

"I've had no trouble with the creative issues," Pedro Luis Ferrer said as we sat in his home studio. "The problem is that, in order to make a concert in a corner of my house, I have to ask permission from the authorities. Where do you expose your work? And with whose permission? That is the problem with our freedom to create."

Pedro Ferrer has been in, out, in, and out with the Castro government for years. He was denied permission to travel abroad to perform and then allowed to travel abroad. He has danced around (and with) his government for so long that he can give masterclasses. He has been a thorn in officialdom's side with his outspoken, clever lyrics that tell about the reality of life in Cuba. He is known as the Bob Dylan of Cuba for his socially conscious lyrics with an edge of political double entendre. He is hugely popular and plays to sell-out concerts in Cuba.

"I can show you a list of songs that are never broadcast on the radio. I have freedom to think, but what radio program will broadcast what I think? I am invited to a radio interview, and afterwards I am edited, and they say, 'Well, you appeared.' There is freedom for creation, but what is lacking is the freedom to expose, to show that creation."

Pedro is a folkie. He plays the acoustic guitar and specializes in *guaracha*, a genre of Cuban music of Spanish origin that is associated with the people of the land. The music is not of country origin, although guaracha has many links with son, a traditional Cuban country music. Like son, guaracha is sung using an alternating solo/chorus structure and uses barbed humor to make its point.

Guaracha first appeared in the clowning, slapstick vaudeville theater known as *buffós cubanos* or *buffós habáneros*. The guaracha – little songs sung by a chorus called *tandas de guaracheros* – were used as bridges between acts, adopted the rhyming schemes of Spanish songs. The biting satire was meant to reflect the idiosyncrasies of the Cuban people and their government, a tradition that Pedro upholds. In the 19th century, guaracha's moral state was considered to be too rude for popular taste, as the songs' subjects were often sexual and "naughty." The lyrics spoke of seemingly trivial matters, but behind that beard were sharp teeth of biting social commentary. Staying true to this form has often landed Pedro in official hot water. It's the ironic, satirical lyrics, rather than the style of playing, that make guaracha. Son is also a sharp-tongued music, but guaracha adds a sense of joy. Pedro's personality is guaracha.

"Our culture has a serious problem: we have the democracy genes," Pedro told me. "That's a deficit of our culture." He is a short, barrel-chested man with a close-cropped beard liberally sprinkled with gray. His large eyeglasses give him a slightly owlish look. He had been up until 3am the previous night working on his newest album in the studio, where we sat. "I'll fix us coffee," he said, perhaps as much to stay alert as to be hospitable.

In Cuba, Spain never attempted to develop democracy, a foreign concept to any imperialistic power. When Cuba became an independent country, after the Second War of Independence (1895-98), the ruling class put on the robes of democracy in order to hold onto power rather than share it with the people.

"There never has been established in Cuba a democracy, despite that we have had elections," Pedro said, returning with two cups of coffee. "We've always had corrupt governments. Then came the Revolution and there was a hope. My parents were revolutionaries. They made the Revolution in the belief to finally find a democracy, to live in a democracy, and to develop a democratic culture with respect for the institutions of law. Then the Revolution assumed the political designs of the socialist countries that weren't democratic. We have a state designed to centralize everything. We are not democratic. We are not democratic to support Fidel and we are not democratic to be against him. Faced with the hostility of the United States to our Revolution, mechanisms of a noncivilian society were institutionalized. They were well intended, but they are not civilian. Cubans have not the notion of the culture of democracy. That's what is happening."

Pedro eased himself into a chair so we sat knee to knee. I glanced around his studio, which is well equipped with a Yamaha keyboard, a computer, a 36-inch TV monitor, and banks of speakers. Pedro can produce an entire album from start to finish here, including the cover art, which he has done in the past. The studio is on the ground floor of Pedro's house, which has a bit of a fortress look, enhanced by the tall, gray stucco wall around it. He and his wife live on the second floor. They will reclaim the ground floor when Pedro's new studio – currently under construction in the back garden – is completed.

"Cuba is a country that, since the triumph of the Revolution, has developed a system that is not a civilian form of government," Pedro went on, taking up a theme that appears often in his songs. "The crash against the United States has served the unification of that order, but not the civilian aspects in our society. The design of our society has been marked by this struggle with the United States that unifies the State, that rules all aspects of our life. When you try to project yourself in independent ways, you have the scratches from rubbing against the State. The way you project yourself – there are your problems in this society.

"It's not that there is not democracy. The problem is that the conception of our democracy is not that of civilian democracy. The difficulties with the bureaucracy are born there. It's not that you are marginalized because you are religious, or because you like rock 'n' roll, or because you are you. I can say that there is not an independent thought of the masses in this society. It doesn't exist.

"To make a political party is the most normal way for people to have a political attitude. If I had decided to create an independent party, I could have been in jail. I have not done that. Instead, I have made songs. And there is no law to take me to jail for that. The government understands that most of the songs made by people like myself are for the good of the social psychology and stability. The songs give a release to the people's strain and bad feelings of things in our society. We have a society where there is no political change, but there are changes of politics. The television, the press, and the radio don't contradict what is established by the power, and we don't have access to the Internet to express ourselves as individuals. I legally cannot have Internet in my home. If I ask for permission to access the Internet, the government will say no. Only institutions or a personality can have access. And suppose I obtain it – the price is not according to what you earn in Cuba. Internet access costs $50 per month, which is double what most people earn."

I met Cubans who had managed to dance around that issue by hacking into the Internet. If you're an artist, a doctor, or a member of nearly any profession, you can get email through a professional affiliation. However, the discussion may not stray from professional issues. A doctor must talk about medical topics and not politics or he will be denied access.

Pedro sees himself as a cultural warrior with responsibilities to his society. "I think that that is instinctive in a man," he said. "It's a natural thing. I think that is a natural projection of the man. I feel that, as a normal human being, the social aspects have to worry me. But I don't feel myself as a social rebel. In Cuba, politics is forbidden. You can only make variations of the themes that are imposed by the power, but politics is forbidden. In order to be a social rebel, you have to implement that which doesn't agree with the established power. In Cuba, a person who doesn't agree with some things is called a *dissentient*.

"Even if I wanted, I think that I can't be a social rebel. Within the establishment, I try to express my points of view that are different. I think that it is very bad for our cultural and our social being that everybody thinks the same and says the same things. On the television, you find people who speak with the same words as the speeches of the party. They are humble citizens, but when you talk with them, they speak with the same text as the government. I struggle in a social way with my ethics, with my art, because these impositions of the government have to be combated in a social way. I think that someday our life will be different, unlike today."

"Why did you choose guaracha?" I asked.

"Guaracha is the link with the joy and the attitude of the Cuban people." Pedro replied. "It's one of the expressions of the joyfulness of the Cuban people in reverse, in that our joyfulness is deeply connected to our sadness. We are a people who enjoy and have feasts and parties, but many times that is its own tragedy. Our reality is full of elements to compose guaracha. It's a reality that is dramatic, and that is joyful. The drama, when you are a dissentient...the drama becomes comical, joyful. You have to understand the Cuban culture.

"We are a people whose main cultural personality developed under the rule of Spain. The African influence brought by the slaves to our country is also a main element of our culture. The slaves, in order to practice their religion under the noses of the Spanish, pretended they were worshipping the Spanish, or Christian, saints. They made their deities in the image of the Spanish saints. In doing so, they projected their joyful festivities with this double speech, the joyful and the sadness. The guaracha has to do with all those things, so it's a deep and dramatic song. When you go to a big party in Cuba, you always see that everyone is doing his own [thing]. The Cuban people are guaracha. They have not abandoned that kind of behavior. If I stop singing to those issues then I simply stop communicating to the Cuban society."

"What good has the Revolution done for musicians?"

"There has been a great increase in educated musicians and an educated audience to listen to them. Since 1959 up to now, the government has been investing money into the cultural education of the people. The result is that there is an oversupply of musicians with a high professional level like you don't find in any Latin-American country. My piano player is a professor in the National School of Arts. In Cuba, you find excellent players of all instruments, excellent musicians, so the money that has been invested in education is well-invested money. What is happening now is that musicians cannot earn a living from the music. There is an overpopulation of professional musicians, and that has cheapened the music market, like lowering the price.

"Then our musicians emigrate abroad. I'm an eventual émigré.

Each eight or nine months, I have to go on tour abroad or I can't afford to buy equipment for my work. What they pay in Cuba for a presentation is unreasonable. I spend money for my concerts. Artists here go abroad to earn money and spend their money here to make a concert. Nevertheless, there are ways. For example, if you are asked to make music for a documentary or you make an orchestration, you make money. In my case, I'm [acclaimed] by the public. My concerts are always full of people. But it's an economical absurdity for me, because the money collected has nothing to do with me. I don't receive it.

"I think the artist and the intellectual need an economic stream to move forward. If the money doesn't come, the artists will be obliged to abandon...to quit their art and to make other things. It's not fair to invest this money in education and then the professional can't do their work. I call that a luxury project. I think that the luxury is dangerous, because our streets are broken, our buildings are falling apart, the schools and hospitals need maintenance, so the money can be put where there is a lack of it."

Pedro's self-contained studio is emblematic of his effort to be an artist of independent music and the producer of that music. He has the technology at his fingertips to create an entire album. But he is not turning his back on the big record companies, instead recording with them now as a way of financing his own personal projects that they reject in fear of taking a financial loss. When he performs at a concert, he sells the records he produces in his own studio.

"Some of my songs have not been broadcast on radio or television, but everyone knows the complete words," he said. "In my concerts, I sing songs that have not been broadcast and thousands of people sing along. How is that? There are people here who record the records from big companies and they sell the copies, as those records are not in the shops. There are people here who have a license to do that. Someone told me, 'Pedro, you don't know how much money I've made with your music.' He told me that to my face. He asked me if I have anything new to publish. They think they are doing me a favor. They say, 'I want something new so I can make money.' I said to one of them, 'Well, if you give me $30,000, you can take it.'

Pedro Luis Ferrer, outspoken performer of *guaracha*, a traditional form of satirical and witty Cuban music

"I won't sign an exclusive contract. What I do is finish my record and then give a company the option for the first buy or I publish by myself. Always it is better if it is sold by a big company and I receive an advance. That's what I'll do in the future."

Pedro has often performed in Miami. His reception by the Cubans in Miami has been mixed, which reflects the way he feels about them. "There is no freedom to express yourself within the Cuban community in Miami. In Miami, I have friends who have abandoned Cuba in order to have more freedom. When I visited...the Cuban community [in Miami], they told me, 'Don't say that. Don't do that, because there will be a problem. You can lose your job here.' The same scam as in Cuba has been imposed on Cubans in Miami by Cubans in Miami. It's the same but a different country. It's a Cuban problem.

"I think part of the constraint to freely express yourself in the Cuban community in Miami serves the people who want to keep the US economic blockade against Cuba. I think that behind this there is a big business. The conflict complements business on both sides, Cuba and the United States. Almost half a century has passed since the blockade and there is [still] no solution. When there is about to be a solution, something happens to stop that. In Cuba, when you disagree with the government, they say you are making the politics of the United States. I think many Cubans who live in Miami – those who make Castro out as some terrible dictator – are doing a big favor to the bureaucrats here in Cuba. Thanks to those Cubans, our government justifies certain policies with the excuse that they are necessary to protect Cuba from the designs of the United States.

"I am worried about what is happening in Miami. There are many tricks that exist in order to cheat and escape the blockade. Millions and millions of dollars move between Cuba and the United States. You can buy Coca Cola and Oreo cookies in Cuba. The direct flights from Miami to Havana are done on American planes, like Continental. There are business interests that want to keep the blockade. There is more money for the conflict than for the peace.

"Many people say that we want to finish with Fidel, but if Fidel is finished, their business will finish, too. I've stopped believing in all those things because I understand that all this is a business. An unfair business.

"Freedom is always an approximation. I think that people are always speaking about freedom, but they don't have a clear concept. The necessities will establish the kingdom of freedom. I think that it depends on the deal you make. Sometimes you choose to accept some parameters that restrain that freedom, but I don't think that...being independent is a warranty for complete freedom. Being totally independent, sometimes you cannot face your economic problems, and that is not freedom, also."

5 My Havana Neighborhood

My daily practical life in Havana bore a close resemblance to that of my neighbors: I always carried a shopping bag; I searched for days for a needed item, such as a face washcloth; I waited in lines; I waited for the water to come back on; I shopped at the local market; I got bored with local television; and I sat in the neighborhood park to enjoy the cool twilight.

I lived in Vedado, a pleasant neighborhood with an egalitarian mix of middle-class, comfortable poor and on-the-margin poor. My street, Calle 6, and the neighboring streets were lined with full-crowned trees that gave some cool relief from the tropical sun. Vedado was created when the wealthy spilled out of walled Old Havana and built their over-the-top houses here. The mansion that served as the model for the palace of the President of Bulgaria was a few blocks from my apartment. The neighborhood also included numerous embassies, government ministries, and cultural institutions. The Straits of Florida were a ten-minute walk from my front door.

My apartment, in an ugly three-story building, had a modest living/dining room, an elemental kitchen with barely enough room for two people to move past each other, a bathroom, and two bedrooms. Attached was an enclosed space that contained two 50-gallon reserve water tanks, a cement basin for washing clothes, and a clothesline. By Cuban standards, it was a fine place.

The apartment belonged to a husband and wife with a five-year-old son. Technically, it was her apartment. She was a dentist by profession. While I rented their place, the family lived at their second apartment, which belonged to the husband, a plastic surgeon. As government employees, the husband and wife received ridiculously low salaries. A central policy of Cuba's socialist government is to provide free medical care to the populace through nationalized medicine. However, the government is severely strapped, financially, and so it makes only token payments to its employees. The plastic surgeon earned $25 a month. The couple rented out the dentist's apartment to supplement their incomes. The plastic surgeon also hired out his car and himself as the driver.

Across the street from my place was a monstrous, 50-foot-high mansion with a grand stairway leading to the entrance. Four 30-foot-high columns supported the portico coming off the roofline. The building had been newly painted a godawful vibrant flesh tone with pink highlights. My neighbors said that it was once a private house that now belonged to a government institute. How else could 60 gallons of paint have been found to paint it?, they asked.

Next to that monumental example of bad taste was a modest house painted a sunny yellow, then a single cement house in need of paint, and, on the corner, what appeared to be an abandoned derelict. People lived in it.

Such a mixture of nice and poor is common throughout Havana. The nice housing is a result of the slowly improving economics, with homeowners now being able to afford paint and repairs. The poor housing is a result of idealistic government policy.

My first visitors were three teenage girls, who knocked on my door before I had time to unpack. The leader, Teresa, asked if she could use my phone. She was a good friend with my landlady, she assured me, pointing to her dental work, who let her use the phone. Teresa made her call and asked if I liked disco. "We love disco. It cost five dollars to get in," she said as a broad hint.

"I think disco music is boring," I countered.

Teresa continued to probe my likes and dislikes, trying to find an opening to my dollars. I denied liking anything but breathing. Over the next week, she often popped in for neighborly visits, always finding a way of asking for five dollars, three dollars, one dollar, which I never gave. One morning, she showed up with a darling two-year-old boy in her arms. Would I give her a dollar for the baby? I didn't want the baby. No, to buy soda for the baby, she said with a laugh. You shouldn't be jacking up a child so young on sugar, I admonished, deflecting her dollar scam.

She became increasingly bold in her search for my dollars. Did I smoke? Drink? Dance? No, no, and no, I said, not wanting to become her mark. She couldn't believe this puritan image I presented. On the fifth visit, she lowered her voice and asked, "Do you like girls?" I thought that she was asking to see if I had any human juice.

"Yes," I replied, somewhat defensively.

"What color? Like this?" She held up her little finger to indicate slenderness.

"I'm here only to work." I tried to sound indignant.

The break in our relationship came two nights later. She came over and explained that her sister was having stomach pains. Did I have anything that might help? Always the prepared traveler, I gave her medicine for stomach gas. We became neighbors at that moment. She borrowed my stomach medicine; I borrowed her matches for the stove. She'd come over just to check on me and chat; I'd ask her questions about Cuban life. She stopped asking for dollars, except on one evening.

"Can I have three dollars? My family ran out of food, and we don't get a new ration card for another of day."

I was suspicious. Three dollars was the entrance fee to the disco, but I knew that the monthly allotment for basic food supplies is meager and hard to stretch over a month for a family. If she needed food, I'd give her food from my fridge. As soon as she left house, she called out in an excited voice, "Mama! Mama! Ham and cheese!", holding them over her head as if they were lottery prizes.

Every night, in the second story of the dilapidated house across the street, a teenage boy practiced hip-hop. I watched him pretending to hold a mic as he went through his moves, singing to a backing track of American rap. He'd launch into a song, stop, rewind the tape, and try again until he hit the accents perfectly. He did not have a good voice. Occasionally, his mother would storm into the room, driven to her wits' end by hours of the unintelligible music, and snap off the tape deck, but most often she compassionately left him alone, for his instincts were good. Music was way out of his poverty and into the world of dollars, travel, a nice car, a good sound system, and a comfortable place to live, so every night the boy in the window with his pretend mic gave voice to his hopes and aspirations. He was Cuban to the core, in that he lived in transit between the dream and the reality.

The neighborhood's day started with roosters crowing at 5am. The sound gave a rural feel to the urban space. Many people kept chickens for the eggs and also grew vegetables in small garden plots, either in their yards or on their rooftops, although their gardens were just as likely to contain decorative plants.

Gaggles of children on their way to the elementary school passed my window at 7.30am, accompanied hand in hand by mothers or fathers. The children wore identical school uniforms of red shorts or skirts, white shirts, and red bandannas reminiscent of the Young Pioneers' outfits of the former Soviet Union. This was to eliminate envy over other pupils' shoes; flashy, satin pro-team jackets; or the latest fashion. All of the pupils of the same grade are taught from a uniform text wherever they attend school in Cuba. There are no elitist schools, or schools for the privileged, with better teachers or materials, which once translated into a leg-up to well-paid jobs for the graduates.

The kids – including the pre-school kids at the daycare center down the block – were extraordinarily well behaved. They were boisterous and energetic, but not rowdy and disruptive. The younger ones entertained themselves with simple toys – cardboard boxes that became trains – and the older ones walked in orderly lines into their classrooms. Everyone was on time. The teachers were openly affectionate with the little kids, giving them hugs and kisses. Such behavior would be subject to censure or a lawsuit in many of the more materialistic developed countries, whereas here the children seemed to thrive. After school, they were always outside playing stickball or other games. I encountered no street gangs or teenagers with badass attitudes and malevolent intentions.

My street was always busy with life. On any given day, people were out sweeping the sidewalks, shouting greetings and queries to each other, fixing cars, untangling their quarrelsome dogs, and in general living life in the sunshine. I couldn't avoid knowing my neighbors; they were interested in me and expected me to be interested in them.

A Cuban joke: schoolchildren there are taught the body parts – head, face, shoulders, arms, hands, plastic bag. I always carried a shopping bag stuffed in my back pocket like a good Scout, prepared to seize an unexpected shopping opportunity. The 42-year-old economic blockade imposed on Cuba by the United States has caused inconveniences and hardships for the Cuban people without achieving the intended effect of bringing down the Castro government. It is a failed policy in this respect.

Consumer goods are in short supply in Cuba. I searched for two weeks to find a face washcloth. I was probably looking in the wrong places, but on my foot journeys around the city I searched in every store that might conceivably have the item – in four-story department stores, in small neighborhood shops, on street stalls, and in grocery stores, which stocked only food, detergent, and a few kitchen-cleaning items. I was sure that face washcloths existed here because, when I asked the clerks, they knew what I was talking about.

One day, in Miramar, the up-scale suburb along the coast west of Havana proper, I went into a groceries/clothing/appliances/sundries store. I spied bath towels. Where there are bath towels there must be washcloths. I made a beeline for the counter, pulling out my plastic shopping bag in expectation. There were only bath towels. I bought one and, at home, ripped it up into washcloth portions. In many regards, I lived like an ordinary Cuban, but an ordinary Cuban would not rip up a bath towel to make face cloths. Too expensive. They'd keep searching for a face cloth.

I waited in lines. Waiting in lines is Cuban meditation, and they do it with patience, forbearance, and grace. The long queues for buses were always calm and orderly. The hot and tired people did not push and shove to board when their buses arrived but proceeded with care for their equally suffering neighbors. They were stoic, too, in the long queues at the bakery. But then, the people in the long checkout lines at my supermarket at home are equally civil to one another. The Cubans don't talk much in the lines. They just wait with the certainty that nothing else can be done.

I waited for the water to come on. It was normal for the city's water supply to be turned off for most of the day, because demand far outstrips supply. Havana has nearly doubled in size as people from the country have flocked in the search of better opportunities. At one point, slums just like the *favellas* that tumble down the hillsides around Rio de Janeiro had threatened to blight Havana. To stop this, the government restricted migration to the city. But the water supply still cannot meet the needs of the population, as Cuba has no major rivers from which to take water. Most of Havana's water supply comes from springs. The government has built dams and reservoirs to store water for residential, agricultural, and industrial use, but these efforts are like trying to inflate a hot-air balloon by mouth.

Tanker trucks deliver water to residences in certain parts of Havana, and men with hand-pushed water carts serve other neighborhoods, but most people wait for the water in their houses to come on. In the morning, I had to be washed and have coffee made by 8am if I was to be certain of having water. In the evening, I waited until after 8pm – when the water was usually available again – to take a shower after a sweating day in the city. At least the electrical blackouts were no longer common.

A block away from my place was a small morning vegetable market that sold tomatoes, onions, black beans, and sweet-tasting finger bananas. The best-stocked vegetable market was six blocks away. For milk, cereal, and a few other necessities, I shopped at a three-story shopping mall with small grocery, appliance, clothing, shoe, and sundry other departments three blocks away. One day, the market ran out of cereal. A week later, there was still no cereal. One morning, when I was in another section of town, I found a store with many boxes of cereal. I bought two. I carried the two boxes of cereal with me all day as I conducted interviews. I was a Cuban shopper.

I often ate from street stands, where food was sold for pesos instead of dollars. I came to know the location of the "cafeterias" in front of people's homes, where I could buy a sandwich or a sweet or an ice-cream cone. Things are so economically tight for the ordinary Cuban that they devise many ways of making ends meet. One of my favorite luncheon spots was the women's hospital four blocks from my house. Entrepreneurs set up their food and drink stands on the corner near the hospital, where they did a bustling business. I enjoyed the company of the women – many of whom were pregnant – as we ate our stand-up lunches.

I could buy a four-inch cheese pizza hot from the oven for 50¢ at the street stands. An ample, thick ham-and-cheese sandwich cost a dollar. An ice-cream cone cost 15¢. I could eat for an entire day on three dollars or less. A cup of thick, sweet coffee served in a demitasse-sized cup cost five cents. Cubans drink a cup in two sips, taken in quick succession. I preferred to linger over my coffee, because I felt very Cuban, standing on the street corner after a ham-and-cheese sandwich which was not very tasty. I imagined myself as part of the scene, unnoticed and, in that, accepted. I, of course, was spotted immediately as non-Cuban. Not because of my skin color – there are plenty of Cubans as white as I am – but because of my shoes. Cubans checked them out first. Foreign-made shoes usually meant a foreigner. Cubans know their shoes as a car buff knows the years and models. Most Cuban shoes are cheap knock-offs, although very fine Cuban hand-made leather shoes are coming back on the local market. My tropical shirt – which I thought very Caribbean – was a dead giveaway. Cubans don't walk around with big green parrots sitting on their chests. And they knew that I was not one of them by how I held myself, how I walked, something about the attitude of my posture.

After six weeks on the island, however, I began to pass. I knew this in two ways: street hustlers stopped trying to sell me fake gold rings, cigars, and girls, and the local taxis, the *botalas* (boats), would pick me up.

The hustlers hissed to get my attention – the usual way in Cuba to call someone's attention, like raising your arm to signal a taxi in New York – or they'd murmur their offerings as I passed on the sidewalk. They were never rude or aggressive. A dismissive flick of the hand or shake of the head would send them away, but they appreciated a polite, verbal 'No.' They weren't rude, so why should they be treated rudely? Eye contact with both men and women was an invitation for a query or comment. If you didn't want the attention, you didn't make eye contact. I came to enjoy this nonverbal communication, for it broke down the isolation, that shield of protection erected so often in big cities. The look or smile could be an invitation or a simple acknowledgment. Either way, it opened up the horizon for inclusion, the possibility of an adventure without danger. Once, when I was walking down the street, my shirt wringing from humidity, a man coming in the opposite direction gently touched my wet shirt in passing. He was just saying, 'It's hot, isn't it? And we're both in this heat together.' That simple gesture lifted my spirits. My spirits were lifted daily as I walked the streets of Havana.

Eventually, I no longer had the aura of looking or of expectation that hustlers everywhere pick up on, like a dog picks up a promising scent. The set of my head and shoulders became more confident, like I knew where to get what I wanted. I belonged. I wasn't a tourist. Perhaps that was what the botalas drivers saw.

There are two kinds of taxis in Havana: the official ones and the unofficial ones – that is, those for tourists and those for locals. Taxis for tourists – new cars, well maintained and distinctively painted – are run on the meter and the government takes a percentage of each fare. The meter rate is reasonable, though, and I never felt ripped off whenever I took such a taxi. It is illegal, however, for a botala driver to pick up a tourist, because that would deprive the government of revenue. A botala driver could lose his or her license for taking such an illegal fare, so they were very cautious about picking up anyone who didn't look like a local. A fare that cost three dollars in a metered taxi cost 50¢ in a botalas.

I liked very much the street attitude of my neighborhood and of Havana. The lack of tension and of aggression made exploring the city an adventure, not a risky dare. I walked everywhere, at any time of day or night, and never felt the need to watch my back. Often, on my walks, I came up behind women on dark streets. They didn't take defensive action, as if it had never occurred to them that they might be in danger. Whenever I met a knot of males of the testosterone-charged age coming down the sidewalk, I never felt it necessary to avoid then, as I might have in many US cities. The knot of boys always untangled to let me through without an intimidating glare, thrown elbow, or challenging slur.

I made it a point to walk the city at different hours of the day or night. Havana at 2pm was a different place to Havana at 2am. But, whatever the hour, there was always life on the streets. The lower end of 23rd Avenue – three blocks of clubs and discos known as La Rampa – is a heavy pick-up zone any time after 9pm. The Prado – the walking street in Old Havana, leading to the Capitolio – is a community hall during the day and a bingo game of many opportunities in the evening, depending on your desires. The Malecón, fronting the sea, is another ongoing scene of action and entertainment. Neumáticos – guys who float on fishing platforms fashioned from tractor-sized inner tubes with webbing strung across their bottoms – launched themselves from the Malecón's seawall. They put air in their tubes at the gas station at the intersection of La Rampa and Malecón. They looked like icons with outsized halos as they carried the inflated tubes on their heads across the street to the sea.

No matter what the hour, I never had to be unduly concerned with the traffic when crossing a street. Even at morning and evening rush hours on the busiest thoroughfares, I jaywalked with impunity. But pedestrians do not have rights; it's the pedestrian's responsibility not to get hit by a car, not the driver's responsibility to avoid the collision. On side streets, I had the street entirely to myself, especially at night.

In the evenings, when I wasn't walking or working, I'd occasionally watch television. Cuban television is dull. There are only two channels, both of which are controlled by the State. The fare includes cultural shows, historic period dramas, comedy skits, soap operas, public-affairs discussion shows, and kids' cartoons, which were as violent as those seen everywhere else in the world. The weekly discussion panel on world politics featured talking heads with predictable opinions. The nightly news program was short on news of substance, but presented long segments of old Revolutionary heroes doing the equivalent of cutting ribbons.

Fidel was on television two or three times a week, giving a speech to one group or another. I expected both channels to be devoted to his appearances, but that was not the case. Once, when he was delivering a speech to social workers, the other channel carried a dog adventure show from New Zealand, sort of like *Rin Tin Tin*, only the star was a Siberian husky and not a German shepherd.

One poignant news segment showed Fidel at a hospital for disadvantaged children. The welfare of handicapped children has always been a personal interest of his. He has established special medical facilities, schools, and work places for the disabled. He has allocated buses to take the children back and forth from their homes to their special education classes. On the live show, he was grandfatherly to the children and solicitous of their parents. This Fidel is never shown on US television, for it runs counter to the image that the United States government has promoted of him, as being an evil communist dictator. Seeing him without that American-made image was one of my wake-up calls about Cuba and the reality of the place.

Baseball games were on television more than Fidel. I've always heard about the terrific caliber of Cuban baseball players, but many of the games I saw had a Keystone Kops quality. Pitchers beaned batters with alarming frequency. Outfielders dropped balls, bobbled the bounce, or simply didn't hustle to make a play. When given the choice, I watched European soccer matches via ESPN.

On Thursday, Friday, and Saturday nights after nine, when children were supposed to be in bed, television carried American television shows of "violence, sex, and dirty language," usually of the detective genre. A Havana joke says that you can find violence, sex, and dirty language without watching the shows, just by riding on the Camels. (A Camel is a public conveyance, a cross between a bus and an over-the-road semi-truck. A diesel cab powerful enough to haul cattle to market pulls this contraption, which looks like a beer can stepped on by a giant, a windowed semi trailer with the middle section indented and the two ends popping up, like a low-flying U. It's said that more people can fit into a Camel than can ride in a 747 plane.)

My habitual evening walk was to the neighborhood park where John Lennon sits. The park fills the complete center of the square block, and the hub – a white cement raised platform with a balustrade, suitable for a band concert, which was probably the original intent – anchors the center of the park. Wide sidewalks radiate from this hub like spokes of a wheel. Deep-green iron benches are spaced around the right-angled periphery and the curved inner ring. The benches bear the three-key Havana city symbol left over from the Spanish colonial days. Old-fashioned globe lights illuminate the park at night, giving the mood of a slower, calmer century.

The park was a family place to me. Youngsters whizzed by on bikes. They were nice bikes – ten-speed mountain bikes like those found in any American suburb. Some kids had roller-blades. There was always a game of Frisbee. Fathers played catch with their sons. Every evening, the same group of boys played a pick-up baseball game in the corner they favored. The bat was a piece of suitable wood. The ball could be a lump of raw rubber or strips of tightly bound cloth. Sometimes they had a tennis ball or a rubber ball or even a real baseball. The scene could have come from any pleasant park in nearly any city in the world.

I was well known as the only North American in the neighborhood. When I'd throw a wayward ball back to a father or to the boys, I got a "thank you" in English. Children practiced their numbers in English with me, but no one intruded. No one attempted to "adopt" me. I felt settled, at home in the neighborhood.

The whole scene struck me as so middle class. The people were nicely dressed, the kids had bikes and scooters, and everyone looked healthy. The phrase "Ike is in the White House" popped into my head. It was like the serene 1950s, when grandfatherly President Dwight Eisenhower patted Uncle Sam on the head and assured us all that the world was at peace and that suburbs were being built. All was well. Eisenhower also declared the first partial economic embargo against Cuba and initiated the plan for the Bay of Pigs, a US-backed invasion of Cuba put into action by President Kennedy on April 17, 1961. Eisenhower was infuriated that Castro hewed a path for the best interests of the Cuban people rather than for the best interests of the United States.

When Castro took over the government, in 1959, after a victorious armed rebellion, he set out certain inalienable rights for Cuban citizens. These included promises of guaranteed housing, of free medical care, of equality in education, and that no one would be without food. These rights smacked of the Red Threat to American administrations from Eisenhower's to the present day's, administrations that would not and could not guarantee such rights for United States citizens.

Castro also proposed that cinemas should be free. Cinematographers hastened to point out that somebody had to pay for the film to make the movies, and there are now no free cinemas in Cuba. Castro once gave a speech to a group of painters urging them to sell their work at low prices so that ordinary citizens could hang culture on their walls. One painter promptly (and loudly) said that a tube of paint cost more than Castro's suggested selling price. Art is one of the few free markets in Cuba.

However, Castro *was* able to deliver on free housing. When he enacted his socialistic policies, which included nationalizing much of the land and key industries, the owners of those properties – often the mansion owners – left the island for Florida. They reasoned that Castro wouldn't last more than a few months. The United States government wouldn't put up with him seizing US corporate assets in the name of the people, which Castro did, primarily in the electricity and telephone industries and the sugar plantations. We'll take an extended vacation, wait for Uncle Sam to apply his big boot, and then go home and take up where we left off, they assured themselves. Forty-two years later, they are still waiting.

Castro even called the big mansions that were left empty "vacationists' houses." "We did not take anyone's house," he said on August 24, 1998 at a meeting of Caribbean heads of government. "Not at all. They went on vacation, and since their vacations were extended indefinitely...the houses are there, preserved and kept at the service of the nation."

Initially, the Castro government gave the abandoned (or

temporarily vacated, depending on your point of view) multi-roomed mansions to the poor who needed housing, while the large single-family homes were subdivided among many families, who were given ownership free and clear, with no obligation to pay rent. Many of the new owners were from the countryside and had no idea how to deal with plumbing, electric lights, toilets, and the other responsibilities of urban home ownership. Plus, they had no money for maintenance, which was their responsibility. The once-grand mansions fell into disrepair – the painted façades faded, crumbled, and the houses took on the look of a slum in the making. People couldn't even afford lightbulbs, and today Havana's houses and buildings primarily use fluorescent lighting, which is cheaper and uses less electrical power.

Government officials saw that their utopian housing scheme wasn't working out as well as they'd hoped, and they stopped giving away the mansions. Instead, they converted them into government-owned buildings for offices and institutions, which is why those old mansions are the best-dressed buildings in the city. The poor occupy the shabbiest housing. There are many nice homes and apartments in Havana, and then there are places where twelve people share a room.

Officially, no one in Cuba pays rent for his or her house. The resident owns the house or the space within a house. When my landlords married, they each kept their houses, which is how I rented one of them. In order to stop land speculation, homeowners aren't allowed to sell their properties, although they can trade houses. However, if you live in an undesirable location and want to move to a nicer part of town, good luck in finding someone willing to trade houses. People who want to marry and get a place of their own, something other than sharing an apartment with parents, also face housing crises. Farcical romantic films are based on this theme. The films are very popular because so many people can identify with them.

Cubans know methods – and the price – of getting around the government's good intentions that fit like a too-tight shoe. An elderly couple, for instance, lives in a run-down house. Someone with means offers to fix the place up and paint it and give the old folks a cash "bonus" in exchange for rights to the house if the folks decide to move, or when they die.

I sat in the park until nearly everyone had gone home for dinner. Well, John, I said to the statue. What do you think?

Give peace a chance.

That's such a cliché, John. Can't you come up with something better?

No.

6 Cayo Hueso

Ramiro de la Cuesta leaned over the rail of his fourth-floor balcony and threw down the keys to the street door. From that distance, he looked a bit like Ray Charles without dark glasses. As a young man, Ramiro was a singer in the group Crusaders. He earned a law degree. He was once the manager of the world-renowned Cuban jazz group Irakere. Now, at the age of 60, he manages a jazz quartet that plays the Havana clubs. He is a jazz dancer. He is the spiritual godfather of the young trumpet player Mario Morejón Hernández, better known as "El Indio," who is widely regarded as the best of the new generation of Cuban horn players. But, most importantly, Ramiro is the godfather of Cayo Hueso, where he has lived for the past 50 years.

Cayo Hueso is a neighborhood of old Havana. If you stand on the grand staircase leading into the University of Havana and look north down the hill towards the sea, you are looking over the shoulder of Cayo Hueso. Physically, there is nothing distinctive about the place, so tourists rarely venture down the streets. There are no trees in Cayo Hueso. The houses abut directly onto the street, as do those in many old sections of European cities. People's living rooms start on the threshold of the street. I learned to knock softly on the street doors because, more often than not, the people are directly on the other side of the door. A knuckle bang reverberates loudly in the high-ceilinged rooms, a bit like someone shouting *"Hello!"* in your ear when a polite nod would suffice.

The houses themselves are in general disrepair, the paint long faded and any charm – if it existed at all – eradicated by poverty.

Cayo Hueso is a *barrio* in both the good sense and the pejorative: there is little traffic, so the people use the streets as a communal yard; kids play stickball or foursquare; mothers gossip while looking after their young; men idle or conduct the business of the day. A palpable sense of community binds the neighborhood. On the other hand, Cayo Hueso is a dead end. There are no employment opportunities. The place is ugly. The streets are riddled with potholes and the sidewalks are broken.

Cayo Hueso is colloquially translated to "Key West," although *hueso* literally means "bone, stone, pit of a fruit." At one time, producing hand-rolled cigars was the neighborhood's chief cottage industry, but the skilled cigar-makers migrated to Key West, Florida (hence the reference). Now it appears that, on the surface, nothing happens in Cayo Hueso. But, under the surface, Cayo Hueso is one of Havana's hot spots. The section has always been home to musicians and continues to be so. It is the Bronx of Havana jazz. What looks like shabby poverty hides richness in creativity. I stumbled across the band Sierra Maestra rehearsing in Cayo Hueso. EGREM, the studio where Buena Vista Social Club recorded and The Afro-Cuban All Stars still record, is in Cayo Hueso.

Across the street from Ramiro's apartment is a gutted manufacturing plant that now serves as the rehearsal hall for a very loud and very hot big band. Bata drums are hand made in Cayo Hueso, as are other traditional musical instruments. Ceremonies and drumming of the spiritual practice Regla de Ocha – more commonly known as Santeria – are very active in Cayo Hueso. None of this is apparent; you have to know where to look or be shown where to look. Ramiro had agreed to show me where to look for an initiation ceremony of the Regla de Ocha ("Rule of the Saints"), the name preferred by the practitioners of Santeria. That's why I knocked on his door.

I caught the keys he threw down but could not for the life of me get them to unlatch the balky door lock. I inserted the key and boldly turned it, as if making a straightforward business deal. The deal refused to be done. I slowly eased in the key, jiggling it seductively, as if trying to impress a lover with my highly attuned sensitivity. The deadbolt didn't give even a sigh of a promise to relent. "Force it!" Ramiro shouted down. I turned the key and shouldered the door, which gave a couple of inches but refused to open. I slammed. I pounded. I rattled. I cursed. I made so much noise that the wheelchair-bound man in the ground-floor apartment – a double amputee – came and opened the door. I thanked him. He took the key and demonstrated how to open the lock, which obeyed him. I thanked him again and, feeling the sting of the reprimand, trudged up the narrow marble stairs to Ramiro.

My friend Jose Antonio Fernández, who was also my indispensable assistant, had introduced me to Ramiro. They had been friends for 40 years, and perhaps it was Jose's recommendation that persuaded Ramiro to be my guide into Santeria. Ramiro greeted me at his door with a hug. Just inside his door was an altar to Yemayá, protector of women, goddess of motherhood, the sea, and rivers. She was Ramiro's personal orisha.

"The ceremony starts at three," he said, leading me out onto his balcony, a mere lip of masonry. In the distance, I could see a sliver of ocean, a cool blue insert between dull gray cement buildings. Below, the brassy big band struck the first chord of its afternoon practice. I looked directly down into the roofless factory across the street, but I couldn't see the musicians. I imagined them pressed against the walls, out of sight, as if pulling a Halloween trick for their own amusement. Ramiro shouted directions to the Santeria ceremony over the horns and drums while pointing out the turns from this block to that, then right for two blocks, then left. "Look for a blue car," he said as we retreated into his apartment. "Listen for the drums. I'll meet you there. I have some errands first."

At the appointed hour, I wandered down the center of San Miguel Street, hoping that there would be only one blue car along the curb. I went one block, then two blocks, past three boys playing stickball with a ball made of wrapped cloth, and then four blocks down the nearly deserted Saturday-afternoon street, past a 1956 Buick fatally wounded by rust and disrepair, before I saw the blue car. I heard no drums until I came directly opposite an open door that led into a private home. Ramiro stood just inside the door.

"Do as I do," he instructed. "No photos. No tape recording. No taking notes."

He knelt to the floor before a pan of water in which floated flower blossoms, as if genuflecting in a Catholic church. He dipped his fingers into the water and touched his moistened fingers to his forehead and to the back of his neck, the equivalent to the Catholic practice of making the sign of the cross with holy water. I copied him. The living-room furniture had been piled in a corner to clear the room. Ramiro and I stood next to a bureau upon which sat two Barbie-like figurines dressed in satin dresses and wearing necklaces of blue and white, the colors of Yemayá. The ceremony was being held in her honor. Yemayá is derived from the Yoruba title *Yeyeomo Eja*, which means "the mother whose children are the fish." Traditionally, she is represented as a beautiful matron with prominent breasts, especially in Brazil, and she is one of the most revered and popular of the orishas in Santeria. She is associated with the Virgin Mary – who also wears robes of blue and white – and with Our Lady of Regla. (Regla is the dock section across the Bay of Havana from the city proper.)

On another bureau across the room stood a doll dressed in a full, deep-yellow dress. The doll represented Oshun, the goddess of rivers, springs, and beauty. Oshun is the divinity of the Oshun River that crosses the Oshogbo region of Nigeria. In Santeria, she is syncretized with Our Lady of La Caridad del Cobre, the patron saint of Cuba. She is the goddess of sexual love, the Venus of the Yoruba pantheon, and has numerous lovers. Paradoxically, she is the patron saint of love, marriage, fertility, and gold, and is the archetype of joy and happiness.

The wall directly opposite us was completely covered with two large pieces of white cloth separated by a narrower red cloth. White and red are the colors of Chango, the orisha of thunder and lightning, the patron saint of drummers. He is the adopted son of Yemayá and one of her greatest loves, in a way that would be unseemly in other religions.

Oshun and Chango also have a personal history. Chango's "legal" wife is Oba, whom he abandoned because of a cruel and bloody trick played by Oshun, who was madly in love with Chango and wanted his fire and thunder for herself. Oba sensed, as wives do, that something was afoot. Not suspecting Oshun, Oba confided in her, woman to woman. Oshun told Oba that Chango would never leave her if she cut off her ears and served them to him in a soup. This she did, but the act so horrified Chango that he fled.

Three empty chairs stood before the red-and-white wall. The sound of drumming came from a back room, a complex, overlapping staccato and seemingly unpredictable rhythms that sounded, to my ear, like an enthusiastically shouted conversation of sports fans comparing the merits of their teams, the respective points clashing and rebounding to create a tangled ball of sound.

"Those are the sacred drums to summon the orishas," Ramiro explained. "Only initiates of Regla de Ocha can go into the back room, where the offerings are made."

People entered the front room from the street, casually greeted one another, and passed through to the back room to pay their respects to the orishas. Then they returned to the front room, which filled with people milling about. After 20 minutes, three men carrying sacred bata drums walked in from the back room. Each drum has two heads, one at each end, which are played simultaneously. The larger head is called the eñu, Yoruba for "mouth," and the smaller head is the tcha tcha, or "anus." In essence, the three drums of a bata set become nine drums, sounding out complex, interweaving rhythmic patterns balanced on each other's beat. The bata drum is perhaps the most musically versatile and potent of the Cuban drums and the most difficult to master. In recent years, bata drumming has crossed over into Cuban jazz, popular dance music, and rock 'n' roll, although in these settings nonconsecrated drums are used.

The drummers (bataleros) wore casual slacks and shirts. They made no show of self-importance, although they were the center of attention. Without the drums, they could have been mistaken as fans in a sports bar. They sat on the three chairs against Chango's colors, placed cloths on their laps, and settled their drums.

The largest drum, the iyá (the mother drum), always takes the place of honor in the center. Four feet long, and with an hourglass shape, this iyá was wrapped in a *banderos*, a colorful beaded shield with a design particular to the iyá drum. Around each of the drumheads was a collar of small brass bells. The drummer was a very pleasant-looking man wearing a blue muscleman T-shirt. He was also a master drummer, having undergone years of preparation and study, not only in drumming but also in the beliefs of Santeria.

Only a master drummer is allowed to play the iyá. There are hundreds of *toques de santo* (literally "rhythms, strokes") to the orishas, and each orisha has his or her own set of drumming patterns. In Nigeria, there are 600 orishas, but in Cuba only 20-25 orishas are active. The bataleros memorize toques that must be played in a specific tempo and dynamic range. The bataleros must know the toques as a heart knows blood.

The toques include invocations to spirits used to precipitate the possession of a believer. The drums invoke the different orishas, even obliging them to "mount" their devotees – that is, to take possession. When someone is "mounted," they are said to be "having a song." The drums, understandably, are venerated.

The iyá, as the lead drum, has the most complicated rhythms. The player is the most knowledgeable of the three drummers, having served his apprenticeship on the other two drums. He has the most freedom for embellishment within the rhythmic patterns set by ancient custom. He may change the level of intensity, but his creativity must remain within the traditional musical standards that were established approximately 500 years ago in west Africa. He is responsible for maintaining the pattern of the chant while simultaneously guiding the other players through the maze of rhythmic complexities. During the ceremony, the iyá player uses all of his aesthetic abilities to call, praise, and appease the orishas.

To the right of the lead drummer sat a small, almost wizened man wearing a red muscleman T-shirt that hung loosely from his narrow shoulders. He played the *okónkolo*, the smallest drum. Approximately two feet long, his okónkolo also had a banderos, but no bells. The okónkolo is the timekeeper and the rhythmic anchor. The drum's stable rhythms sound the main metric pulses and the ostinati. The okónkolo's rhythms are the least complex, with the shortest cycles and the least variations.

In its traditional place, to the left of the iyá was the *itótele*, the middle-sized drum. This drum is the energizing force and works in close partnership with the iyá. The itótele drummer interprets the iya's playing. He must be constantly alert to discern between the iya's calls (which demand a response) and the embellishments that the iyá drummer may throw in. The itótele's response must be exact in order to fill the proper rhythmic answer to the iyá's call. With this call and response, the drums hold a conversation as automatic as natural speech. The iyá drummer can test the itótele drummer's ability to answer correctly, making a game of musical knowledge.

A singer dressed in an Adidas blue-nylon warm-up suit sat to the side of the drummers. He began a chant in Yoruba in the nasal, high-pitched style made popular by the famous Cuban singer Lázaro Ros, who was the lead soloist for 30 years with The Nacional Folkloric Ensemble and set the standard for singing the Yoruba chants of Santeria. In the 1970s, Ros decided to take the chants into secular music. He was instrumental in founding the Cuban Afro-rock band Sintesis and also recorded with Mezcla, as well as recording a number of solo albums.

The singer and the drummers worked their way through toques calling for individual orishas to be present. When 'Meta-Meta' was played, Chango's "children" approached the iyá drum individually with a slow, side-to-side, one-two/one-two shuffle. Each person did a full-body prostration on the floor – arms straight back along the body, palms up. When 'Rumba Llesa' was played (Oshun's toques), some of the women prostrated by lying on one side with a hand cocked on their hip, then turned to make the gesture on the opposite side. As each person prostrated on the floor, everyone in the room bent to touch the floor with one hand. Then the person rose, crossed both arms across his chest, and bowed to touch his forehead to the drums. Then he kissed the drums – first the iyá, then the itótele, and then the okónkolo. An offering – usually a ten-peso note (50¢) – was left in a basket at the foot of the iyá player. Sometimes a separate note was given to the singer. The singer and drummers weren't getting paid for their services, so the offerings were divided between them, in the spirit of a church collection.

This ritual of calling the orishas, welcoming them, and making an offering to them took about an hour. Then the first initiate – a young Cuban woman – was led into the room, preceded by a woman sprinkling water with her fingers from a bowl to open the way for the initiate to enter. Then came the singer, walking backwards, facing the initiate. She wore a red tunic and white pantaloons – the colors of Chango, her chosen orisha – and carried a live chicken in one hand. (A chicken or dove is a symbol of cleansing.) Assistants balanced a 20-pound stem of bananas on her shoulder as an offering.

Two senior santeros – a man and a woman – guided the novice through the ceremony. She laid full length on the floor before the iyá drum and then stood. People danced a circle around her as she turned within the circle. Then she danced alone before the iyá drum. The drumming increased in tempo. The two assistants ran the initiate twice around a tight circle to gain momentum for the exit through the crowd and into the back room.

This same ceremony was repeated for the second initiate, a man from Spain. He was dressed in a white satin jacket and pantaloons and wore a white crown made of cloth. His orisha was Obatala, the King of the White Cloth, who represents peace and purity. (He is also the father of mankind and the messenger of Olofi, one of the Yoruba names for God.) Obatala is believed to control the mind and all thoughts. He – who can also be a she – is generally identified with Our Lady of Mercy. Many North Americans and Europeans – notably Scandinavians – are becoming initiates in Santeria. New York has a large and active Santeria community.

Two and a half hours of drumming and chanting followed the initiation ceremonies. The 50 people jammed into the 14-foot-square room formed lines, like those in line dancing, and did a one-two shuffle to the right, a one-two shuffle to the left, their arms moving back and forth, elbows out, a bit like the funky chicken. The room was thick with cigarette smoke. The people sang chants in Yoruba at the tops of their voices. The drumming increased to a point at which it seemed humanly impossible that the bataleros could play at such incredible speed. The room filled with a cacophony of what seemed like blurred sound, and yet every note was precise and exactly in its place.

The drum vibrations penetrated me so deeply I'm sure that my DNA helix swayed to the beat. After hours of playing the drums on their laps, bataleros often urinate blood because of the vibrations pounding their kidneys. The chanting and the drumming became deafening, which was part of the intent. All other sounds, all distractions, were to be driven from the mind so that the person was filled with the spirit. People were laughing and smiling, feeling the cathartic, cleansing vitality of the dancing, the drumming, the chanting, the energy of the orishas. The room became hotter and hotter as the dancers went faster and faster, shoulders rolling, hips swiveling, hands clapping.

A young man seemed to be going faster than the others, his head arched back further than the others. He twirled in place. His arms swung wildly, as if they were helicopter blades that had stripped their gears. An elderly lady eyed him, her expression one of anticipation, as if expecting something to happen, perhaps a "mounting" by an orisha. The man's eyes widened and became a fixed stare.

According to Yoruba belief, which is the basis of Santeria, a fixed expression, with the eyes wide and radiant and the gaze seemingly magnified, reflects *áshe*, the brightness of the spirit. The gods have "inner" or "spiritual" eyes with which to see the world of heaven, but they also have "outside" eyes with which to view the world of men and women. When a person comes under the influence of a spirit, his ordinary eyes swell to accommodate the inner eyes, the eyes of the god. From these widened and protruding eyes, the god can see all of the devotees and all of their experiences.

The man blinked. A normal expression returned to his sweat-drenched face. At that moment, a large woman dressed in white suddenly began to spin in a dizzying circle. She staggered for balance as the trance overtook her. A couple of people caught her by the elbows and guided her to the back room, very casually and respectfully.

"The saints eat hearts" is a Santeria saying meaning that the orisha sees into a person's heart and divines his true intentions. The orisha's primary interest is the intention; how that intention is enacted is secondary. Four and a half hours after the ceremony started, I staggered – literally – back out onto the street. My heart felt thoroughly gnawed upon. My brain felt bruised by the drumming, swollen in its now-too-tight cranium.

Ramiro was at my side. "Are you all right?"

I wanted to tell him never to do that to me again, but I stopped myself. I nodded yes. He took me gently by the elbow and we walked down the middle of San Miguel Street on a warm Havana night. "I understand," he said.

I wanted to walk off the Santeria. I thanked Ramiro at his door and set out for the Capitolio, a 20-minute walk away. The Capitolio area of Old Havana is one of the city's hot spots. The Capitolio building, itself modeled after the US capital in Washington, DC, is the former seat of the Cuban Congress, which no longer exists. The government's buildings are now grouped around the Plaza de la Revolution, where Castro works in a huge, nondescript, Soviet-block-style building. Now a beautifully restored tourist site, the Capitolio houses the Museum of Natural Science, the Museum of Science and Technology, a café, and a cyber café, complete with email access. The street in front of the Capitolio is the central hub for the botalas. Each botalas has a prescribed route around the city, much like a bus route, which begins and ends at the Capitolio, where you can transfer to another taxi to take you to your destination, if necessary.

The botalas, parked two deep in the middle of the broad avenue, are an amazing collection of vintage American cars, most of them rolling junk-heaps. American male tourists of a certain age get goo-goo eyed at the sight of the old cars, perhaps because the cars trigger flashbacks of teenage nights in back seats. However, the cars are a major contributor to Havana's air pollution, which can be considerable, and the drivers don't harbor a romantic sentimentality for the cars, which can be a nightmare to keep running. One botala driver complained mightily to me about the cost of keeping his 1947 Chevy on the road. "You know what one piston cost? You know?" he exclaimed. "I could not buy a piston for this car so I had to get one made. You know, machined special. You know what that cost?

You know?" The very thought worked the guy into a foam. "Seven thousand peso!" He slammed his hand against the steering wheel. "A piston for a new Mercedes doesn't cost that much!"

The botalas drivers are creative geniuses in keeping their livelihood operating. They fashion new parts out of scraps of whatever, including spoons, discarded strips of metal, and wood. Many of the drivers are from the countryside and their farm work has made them well seasoned in the ingenious skill of keeping machinery running. When the price of gasoline far outpaced diesel fuel, they took the diesel engines out of tractors and installed them in their cars.

The botalas drivers are a free enterprise, which, I was told, is a pain in Castro's ideological neck. The drivers are wealthy compared to many professionals stuck on a government salary. By law, a person can only own one car in Cuba, so a botala owner buys a car for his wife, one for his brother, one his cousin, and one for his six-year-old son, and he has a taxi fleet. The botalas are absolutely necessary to the transportation needs of Cubans, so the government can't put them out of business or take a cut of their fare, as with the official taxis, because that would drive the fare beyond the means of the ordinary Cuban. The botalas drivers are the government's Catch 22.

Vintage cars are exclaimed over by foreign visitors, whether they are beautifully restored or rolling deathtraps. However, not much attention is given to the new mid-priced Japanese, Korean, and French cars. If the number of late-model cars – including expensive American SUVs, BMWs, Mercedes, and Audis – on the streets is accepted as an economical indicator, then the Cuban middle class is re-emerging. However, bicycles and motorcycles with sidecars are a very common form of transportation on Havana's streets. When the devastating economics of the Special Period made gasoline a luxury item, 100,000 bicycles were imported, and many of these vintage bikes are still on the road. American male tourists of a certain age do not goggle at the bikes.

There are two hot-spot walks that converge at Capitolio. One starts at the Malecón and goes up Paseo de Martí, better known as the Prado, an elevated classical-Spanish promenade that runs down the center of the street. This broad, lovely walkway with narrow traffic lanes on each side was completed in 1852. I felt classy just walking under the canopy of shade trees. I'd sit on the benches in the side nooks, a *flaneur* elegantly sprawled, to watch the parade of people pass. A favorite watching spot was midway up the Padro between Calle Colon and Refugio, where people gathered for the informal Se Permuta ("For Exchange") to trade information on available housing and to arrange swaps.

At the end of the Prado is the Parque Central, a shady square flanked by five-star hotels. This is the starting point for the other hot-spot walk, down Calle de Obispo to Plaza de Armas, a walk that cuts right through restored Old Havana. The El Floridita bar/restaurant, made famous by Hemingway's drinking habits, sits on the corner of Obispo and Monserrate, across from the tiny Plazuela de Albear. The Floridita is rather staid, and in that it's hard to imagine Hemingway in there raising hell. I had expected something scruffier, more working-class Cuban, which it might have been in Hemingway's time. Now the place has glass doors that open onto a pleasant, up-scale bar with tables bedecked with white linen tablecloths. A dining room hides behind red velvet curtains. A trio often plays soothing music. I've been to such places in Chicago suburbs.

Down the block from the Floridita, along Monserrate Street, there are a couple of much livelier bars. The Monserrate bar is not sealed away behind glass doors; it is without pretensions and designed not to suffer damage if the good times became too rambunctious. The outside walls are open latticework, which allows the live music – Cuban dance, salsa, timba, and rumba – to pour out and the people standing on the curb to peer in. Dancers crowd the middle of the room. This is where I would expected to find a hale and hearty Hemingway, half lit on *mojitos*, boisterously backslapping friends and strangers alike.

Calle de Obispo, a narrow walking street lined with attractive shops, is a comfort zone for tourists, familiar and yet foreign. I preferred Obispo's night life to that of the more touted La Rampa. La Rampa has a big-city-edge feel, a place where indulgences are offered and easily purchased. Obispo has more charm and atmosphere for a hand-in-hand stroll. Small, intimate bars along the street feature live music popular with the locals as well as visitors. The bars have a neighborhood hang-out feel, an old glove that an outsider can slip on and feel as though they're wearing a natural part of the Cuban costume.

The Hotel Ambos Mundos, where Hemingway stayed while he thought out the plot of *For Whom The Bell Tolls* (according to the guidebooks), is at the lower end of Obispo, a block from Plaza de Armas. Like the Floridita, the hotel has been refurbished with genteel respectability, which is not a put-down. Genteel respectability is comfortable, pleasant, and great for a good night's sleep. The open lobby is inviting and the hotel bar an enjoyable place to take a break. The building was the first photography studio in Havana, founded by George Washington Halsey in 1841, according to the plaque on the wall.

Before reaching Plaza de Armas, I took a right turn on Calle de Mercaderas. Several square blocks surrounding this street are a fine example of the Ministry of Tourism at work. Calle de Mercaderas, populated by several very Cuban restaurants and hotels, has reclaimed the colonial feel of Old Havana and has not been littered with tourist traps. Mercaderas ends at Plaza Vieja, which was one of the four main squares of Havana when the Spanish still ruled. Once a market for peasants and free negroes, the spacious square is currently under restoration. The large fountain in the center was rebuilt after the original was demolished in the 1930s to make way for an underground parking lot. Several of the grand buildings that ring the plaza are being brought back to their former grandeur.

I wandered back to Plaza de Armas, thinking about treating myself to a cappuccino at one of the two outdoor cafés that had live music, but the cafés were full of a mixed lot of Cubans and tourists. A block away was another café with music, at the entrance of the short, narrow passageway leading to Cathedral Square. I decided to try the outdoor café in Cathedral Square for its European atmosphere, but it, too, was full. Against one wall sat a group of old men playing son. They looked like a tourist's snapshot.

I wandered on across the Malecón to admire the fortress across the bay. It was a thoroughly enjoyable walk, full of history and music and atmosphere. I decided to try my luck with a botala for a ride home. Within a minute, one pulled over for me. I gave my address to the driver, the only female taxi driver I encountered in Havana. I was most puffed up with myself now. I had been to a Santeria ceremony, walked the old city like a native, heard at least eight bands as I wandered about, and had now flagged down a botala. I felt very Cuban. As soon as I got in the car, the driver said, "You're North American, aren't you?"

"United States," I admitted.

"That's good," she replied in perfect English. She looked like a matronly housewife who had surreptitiously sneaked out in the family car to earn extra pesos. As it turned out, she was a retired economist who didn't want to stay at home. "I've always had my own money," she said. "My children ask, 'Why do you drive, Mama? You don't have to.' But I do have to."

Driving a taxi was her best option to make money. "But you know how much it cost just to turn this car on? Fifty peso. That about $2.50 for you. And then it breaks down, and I'm not a mechanic, like those clever men from the country, and neither is my husband, a doctor, who is going to retire soon. And then what will he do? He says that he wants to drive, too, but there are no more botalas licenses available. He's says that he will drive illegally, because we'll need the money when he retires. If he gets caught, it's a 10,000-peso fine. He's says that he'll take the risk."

We pulled up at my house. "There can be so many problems in Cuba," my driver said. "But it's a good place, isn't it?"

7 Bata Drums

Tradition says that Chango, lord of lightning, fire, thunder, war, and virility, made the first set of bata drums, although Anyan, the deity of the drums, presides over their actual playing. Chango was also the legendary fourth (or third, depending on the source) *oba* ("king") of the Yoruba city of Oyo in Nigeria. His reign purportedly lasted seven violent years.

According to legend, King Chango was fascinated with magic and personally possessed great magical powers. He didn't do parlor tricks, such as making alligators leap from empty bags, but instead had grander visions, like changing the weather. One day, he inadvertently caused a thunderstorm that destroyed his palace, killing many of his wives and children. King Chango was so sorrowful and full of remorse that he abdicated and hanged himself.

When he was confirmed as safely dead, his enemies gleefully rejoiced at his disgrace. They vilified his name, heaped scorn upon his memory, and smeared his reputation with every creative invective imaginable. They consigned him to the dungheap of history reserved for especially nasty people. Shortly after this orgy of vengeance, a series of very violent thunderstorms devastated large parts of Oyo. Many of Chango's superstitious former followers attributed the storms to the dead king's anger. They cried out, "Oba ko so!" ("The king did not hang!") and made many sacrifices in his honor. He was proclaimed an orisha and is worshipped to this day.

Chango's mythic thunder and lightning may be traced to Jakuta, a Yoruba solar deity. Jakuta, the stone-thrower, was a guardian of morality and goodness. Whenever people did evil in the eyes of

Oloddumare, the Supreme Creator, Jakuta would hurl stones of fire from above at the offender. Chango's attributes include retribution and justice.

With a role model like Chango looking over their collective shoulder, Cuban drummers take their music very seriously indeed. Chango is a party-hardy guy who loves to dance, is an incorrigible skirt-chaser, and has an infamous reputation as a passionate lover with a gargantuan ego. His vanity matches that of any self-delusional diva queen. It's understandable why Chango has a cult following among Cuban males, whether they play the drums or not. The central theme of Chango's cult is power, be it procreative, authoritative, destructive, medicinal, or moral. He symbolizes raw power and control over general difficulties and enemies, both physical and spiritual. Playing the bata drums denotes the grandeur of a man capable of conquering enemies. I am not suggesting that every Cuban drummer is a wild man, a Chango waiting to be unleashed; they just play like wild men.

Many Cuban drummers – especially those who play the bata drums – are initiates into Santeria on at least the elementary "necklaces" (*collares* or *elekas*) and "warrior" levels. The necklaces are five strands of beads in the colors of the five major orishas that can protect the wearer against all forms of evil. It's common to see Cubans wearing bracelets and necklaces in the colors of their orisha – for example, blue and white for Yemayá, red and white for Chango, and yellow and green for Orula, the Lord of Divination.

Regino Jiménez Sáez is a santero and a master bata drummer. He is one of five men in Cuba allowed to hand-make sacred bata drums. He teaches drumming and has been a guest lecturer at several universities in the United States. I met him at the initiation ceremony. He invited me to his home, and several days afterwards I took up his invitation.

The front door of his house in Cayo Hueso opens directly onto the street. I knocked softly. The door was opened by Regino's youngest daughter, a teenager. Her father and mother were not at home, she said. It was her mother's birthday and they were out shopping but would be back shortly. I was welcome to wait inside.

The rooms were spacious, with 14-foot-high ceilings. The floor was of white tile decorated with green and red floral designs. On the back of the front door hung a string of garlic to keep malevolent spirits at bay. Above the television was a velvet painting of a stag against the background of shimmering, icy mountains.

I sat on a couch in the living room. The daughter sat on the other couch and read movie magazines, obviously bored. Her older sister was in the other room soaking her feet in a pale-blue bucket to soften the calluses on her heels so that she could scrape them off more easily. Hanging on one wall were four consecrated, sacred drums made by Regino. In a corner was a three-foot-high altar to Chango. On the altar stood Chango's staff, about three feet long and completely wrapped in red and white beads, with only Chango's dark, hawk-beaked face uncovered, a face with remarkably Inca features. A double lightning bolt – Chango's symbol of power – came out of its head. On the floor, a wooden, double-bladed ax rested against the altar, one blade white and the other red. (Double-edged power can create or destroy.) A figurine of St Barbara in flowing Catholic robes stood on the floor next to the altar. (St Barbara is Chango's Catholic beard. Her goblet is a symbol of Chango's mortar, the vessel in which he prepares his powerful spells. The sword in her left hand represents Chango's double-edged ax.) A small, black-skinned doll in a ruffled blue dress – the kind of toy a small girl might play with – stood on the other side of the altar.

Regino and his wife arrived laden with packages, all practical household stuff. He was a dark, handsome man with the slightest of gray showing in his short black hair. I felt that he had empathic eyes capable of seeing the emotional person under the physical trappings. His most impressive feature was his rounded, powerful shoulders. After a flurry of putting things away, he sat on the couch beside me and talked about the sacred and the secular bata drums.

"The sacred bata speaks between man and God. Through the organized sound, the chants and drumming patterns, we communicate with the orishas and with the spirits of the dead, our ancestors. In ceremonies, the spirit of an orisha can possess people, as you saw the other day. The chants, the language, the communication of the bata drums open the way to communicate, to ask assistance of your orisha, and to give respect to the orisha. It is believed that Ána, the messenger of the gods, lives inside the bata drum. In the ceremony known as *oru del igbodu*, the drums speak with the voice of the gods."

There are two types of bata drums, Regino explained, the *aberikula* and the *ána*. The aberikula is not consecrated. It is made differently from the ána, the baptized drum. The aberikula can be played by anyone. It's the bata drum played in popular music, in jazz bands, or in any entertainment event. The ána, played exclusively in Santeria ceremonies, can be played only by bataleros who have gone through the special Santeria initiation.

"The drummers you saw at the ceremony were not just musicians," Regino said. "They have had long and special training in the rituals of Santeria. For them, playing the bata is a spiritual and sacred experience. The music is not danced to for enjoyment only. The music is how you talk to the gods. The ána has active sacred principles. You have to do a ceremony for the drum and for the person who is going to play the bata drum. To be initiated into the drum, you have to ask permission of the drums. Not everyone can be initiated, and only men are initiated bata drummers. The bata is a family. The iyá drum is the mother and the bataleros are part of her family. They are called *omó Ána*, 'children of the god of the drum.' Kinship relations and the male/female polarities are essential to bata symbolism."

Bataleros memorize toques, the rhythms for each song associated with a specific orisha. "A toque, the 'beat,' has a standard rhythmic phrase," Regino explained. "Many toques derive from African religious drumming, in which particular rhythmic patterns are used to summon individual gods. These patterns have been set for hundreds of years and cannot be changed. A Cuban percussionist is judged not by his energy level but by his knowledge and use of standard toques and variations in his improvisations and in support of the band. There are hundreds of toques to learn. People have played the bata drums for 40 years and still not mastered all the toques. There is bata music for war that applies to battles between good and evil. There is a rhythm for a hunter that mimics the stalking of the hunter. There is always something to learn."

A batalero must learn three types of phrases: *conversaciones* ("conversations"), *llames* ("calls"), and *viros*. In conversaciones (also called *lenguas* in Cuba), the drummer is said to be talking to the orisha. The iyá always speaks to the itótele while the okónkolo marks the beat. The iyá is the only drum that "asks" for changes in the rhythm or toque.

Llames are played by the iyá as a cueing device for the two other drums. For each llame, there is an appropriate response, or *respuesto*. Llames are played at the start of each toque, or in the middle, to indicate the start of another pattern or a conversation. Like the conversaciones, the llames occur at precise points in the ritual or in the development of the music, not at the whim of the player.

Viros (also called *vuelta*) are various successive rhythms in a song that pass from one drum to another. The viro can occur when dancers are portraying a different attribute of an orisha. These bata patterns are also used in secular music.

Practitioners of Santeria believe the bata drums' rhythms to be sonic representations of divine principles. If the sounds are properly organized throughout the chanting, drumming, and recitation, the gap between the physical and spiritual worlds can be bridged. This manipulation of ritualized music is the key to opening the door between man/woman and the orishas. The rhythms are based on a drum language that represents the tonal changes and speech patterns of the Yoruba language. The drumming patterns are not written down but are passed on orally from generation to generation of bata drummers.

"Several years ago, I was in Nigeria, in the land of Oyo, of Chango," Regino said. "We were there to investigate what we were doing with the music and to study, as this drumming is very ancient. When we were drumming, the Nigerians could hear that it was Cuban drumming. Our Cuban accent makes the Yoruba language sound a little different than that in Nigeria. We went to the Yoruba temple, where the king of Oyo listened to us. He could distinguish the rhythms and the chants and the language. Though the phonetics were different, he understood what we were transmitting, communicating the Chango rhythm and chants, the dancing.

"The language of ancient Yoruba in the drumming has been maintained in Cuba more than in Africa. In this, the African traditions are being reinvented in Cuba. The African slaves brought their traditions with them, but in Africa many of the traditions have become lost. But in Cuba, many of those traditions have been maintained. Yes, it has been transformed, but we have maintained this through the centuries, so it's the closest to the African traditions."

Other drums besides the bata used in Cuban music trace their ancestry back to Africa. The *yuka* drums, which are the mainstay percussion of rumba, are of Bantu (Congolese) origin. Three types of long, cylindrical drum make up a yuka set; the large *caja*, the medium-sized *mula*, and the smaller *cachimbo*. The caja is played with bare hands, while the mula and cachimbo are played with one hand and a stick. The word *yuka* also refers to a style of music created by the slaves on the sugar plantations in Cuba. When the African slave music melded with the slavemasters' Spanish decima, the basis for rumba was born.

The conga drum is integral to Cuban salsa music and is believed to derive from the Bantu *makuta*. The largest conga drum is called the *tumbadora*. The basic pattern for the conga in salsa is called *tumbao*, from the Spanish verb *tumbar* ("to tumble, fall, knock down, throw down, heave down"). In colloquial usage, it means "to inebriate, overpower, stun." All of these terms can apply to salsa.

The middle-sized conga drum has various names: *conga*, *segunda*, and *tres golpes*. The smallest conga drum is called the *quinto*, from the Spanish *requinto*, a name also given to the similarly high-pitched drum used in Puerto Rican *bomba* and *plena* music.

The conga drum should not be confused with the bongo, which is a Cuban original. The bongo was invented in eastern Cuba and was essential for playing son music, which also came from that end of the island. The basic bongo rhythm, the *martillo* ("hammer"), is a steady, eighth-note pattern played with alternating hands. Beats one, two, three, and four are stressed, which produces a hammer-like sound.

All of these drums have found their way into Cuban popular

Three young conga players making their debut at a rumba party

music. "A lot of music groups are now using the bata," Regino said, "but the bata drums of secular music have only one sound, in part because they are played by only one person, compared to the complexity of the bata played in Santeria ceremonies. It takes three people to play the bata drums, but most bands cannot afford three drummers only for the bata. But one person playing cannot achieve a lot of the [richness] and connotations. With only one person playing, that causes changes in the rhythm pattern. For example, there is a toque that goes *a-cha-cha-la-ca-fula*, a very fast rhythm. When three players play it, the rhythm has a lot of conversation. Only one player cannot do that. In popular music, the bata is stripped down, made simpler. The rhythms of the orishas [are] in popular music, although only some of the toques. Not all of them. The rhythms for the orishas are fast, and so they can be adapted to the popular music. Bata has come into popular music because of the orishas. They are very strong."

Batarumba, a fairly recent development in Cuban music, uses two congas, guitars, and bata drums. The bata has been created inside the rumba because the rumba has musical connotations and everything – like the bata – can be inserted into the rumba. "It was a controversy among the bata and the people talking to the congas," Regino said. "It's a popular thing now."

The clave is at the root of bata drumming, as it is for all Cuban music. *Clave* is a Spanish word that translates as "clef, key, or keystone." In Cuban musical terminology it means either a pair of sticks for playing rhythms, the specific pattern played, or the underlying rules that govern this pattern. Clave is a two-measure pattern in which each measure is diametrically opposed. The two measures are not at odds, but rather they are balanced opposites, like positive and negative, expansive and contractive, or the poles of magnets. As the pattern is repeated, an alternation from one polarity to the other takes place, creating pulse and rhythmic drive. Were the pattern to be suddenly reversed, the rhythm would be destroyed, as with reversing one magnet within a series.

Bataleros know the starting points for their parts in a particular toque by its relationship with the clave pattern. The length of the part is judged by how long it takes for the part to be synchronized with the start of the clave, or how many repetitions before it lines up again with the start of the clave. In bata drumming, the patterns are held in place according to both the internal relationships between the drums and their relationships with the clave. This double fit is a natural and integral part of the bata rhythms.

Bata drums made their first public appearance in 1937, when the Cuban social anthropologist Fernándo Ortiz presented them at a performance of traditional music, but it wasn't until the 1950s that bata drums moved into secular music, when the well-known sacred bata drummer Jesús Pérez made that bold move. This caused a huge controversy between the traditionalists and those who found nothing wrong in bringing spiritual music out to the people, a bit like taking gospel out of the church and onto the stage. Pérez took a lot of personal heat for his "heresy," although he was eventually forgiven, because he is such a nice, well-respected man. Since the early 1970s, bata drum ensembles have been included in the renowned Cuban jazz band Irakere, Jerry Gonzalez's Fort Apache Band, and the Puerto

Rican groups Batacumbele and Zaperooko. Pablo Menéndez uses a bata set in his band, Mezcla. It is no longer unusual for the bata to be part of a popular-music band.

"The sacred bata, the *fundamento de santo*, or 'fundamental drum,' is constructed differently from the secular bata," Regino said. "The sacred bata is made by hand. Now there are factories that make the secular bata. The ordinary bata uses metal pegs for tuning and can be made out of strips of wood. The ordinary bata does not have bells around the heads, either. The sacred drum has strips of leather to tune it. The sacred drums are more melodic and have more sounds. The fundamental drum must be made out of a single piece of hardwood, either cedar or mahoe, because the bata is a symbol of unity. I use an ax to hollow out the piece of wood. The drums have very specific sizes and must be measured carefully at every stage. What is inside the drum cannot be seen and cannot be lost. That is fundamental. For the drumheads, we use the skin of deer, goat, or cattle, but the males only. The skins also receive a ceremony before they are put on the drums.

"You have to have a wide knowledge of the proper bata in order to make a fundamental. I do a certain ceremony when I make a drum, and there is a ceremony for the person who will play the drum. To make a drum, I have to know the person well. It has to be a real man to contain the power. I have to know that the man will not be offensive and will be careful. You can't make a drum for just anyone. There is a lot of demand for bata drums, but I don't make drums for a business. Nowadays it has become commercialized, [it's] becoming a business, but that's not correct. To make the bata as a business will lessen the meaning of those drums. The drums have a lot of value for the santeros and the Santeria religion."

8 Santeria

It's said that, when a santero or santera wants to harm an enemy, or have a favor granted, or call down a benefit, he or she goes to a ceiba (silk cotton) tree at midnight, removes his or her clothes, and walks around the tree several times while touching the trunk. The petitioner sweetly murmurs to the tree, which is considered sacred in Santeria and is the basis of the greatest magic in the religion. The person sings softly to the tree in order to persuade the spirit to grant the wish requested. The ceiba can assist in the casting of great beneficial spells for love and increase. The tree can also be an accomplice in spells for death and destruction.

The tree is so highly respected that a santero will not cross its shadow without first asking permission. The spirit represented by the tree is very sensitive and easily offended. If offended, the ceiba will not give its protection to the santero, whose spells will be ineffective without the sanction of the tree's spirit. The tree does not discriminate between good and evil as long as its service is paid and full respect is shown during the transaction. Santeros believe that even lightning respects the ceiba. (In reality, the tree is seldom struck by lightning.)

The trunk of the ceiba can be used to cast evil spells, and the earth around the tree is used in black magic, while the tree's shade attracts the spirits. The shade itself gives supernatural strength to all of the spells buried beneath it. The ceiba also has a very positive practical use: the roots and leaves have medicinal value. Bush doctors in various countries use the ceiba's leaves to treat venereal disease and difficulties in the urinary tract. The leaves are also reputed to be excellent in the treatment of anemia, while the bark is brewed into a special tea to help barren women conceive.

A ceiba tree used for Santeria purposes stands in the northeast corner of the Plaza de Armas, the oldest plaza in Havana. Offerings – fruit, rum-soaked cakes, pastries, and money – are purportedly buried under its roots and are strewn about the trunk, although this may be an urban myth. I went to check it out.

The tree stands behind a black iron fence. A man sat on a folding chair inside the gate. I thought he was there to collect an entrance fee, but no such fee was asked. Instead, he offered advice on the proper procedure for asking the tree for a blessing. "Walk counter-clockwise around the tree with your hand on the trunk, stating a request on each circuit," he told me, as if giving directions to a local restaurant. I did as instructed. I took care not to trip on the gnarled roots underfoot while looking for signs of turned earth, so as not to step on buried offerings. The tree was perhaps four feet in diameter, and the path around it was packed down hard. My fingertips traced the narrow band made shiny by thousands of wishes brushed on the gray bark. First time around: may my friends and loved ones enjoy good health. Second time around: may my friends and loved ones have prosperity. Third time around: may I be free of the desire to have desires. After the third circuit, I threw a few coins down among the scattering of others at the tree's trunk. Then I added a bill as a little extra incentive for my third wish. That one would take a miracle.

In Cuba, the ceiba stands in for the iroko (*Chlorophora excelsa*), a species of African mahogany. As the iroko does not grow in the Caribbean, the Africans transplanted to Cuba by slavery substituted the ceiba. The ceiba is worshipped throughout the Caribbean where west African peoples were forced into slave labor. When plantation owners instructed their slaves to cut down the ceiba to make way for new fields, the Africans made sure that the tree understood that it was the master who ordered such a desecration. The iroko represents one of the African aspects of the Conception of Mary and is venerated by many Africans along the coast of Guinea. The Kongo people call the tree *nkunia case sami* ("the tree of God"),

Mamá Ungunda, and *Iggi-Olorun*. Santeros believe that the ceiba is a female tree with an essentially maternal spirit.

There are also stately Royal palms in the Plaza Armas. In Cuba, the palm is almost as spiritually powerful as the ceiba. It is believed to be where Chango lives, the orisha of thunder, lightning, and fire. This is based on the fact that the palm is often hit by lightning bolts, which are weapons of Chango. When lightning hits a palm, that is Chango coming home.

Here's one of the legends behind the palm and Chango. Chango, an incorrigible woman-chaser, asked a small lizard to deliver a present to one of his lovers. The lizard put the gift in its mouth and scurried towards the beloved's house. On the way, the lizard stumbled in its haste and the gift became stuck in its throat, which explains why the skin of a lizard's throat is distended. Because of this unfortunate *faux pas*, the lizard was unable to deliver the gift. When Chango discovered this, he became enraged and verbally reamed the lizard a new you-know-what. Great balls of fire blasted from Chango's mouth with every word. The lizard couldn't utter a word in its defense, because it was scared speechless and also because the gift still blocked its throat. In fear of being roasted alive, the lizard ran up a palm tree. Chango threw a lightning bolt at the tree. Ever since, the palm tree has been the object of Chango's anger – and his lightning bolts – because the lizard still hides among the branches to protect himself from the orisha.

In the northeastern United States, around New York, where Santeria has a wide following, the elm tree is said to belong to Chango. Santeros use the elm to cast their spells, because neither the ceiba nor the palm grow in the cold climate.

The Santeria religion originated along the Niger River among the Yoruba people in what is now Nigeria and Benin. It was transported to the Caribbean along with the west African slaves. Yorubaland, as the home territory was known before the modern states were created, was a series of kingdoms with powerful and complex social structures. The most important of the kingdoms, Benin, existed from the twelfth century until 1896, when English imperialists took control. Benin was a theocratic autocracy in which the king, or *oba*, had absolute power.

The people had a very advanced culture, as can be seen by the bronze and ivory artworks, dating from archaic times up to the 17th century, that are now in museums throughout the world.

The downfall of the civilization began at the beginning of the 17th century, when the Ewe people invaded the region of Dahomey and the neighboring kingdoms. The Yoruba tribes fled to the Nigerian coast, where rival African chiefs, Arabs, and European slave-traders captured many of their people and shipped them off to the New World.

For four centuries, seaports in the wide scoop of the Gulf of Benin were the epicenter of the slave trade. The Yoruba shipped to Cuba and other Caribbean ports most certainly left their homeland from these seaports. In Cuba, the Yoruba became known as the Lucumi. (The word *lucumi* means "friendship.") Some researchers believe that the word derives from *akumi*, which means "I am Aku." In Sierra Leone, where the Yoruba also live, they are known as the Aku.

The Lucumis in Cuba adopted Catholic imagery for their deities in a subterfuge to protect their belief system from being destroyed by the Spanish slavemasters. Chango is identified with St Barbara; Oggún – a god of war and patron of blacksmiths, as well as Chango's brother – is associated with St Peter; Olofi (or Olorun) is syncretized as both the Eternal Father and the Holy Spirit; while Oyá, mistress of the wind and lightning and queen of the cemetery, the guardian between life and death, is disguised as St Teresa of Avila.

The term Santeria is derived from the Spanish word *santo* ("saints") and literally means "the worship of saints." Although Santeria is the most widely accepted term, and not disputed, many santeros prefer the term Regla de Ocha.

Today in Cuba, Lucumi and Santeria are synonymous. Santeria is practiced primarily in western Cuba, focused in Havana and Matanzas, where Yoruba were settled as slaves for the sugar plantations. The eastern end of the island, Oriente Province, is today much more predominantly black, but the slave population there was from Konga and Santeria did not have the cultural base to flourish there.

There was a time when Santeria had to hide behind the skirts of

Catholicism, but that has changed. Up until 40 years ago, Santeria was a persecuted religion and its adherents were actively chased down and jailed. Its practitioners were portrayed as people who believed in black magic and blood sacrifices and were ostracized, socially marginalized, and – perhaps worst – treated as some colorful aberration, a quaint remnant of the uneducated, primitive African past. But the religion lived underground and, even from that position, influenced the society and culture, largely through music.

When Castro took over the government in 1959, he instigated policies that brought Cuba's African heritage to a position of equity – at least as far as a government can encourage through policy. The African-based music and the arts moved more into the mainstream, and so did Santeria. The religion was no longer outlawed. But it wasn't until 1992, the Special Period, that Santeria really burst into the open.

Santeria is a very practical religion. If you need money or food, you go to your orisha and ask. If you want a love match, you conduct the proper ceremony to your orisha. When the Special Period hit, nearly everyone needed food and money. They needed to get school uniforms for their children or an extra carton of milk or their cars fixed, so they came right out with Santeria and asked. People no longer felt it necessary to be Catholic and go to Mass, as was once part and parcel of Santeria. They wore the colors of their orishas and openly practiced their rituals.

The power of an orisha is not an intangible, mystical force nurtured by the faith of the believers. It is not something sublimely ethereal that sustains the "should and could" through faith. It's raw energy, an awesome power, visually and materially discernible. One does not pray to God through the orishas on bended knees and hope that the orishas will convey the message to the godhead; the orisha is a direct manifestation of God. The orishas are not gods *per se* but children and servants of Oloddumare, the central creative force. Every individual's life is overseen by orishas, who are much like the guardian angels of Christendom. An orisha can say at once whether or not a wish will be granted.

However, the orishas are not mere pawns of human beings in their search for wealth and power. The orishas are the mouthpiece of the godhead, and through them God makes his wishes and designs known to mankind. An orisha is always willing to help and to guide but is ready also to chastise when God's laws are broken. The worship of the orishas is not easy, because they demand strict obedience and total surrender to their will. Santeria is a highly ritualistic religion, in which strict protocol is observed.

Although many of the west Africans who came to the New World as slaves may not have spoken the same language, they nonetheless shared a basic fundamental belief system, based in nature spirits who can intercede for man with the gods, who are too powerful for mere mortals to address directly. This concept is also found in Catholicism when people pray to a saint, such as St Mary, to act on their behalf with the Supreme Deity. The west Africans – the Fon, the Nago, the Kong, the Bantu, the Ibo, the Dahomeans, and other tribes – mixed together as slaves, borrowing and adapting from each other's belief systems. Voodoo, from the ancient Haitian ritual of Vodun; the Obeah of Jamaica; the Umbanda, Macumba, and Candomblé of Brazil – all of these share similarities and even some of the same deities. Chango and Yemayá are familiar figures in Candomblé. In Voodoo, Santeria's Oggún is known as Oggou and Eleggual is called Legba.

Orishas have great power and magic, yet are believable and human in their behavior, and Chango is a prime example of this. The gods of the Yoruba pantheon share many of the characteristics of the Greek gods on Mount Olympus. Their behaviour, for instance, is very human – lustful, fallible, humorous, jealous, vain, egotistical, power hungry, generous, loving, angry, protective, and vengeful. They are equally capable of being benevolent or nasty dictators. However, an important difference between the Greek and the Yoruba deities is that Zeus *et al* are consigned to legends and books on mythology while Chango and his crowd are very much alive and active today in the affairs of mankind. When was the last time you heard of someone worshipping, in all seriousness, at the altar of Zeus? There might be a classicist throwback out there doing something like that, but thousands upon thousands of people in many countries include the orishas in their daily lives in a very real way.

The exact etymology of the word *orisha* is uncertain. It may derive from the word *asha*, meaning "religious ceremony," or from the roots *ri* ("to see") and *sha* ("to choose").

In Santeria, God is known as Oloddumare. Oloddumare is not created; he always existed. Oloddumare is immanent, omnipotent, and omniscient. There are other names associated with Oloddumare, too. Olorun is the owner of the *orun* ("heavens"), as well as the deity who lives in heaven, and is identified by both heaven and the sun. To the santeros, Oloddumare is God as the Almighty and Olorun is God as the Creator of the material world. Olofi, or Olofin, meanwhile, is a common name used to refer to God, and is syncretized as Jesus Christ, while Eledda is the spark of life in each human being, often associated with one's guardian angel. The orishas were created by Oloddumare to manifest his will and to express his essence in nature.

Santeria's fundamental belief is that destiny begins before birth in Ile-Olofi, "the house of God," or heaven. The Yoruba believe that we are the children of the gods. Race, language, and place of birth are of no importance to the orishas, who encompass the entire world with their divine powers and claim all human beings as their children. The Santeria priesthood perceives the orishas to be their universal parents, and the orishas are felt to be part of a devotee's extended family. That extended family includes dead ancestors.

The *eggun* are the spirits of one's ancestors. This may include the elders who belonged to the same Santeria "house" or "family" in which one has been initiated. It is important to ensure that the eggun are happy and enlightened so that they may be able to grant their protection to their devotees. Ancestor worship and belief in the powers of the eggun in Santeria can be traced to a similar belief among the Yoruba. In Nigeria, the spirits of the ancestors are believed to take possession of the living.

Ancestral spirits are considered to be relevant to the welfare of a descent group or its members. The spirits of the ancestors of a kin group are looked to for assistance in economic and social matters, and some misfortunes – famine, poor crops, personal losses – are ascribed to failure to have performed the appropriate rituals or to having misbehaved in some way. Everyone will become an ancestral spirit, as that is part of a person's development. Death is not a terminal stage but rather one among many steps on the road to accomplishing purpose.

The holy city in Santeria is Ile-Ife, probably the oldest town of the Yoruba people, and is considered to be the ancestral home of the Yoruba people. (The word *ile* means "home.") The Yoruba also honor Ile-Ife as a holy city and the legendary birthplace of mankind. It is regarded as an oracle city, very much like Delphi in ancient Greece, and it's a pilgrimage center for all Yoruba. For the Yoruba, Ile-Ife is Rome, Mecca, Bethlehem, and Jerusalem. Also called Ife-Loudun (population approximately 300,000), Ile-Ife is in the State of Osun in southwestern Nigeria at the intersection of roads from Ibadan, Ilesha, and Ondo. It is primarily a city of town-dwelling farmers who cultivate palm oil and kernels, yams, cassava, maize, pumpkins, and kola nuts for the local markets. The city is a major collecting point for the cocoa and cotton grown in the surrounding area, and is also the home of Obafemi Awolowo University (formerly the University of Ife), founded in 1961 and one of Nigeria's major centers of education. The university operates a teaching hospital, an observatory, and a major library, and is affiliated with the Institute of Agricultural Research and Training.

The Yoruba constitutes one of the major ethnic groups in Africa. They number approximately 25 million, and their cultural history spreads across a large area of west Africa. In Nigeria, Yoruba culture covers all of the states of Lagos, Ogun, Oyo, and Ondo, as well as the Ilorin and Kabba regions of the Kwarea State. In neighboring Benin (formerly Dahomey), the core of the Yoruba culture covers the area between the Weme River and the Nigerian border, while the Ana and Fe (Ife) subgroups of Yoruba culture occupy the Atakpame region of the neighboring Togo Republic. Influences of the Yoruba culture are found in Cuba, Haiti, Brazil, and most Caribbean islands as a result of the slave trade. (The Yoruba were the largest single group of African people in the African diaspora.)

The exact date of the founding of Ile-Ife is uncertain, but according to a monograph entitled "Edo: Origin Of Ile-Ife Monarchy," compiled by Nowamagbe A Omoigui, MD, MPH,

FACC, the story starts in around AD 1068, when Ogiso Owodo, the last *ogiso* ("king") of the Kingdom of Igodomigodo, ascended the throne following the death of his father, Ogiso Arigho. His capital was the city of Ile.

Owodo was a hermaphrodite with fully developed male and female sexual organs, which gave him conflicting emotions, causing rather erratic behavior and character. He murdered his mother, an act which was covered up by his father, and had a strong passion for his late father's senior wife, Esagho, and fell under her influence. According to Omoigui's account, Esagho was a huge lesbian who was believed to be also a witch. Owodo married Esagho and ten other of his late father's wives, murdered two of them, and banished the rest from the palace. Owodo's often violent and erratic behavior became the source of a great deal of strife and consternation in the kingdom.

The Edion Uzama Council, which had the responsibility of the wellbeing of the kingdom, consulted the oracle of Iso Temple. They used their mystic powers to invoke the god Belial to send Osagan, a herbivore beast, to their service. Osagan was directed into the forest, where he ate clear a large area. He then went about the region, capturing and transporting people to the newly created space. Much of the population of Ile went to this new settlement, and yet, beset by his personal problems, Owodo paid scant attention to the dwindling population of the capital. The forest clearing soon developed into a major market center. According to the story, that is how Ile-Ife came into being, in about AD 1075.

While all of this was going on, Owodo fathered one child, Ekaladerhan. However, the lack of the customary large brood posed a big problem for Owodo, and he was persuaded to consult the oracle Obiro. In his place, he sent his wife Esagho and three men. Obiro instructed that Esagho be executed. She bribed the three men to report that Owodo's young son, Ekaladerhan, was the cause of the problem, and that he should be executed. But Ekaladerhan, a powerful mystic, was also Prince Ekaladerhan and had numerous allies. Prudently judging outright murder as being too risky, Esagho urged Owodo to banish Ekaladerhan and his mother to the forest. This happened in around AD 1084.

Eventually, Owodo realized that he had been misled into sending his only child away. He sent soldiers to capture Ekaladerhan and bring him back from Ughoton, where he had settled, but the soldiers did not return. This increased Owodo's distress and triggered abnormal fits. He started executing people at random, especially pregnant women. During one of his fits, in around 1091, he executed one pregnant woman too many, and this led to a popular rebellion against him. He was driven from the palace and banished from Ile, the capital of his kingdom. He fled to the village of Ihinmwirin with only three of his old wives, where he died in misery as a farmer.

There is another story about the creation of Ile-Ife, one which is tied to the creation of the world and mankind. According to this legend, when Olofi (or Olofin, one of the several derivative names in Yoruba and Santeria for God) decided to create solid ground, he assigned the work to Obatala, a symbol of intellect and purity, the father and creator of mankind on the physical level. Obatala was given an assistant, Orúnmila, the personification of wisdom, who could divine the future of mankind by casting 16 palm nuts. Orúnmila consulted his oracle and told Obatala that he needed loose earth in a snail shell, a hen, a cat, a palm nut, and a long gold chain.

The gold chain was dropped from *orun* ("the heavens") and Obatala descended to the marshy ground below. Clinging to the chain with one hand, he spilled the loose earth from the snail shell onto the marshy ground. Then he immediately dropped the hen onto the ground. The hen then started to scratch at the earth, scattering it in all directions. The dry, loose earth transformed the marshy earth into solid land. When sufficient land had been created, Obatala let go of the gold chain and stepped onto Earth.

But that was only half the job done. Olofi instructed Obatala to create mankind by molding male and female figures from clay. When the clay dried, Olofi would come down and breathe his life-force into the inert figures. Obatala set about his task, but he soon became thirsty and drank some palm wine – a bit too much palm wine, as it turned out. Clumsy from the effects of the wine, Obatala's new figures were twisted and malformed. Still, he set them out to dry next to the well-formed figures. Olofi, who trusted Obatala, did not examine the figures before he gave them life. That is why there are deformed people in the world.

There is also the prosaic textbook history of Ile-Ife. Scholars postulate that a political crisis in Arabia after the rise of Islam forced the Yoruba to migrate to their present homeland in approximately AD 600. Whatever the reason behind their arrival, a large region of west Africa became known as Yorubaland, a patchwork of independent kingdoms headed by Yoruba kings. Yorubaland was a highly civilized, wealthy, and well-organized land. By the early eleventh century, Ile-Ife (possibly named for Ifa, the god of divination) was the capital of Oduduwa, a well-established kingdom, and by the late twelfth and early 13th centuries the region was famous for the highly refined naturalistic terra-cotta heads and bronze pieces made there by the lost wax process. Ife exercised great political and cultural influence over the Edo kingdom of neighboring Benin.

Later, Benin and another kingdom, Old Oyo (Katunga), became more important political kingdoms than Ile-Ife, although the city remained the chief religious center for the Yoruba. The *alafin* ("king") of Oyo had promised not to attack or conduct slave raids on Ile-Ife in return for the *ida oranyan*, the "sword of state," which symbolized spiritual authority. However, in 1793, Alafin Awole launched a slave raid that failed and brought on a series of wars that destroyed the Oyo empire. In the 1820s, Ile-Ife became a haven for refugees fleeing the Muslim Fulani slave raids in other parts of Yorubaland. In 1882, Ife declared a disastrous war against Ibadan and Modakeke, whose combined armies defeated Ife and nearly destroyed the city.

However, the city rebounded and flourished. Some 49 kings have presided over Ile-Ife's affairs. The present *oni* or *ooni* ("king") is both the temporal and spiritual head of the Ife kingdom. He is believed to be the direct descendant of Oddudua, the orisha founder of Ife and one of the three deities sent to Earth by the Creator, Oloddumare, to oversee the destinies of mankind. He is a divine king from whom all other Yoruba kings receive their right to wear the beaded crown that symbolizes their power. He is the supreme leader, and the day-to-day administration of the city is vested in his prime minister, the Obalufe (also known as Orunto), head of the temporal lords of Ile-Ife. The center of modern Ile-Ife is the *afin* ("palace") of the present oni, who has custody of the sacred staff of Oranmiyan (a king of Benin), an 18-foot-long granite monolith in the shape of an elephant's tusk.

Ranking above the oni is the *araba* of Ile-Ife. From his photos, the present araba, Aworeni Adisa Mokoranwale, is a large, affable man. He is the supreme spiritual leader and head of the Ife tradition worldwide, the retainer of Odu and the Divine Personages of orisha in this world. He is responsible for ensuring that the teachings of Ife are properly respected and truthfully enforced. All of the "ceremonies" to the orisha are performed and sanctioned by him. The araba bestows his sanction upon the oni of Ife before he can be seated on the throne.

The image of Santeria has been tainted by the practice of blood sacrifices and association with magic. Migene Gonzáles-Wippler, in her book *Santeria, The Religion*, describes sacrifice as "a universal panacea to cure the ills of mankind and to redeem its sins. Every human society has practiced it at one time or another. Sometimes sacrifices are minimal, a candle lit in church. Or apotheosic, like Christ's death on the cross." She goes on to say, "sacrifice is the means by which human beings acknowledge their inabilities to cope with the challenges of life, and ask for help in meeting that challenge [*sic*]."

The importance of blood sacrifices to deities is well documented in history, ranging from the ancient Hebrews to the Incas. In Santeria, there are three types of animal sacrifices: ritual cleansings, in which the animals are believed to take on the negative vibrations surrounding an individual; offerings to the eggun (ancestors) or the orishas; and initiation offerings, in which blood is given to the saints. The animals used in the ritualistic sacrifices are fowl – chickens, doves, ducks, guinea hens, pigeons – known collectively as *plumas* ("feathers").

Sacrifice does not always require a sacrificial victim. Fruit, money, flowers, candles, or an orisha's favorite food are commonplace offerings in Santeria. Blood sacrifices are reserved for the really big problems, like if a person's life is in danger. In New York, santeros were frequently arrested for performing blood sacrifices, not because they were committing a criminal act but because of the cruelty they were inflicting on the animals. One such case went to the US Supreme Court, which ruled that the practice was protected by the First Amendment as freedom of speech.

Sacrifice contains the concepts of *ashé* and *ebbo*, which are part of the ancient Yoruba tradition. In Yoruba, ashé means "so be it," "may it happen." It is the power with which the universe was created. Everything is made of ashé, and through ashé everything is possible. Ashé may be present in a drop of semen or a drop of blood.

Ebbo, in the context of sacrifice, is the way in which the orishas are propitiated so that they will give up their ashé. Ebbo is also associated with magic, although magic within Santeria is a loose term and construct. Many santeros do not consider ebbo as magic. There is nothing magical in Santeria, they maintain. It is all the work of the orishas and the gods.

In her book, Gonzáles-Wippler offers interesting insights on magic and the subconscious. "In many ways, Santeria is jungle magic adapted to city living," she writes. "Its ritual practices are based on sympathetic magic, based on what Scottish anthropologist Sir James George Frazer, author of *The Golden Bough* (1890), which had a great impact on 20th-century anthropology, called the laws of similarity and contact."

According to Frazer, the law of similarity may be expressed by the magical principle that "like produces like." Magic that hinges on this is called homeopathic magic. In this system, the magician believes that he can create virtually any kind of natural phenomenon by acting it out beforehand, often by using natural objects that are in a sympathetic alliance with the purpose of the ceremony. The most familiar example of this type of magic is that of a wax doll that has been molded in the image of the person to be affected.

To paraphase Gonzáles-Wippler, contagious magic assumes that things that have been in contact with each other are always in contact. It is thus possible to exert influences on a person if one can only procure something that has been in contact with that person.

All forms of sympathetic magic assume that things act on each other at a distance, through an unidentified and unexplainable attraction, the initial contact being sparked by the will of the magician. This belief in the sympathetic influence exerted on each other by objects or individuals separated by distance is of tremendous importance in Santeria and in any form of natural magic. The law of contact states, "Things which have been in contact with each other continue to affect each other long after the physical contact has been broken."

The English writer and magician Aleister Crowley defined magic as the ability to effect changes in consciousness in accordance with the will of the magician. This definition agrees in principle with the magical practices of Santeria, but one must also have the faith, the burning conviction, that the magic will work.

In Santeria, this faith is firmly placed in the mighty powers of the saints, the orishas. The supernatural powers of the orishas, in close alliance with the sympathetic magic of the santeros and their strong determination to succeed, bring about the changes in consciousness described by Crowley.

Santeria is largely natural magic, Gonzáles-Wippler states. But, more than that, it is a system that seeks to find the divine in the most common, ordinary things. It is childlike and often naïve, but it is this simple and total faith that makes it so powerful. There are no sophisticated tenets in Santeria. Its wisdom is the wisdom of the earth. All that Santeria wants to do is embrace nature, but in doing so it embraces the souls of all things.

To explain the validity of the magical claims of the santeros, Gonzáles-Wippler wrote, "I believe that saints are just so many points of contact with the subconscious mind, each one controlling an aspect of human endeavor. Unshakable faith and strongly concentrated will could tap the vast reservoir of power which is the unconscious mind at exactly the point desired by using a simple key word: the name of the orisha that controls that particular area. I believe this is exactly what the santero does when he invokes an orisha. The spells and the magical rituals he uses are simply additional fuel for his already unwavering faith and determination.

"The key word in the practice of Santeria is *ebbo*, magic, specifically sympathetic magic, which is a way of life to most Latinos. There are cults and magico-religious practices from Argentina to Mexico, and mystical figures with miraculous powers from Maximon in Guatemala to Maria Lionza in Venezuela. But whenever syncretism takes place between two or more belief systems, the magical or supernatural aspect is always the principal link."

9 Hamel Callejón

On Sunday, I went to Hamel Callejón, the most phantasmagoric place in Havana. *Callejón* means "back street," and Hamel indeed is a short street tucked away back in Cayo Hueso. When I turned the corner from Calle Hospital onto Hamel, there was only a playground. Nothing extraordinary. I walked another 20 yards and the street took a slight dogleg to the left. One step around that dogleg and my reaction was, *Na-a-a-w!*

I had walked smack dab into the mind of an artist, or artists. I had a flash of embarrassment, as if accidentally opening the wrong door and seeing entangled sheets heaving to and fro. But the sight before me was more thrilling than any titillating voyeurism. This was witnessing audacity giving a most energetic "up yours" on a grand scale.

The buildings on both sides of the street, from the ground floor to three stories up, were completely covered with swirling, painted designs – totemic figures, African motifs, mystical symbols, abstract cubes, Cuban patriotism, cultural exhortations, post-modern wit, and clear, bold statements of "this is who we are." Steel constructs stood in the street saying, "Puzzle this one out." Potted palms stood on 15-foot-high Ionic columns. A silver-painted bathtub on wheels was suspended on rails over the street. A bright-yellow, fantastical, modernistic warrior stood with one foot poised on a tire rim, ready to hurtle a miniature spear into the head of anyone walking beneath him. A quote from Fernándo Ortiz read, "A people who denies themselves is going to commit suicide [*sic*]."

As I walked around in a wonderment of discovery, I bumped into

The buildings on Hamel Callejón in Havana, painted by local and internationally renowned artist Salvador Gonzales Ecalona, who has adopted the locale as a community project

a man holding a big cigar held rakishly between his fingers. He stood about five feet seven inches tall, was compact, solid, and Hollywood handsome, with a full head of brushed-back silver hair. He was dressed stylishly in a double-breasted jacket, dark-red shirt, and black tie with silver highlights. His loafers were highly polished. He seemed slightly removed, like an overlord surveying his fields. When I apologized for bumping into him, he was polite and courteous in the Old World sense.

"What is this?" I gestured around me.

"I created it," he replied. "I'm Salvador Gonzales Ecalona."

Salvador Gonzales Ecalona, I later discovered, is an internationally respected painter. His public works are in Los Angeles, Philadelphia, Chicago, and Rome, to name a few places. Museums and private connoisseurs collect his art. Hamel Callejón is his private community project. All of the paintings in Hamel Callejón are by his hand.

I remarked that much of the street reminded me of found art.

"This is not found art in the sense of the Found Art movement that became popular in New York at one time," he replied. "That movement had an element of rediscovering ordinary objects, the things thrown away, as material for art. There was an anti-snobbishness to the attitude, a chiding of the affluent society. Here, in this neighborhood, we don't rediscover the beauty in the ordinary; we never lose sight of the beauty. Everything is precious because there is so little of it. These people are poor. They don't have the luxury to discard things. Everything is used, not only the material things but cultural attitudes and values."

The street is a community center. On Saturdays, there are activities for the local children, including art lessons. Adult volunteers teach, supervise, and keep the street clean. They are very aware that police keep a close eye on Hamel Callejón, because the locals sell herbal medicines and illegal rum to make money. The street is seen by authorities as a potential trouble spot, but they are not sure how. Salvador works hard to give the authorities no excuse to close down Hamel Callejón.

The highlight of every Sunday on Hamel Callejón is rumba, and by noon a large crowd had gathered as musicians set up their drums. The "house band" is Clave y Guaguancó, one of the best rumba groups in Cuba. Clave y Guaguancó, Yoruba o Andabo (a group started in 1961 by stevedores from the Havana wharves), and Los Múnequitos De Matanzas have long been the top rumba bands in Cuba. Clave y Guaguancó has been in existence for 56 years. When they are unavailable for the Hamel Sunday gig, other folkloric groups stand in. The entertainment is not advertised, as it is primarily for the local neighbors, although some outsiders – including tourists – do find it.

There is a popular saying: "Without rumba, there is no Cuba; without Cuba, there is no rumba." Rumba is Cuba's only indigenous music, neither Spanish nor African but an original that came out of the mix of those two cultural influences, like mixing yellow and blue to get green.

The Spanish words *rumba* and *rumbón* refer to a collective festive event, a gala meal, a carousal, or a high time. The words are synonymous with some Bantu and other west African words used in Cuba, such as *tumba, macumba,* and *tambo,* all meaning a social, secular gathering with music and dancing. Fernándo Ortiz, a Cuban ethnologist and major scholar of Afro-Cuban folkloric traditions, defines the verb *rumba* as "to gather and dance," "to have a party."

The dance ancestry of rumba can be traced to western and central Africa, particularly to tribes of the Kongo, Lunda, and the Luba of Zaire. Those people have historically shared dances that focus on the gradual closeness of male and female dancers and the touching of thighs and bellies. Dances like the makuta and yuka, rumba's antecedents, still survive in Cuba. The distinct characteristics of those dances include the dancing pair moving in a circle, the dancers independent and yet in relation to one another, and dancing to drums and a wooden box, and are seen in the evolution of the rumba style and form. The dancers bumping off each other and the gestures toward the navel are an obvious link between the rumba and the African dances. The Bantu words *mkumba* and *mukumba* – meaning "navel" and "belly-button" – can be heard in the names makuta, yuka and rumba.

The famous rumba band Clave y Guaguancó, who perform at Hamel Callejón every Sunday at noon to acknowledge their roots

In Cuba, the rumba developed during the 1850s and 1860s in places where free blacks gathered and enslaved Africans were permitted to congregate after work. Musically, the Bantu Congolese yuka of the sugar plantations and the Cuban traditional son, a country music with strong Spanish overtones, met and began to dance with each other. There was the Spanish flamenco style of rumba, *flamena* ("gypsy rumba"), as well as the African rumbas. Merged with the son, the rumba formed the backbone of modern Cuban dance music, according to Leonarda Acosta, a scholar of Cuban music. Rumba gave new life to son. Benny Moré, perhaps the best-known Cuban musician outside of Cuba in the 1940s and 1950s and generally associated with son, trova, and bolero, was an ardent *rumbero*, as reflected in his style of improvisations and refrains.

In the late 1880s, after the abolition of slavery in Cuba in 1888, poor Afro-Cubans, *los negroes humildes*, moved to urban areas and joined poor white Cubans looking for jobs, which were plentiful near the ports. The rumba has its roots in the Cuban countryside and in the ports, particularly those of Havana and Matanzas, both of which have distinct rumba styles.

In the crowd gathering for the rumba, I spotted my friend Ramiro de la Cuesta, the godfather of Cayo Hueso, who lives a couple of blocks from Hamel Callejón. After a big hug, he gave me some background on the rumba. "The workers in the harbours, most of them negro stevedores, during their resting time made rumba on boxes of imported candles of different sizes to obtain different sounds," he said. "The boxes used to pack fish or candles gave a good tone. They played whatever was at hand – frying pans, spoons, backs of chairs, cabinet drawers, crates, whatever. Later, the rumba began to be played in the solares. The solares were large houses divided into crowded living quarters where poor Cubans were forced to live. They also served as a meeting place to relax, to play, to sing and dance, and to read poetry."

The musicians arrived as we spoke. Ramiro grabbed a big fellow wearing an ersatz New York-style baseball shirt and a straw hat. "This is my old friend Amado Dedue Hernández, the director of Clave y Guaguancó." Amado looked like a corporate lawyer relaxing. He was six feet tall and had a generous parabolic curve to his portly belly. His hands were small and fleshy. He had a round, well-fed face and wore thick eyeglasses with fashionable red frames flecked with gold-colored flakes. His white hair was curled forward in the style of a Roman emperor. He held himself with utter confidence. In a courtroom, his size and attitude would be intimidating. Rumba is an energetic music suitable for lean, whippet bodies that can move with speed and grace. One would never at first sight mistake Amado for a rumbero.

"This afternoon, after here, the group is going to the Cubadisco awards, which are like the Grammys," said Ramiro. "They have been nominated in the Folkloric category."

I expressed surprise that such a successful group would be playing for free on an obscure back street.

"We have a philosophy," Amado answered. "We cannot forget our origins, our roots. Most of us in the band were born in the solares, and we were born influenced by the rumba. No matter what success we may have, no matter the fame we can have, we cannot forget our origin. That's why we are in the Hamel."

The band's drummers edged past us to put their instruments in place. The rumba uses three basic drums: conga, segundo, and quinto. The name *conga* acknowledges the drum's Kongo-Angolan forerunners, which had the same long barrel shape. Also known as the tumbador and the "opener," it is the first drum to sound and opens a song. It is also the deepest-sounding drum and anchors the ensemble in pitch and in an ostinato, or repeated pattern. The middle-register drum, the second to come in, is the *segundo* ("second" in Spanish), or *macho ormale*, or *seis-por-ocho*, a name which gives reference to the 6/8 rhythm it keeps. Also known as the *tres-dos* for its 3/2 beat, it complements the conga. Meanwhile, the third and smallest drum, the quinto, improvises and is played at a counter-tempo.

Clave y Guaguancó drummers also play boxes, even those that they sit upon. The boxes symbolise a return to colonial times, when slave-owners prohibited the use of drums by their slaves. The masters, perhaps paranoid about owning other human beings against their will and profiting from their labor, feared that the drumming might contain messages of rebellion and signal a revolt. Drumming was essential in African-based festivals that attracted large crowds of slaves, and so the festivals were banned when the slavemasters' fear levels ran high. But the enslaved Africans applied ingenuity to create drums that didn't look like drums. Boxes and crates were dismantled, sanded, and reassembled without cracks. They still looked like boxes, but they were improved boxes with greater resonance and drum-like qualities. Dresser drawers, sides of wardrobes, and closets were pressed into service by rumba players.

Other members of Clave y Guaguancó took their places. One tapped out a few notes on *la guagua*, a drum struck with two sticks. A fellow picked up the shaker, a large and beautiful gourd with a deep-red luster fixed to the outside of which was a net with small cowrie shells woven into it. The generic name for the shaker is *guiro*, but it is also called *chequere* or *chekeres*. The guiro gourd, which grows on the guira tree, was also used as a drum substitute when drums were outlawed.

The band stood ready. The only essential instrument missing was the clave, consisting of two sticks struck together. The clave is the very heartbeat of all Cuban music, whether the instrument is actually played in a band or not. Without an internal sense of clave, the musicians say, it is impossible to play Cuban music. If you don't have the clave, you don't have the beat. The clave beat itself is a two-measure rhythm consisting of three percussive strokes in one measure, followed by a measure with two strokes. A variation on this is melodies of two/three. The style originated when Cuban blacks marked the time when different choral groups harmonized various vocal lines of the same song. Guitars and an unstrung banjo, something like a frame drum, that was struck with clave sticks accompanied the groups. The Cuban ethnologist Fernándo Ortiz claims that the word *clave* is derived from *clavija*, meaning "wooden peg."

The clave player and lead singer of Clave y Guaguancó is Amado, who continued to talk with Ramiro and me as the band waited. "The rumba is not a study. The rumba is in the streets. The rumba is the

Amado Dedeu Hernández, the director of Clave y Guaguancó

daily experience of the people," he said, finishing our discussion of the music. He eased through the crowd of about 100 people jammed shoulder to shoulder in a U around the band. He took his place before the mic, surveyed the crowd with a satisfied smile, and struck his two short wooden pegs together twice. The conga player picked up the beat, set the rhythm, and, without warning, devastation tore through the crowd.

Rumba is a cluster bomb – all of the parts explode simultaneously. Bomblets of music rained down on our heads and shredded inhibitions. Stiffness was ripped off knees and hips, leaving the victims of the rumba assault trembling like raindrops sliding down a windowpane. People were tossed into the air. At least, that's what it looked like as the crowd rose on the wave of music, their shoulders shaking, buffeted by the blast of rhythm.

A man began to stalk a woman. She kept her distance but teased him. His intent was graphically clear by his lewd pelvic thrusts. She covered her vulnerability with her hands but did not flee more than a few steps. He approached again, not in a violent charge, but seductively, waving his grace as a flower waves its stamen. He came from behind, nearly touching her as she glanced over her shoulder, hips jutted backward. The guy thought he was about to put one up on the scoreboard when she laughingly moved away. He shook his head in disgust and danced away from her.

"This is the *guaguancó*," Ramiro said in my ear, "one of the three dances in the folkloric rumba complex. The man tries to vaccinate the woman, the *vacúnao* – you know, the man/woman thing."

Amado had established the melody in his introduction. Then he sang the basic narrative, the *tema*, which the dancers acted out. All of the band members sang the chorus, the *estribillow*.

The couple kept their distance from each other. Their dance resembled the stylized movements of a rooster and a hen. He puffed out his chest and strutted. She pretended not to notice while pecking away, head down and forward, elbows up and out. He began to circle again and she greeted him with an open dare – give it your best shot. The drumming rhythm was medium by rumba standards, with the dancers timing themselves to the quinto drum. He tried subtlety, signaling his intention with a hand and then a foot. The woman was coy. He tried to dazzle her with fancy footwork. She showed her dancing skills with evasion while still being alluring and almost available. It was a delicate balance, just like a real-life courtship. The guaguancó evolved out of the yuka, which has its roots in a Congolese fertility dance. The drumming pace increased, and the man came on more aggressively, determined to dominate. The woman had a choice: surrender or evade.

"The dance is just like real life," Ramiro commented with a laugh. "It appears that the man has the power, but it's the woman who ultimately decides. It looks like the man is trying to sexually possess the woman, but if you notice closely it's the woman who provokes the sex. How she entices and evades is in her dancing skill."

Politically correct critics decry the guaguancó, the dance most favored of the rumba complex by dancers, as sexist, a flagship for macho social behavior and values that keep women in a secondary and passive role, to which rumberos answer, "Think less. Dance more."

The dance's climax was fast approaching. Would he? Would she? The dancers were within a fraction of each other, arms held high, exposing their full bodies, shoulders shaking in a sexy shimmer, their pelvises prancing in heat, as if trying to cross hot sand barefoot. The dancers were grinning, and the crowd was clapping and shouting and grinning, and the drummers' hands were flying faster than hummingbirds' wings, and the music – layers upon layers of sound pulsing against one another – kept pounding the living daylights out of us. In the end, the dancers were just friends, but what a way to show friendship!

It's no wonder that the rumba has gained popularity in the past 40 years. In the 1800s, before the abolition of slavery in Cuba in 1866, rumbas were danced and played in slave barracks and in certain festivals tolerated by slave-owners. With the end of slavery, the music and dance belonged strictly to the black and mulatto lower working class. The "white" bourgeoisie denounced it as licentious, immoral, savage, and primitive, which perhaps isn't an entirely false representation. The rumba had a vital role in proletarian culture and, by extension, in modern Cuban culture as a

A staged performance of rumba, re-enacting the three styles of rumba and their historical settings, is performed every Sunday afternoon by Gran Planque in Havana

whole. One description called the rumba "a popular dance cultivated in a certain licentious ambience by happy people." That was certainly what was going on in Hamel.

Before the music had started, Amado had voiced the opinion that the increasing popularity of rumba was related to the cultural development of the Cuban people. "Because one time the rumba was discriminated against for racial bias and prejudice, we can say that the people were ignorant, no matter their level of education," he said. "They rejected a popular genre that I think identifies us. But now our culture has more culture, so to speak, in that people are more accepting of all our cultural heritages. The rumba is the seal of our identity because of the mixture of the Spanish and African, of which the result is Cuban. We are a mixture, a mingle, and the rumba is the same. For me, our identity is in the rumba. The rumba is also popular because it is not religious. Some of our music, like the bata, has a religious base, and there is not a great deal of participation by the general public for this reason. The people were not initiated into the rites of those religions. Rumba is more profane.

"Now the rumba has lost its racial connotation. After the Revolution, there have been greater open possibilities in accepting the rumba. The government has gone to the rescue of all culture heritages, and the rumba has been given more space. Politicians have used the rumba and the congas in their campaigns."

The band started another rumba, this one a slower 4/4 beat played primarily on the boxes. An old man with a grizzled chin emerged from the crowd and began to dance at a tai chi pace but with none of the solemnity of the warrior discipline.

"The *yambú*," Ramiro said. "Also called the *rumba de cahon* ['box rumba']. It's the oldest of the three rumbas and comes from the countryside around Matanzas. But there are a lot of steps from the Abakuá, the secret men's society that is strong in the port areas here. Abakuá also has religious connotations that reach back to Nigeria."

A young woman stepped from the crowd to dance with the old man. Ramiro laughed. "These people know their rumba," he said. "It's said that the yambú is slow so the older people can follow the steps, but it's really about age and youth...and seduction."

The young woman, clad in tight Spandex, had long, erotic black hair. She flashed the man a smile that would puddle a younger man, but the old fellow was seasoned. He ignored her and stayed with his dance. She danced closer, offering one fetching shoulder, then the other, and shaking what was in between. The old man noticed. He turned toward her and then, in a poignant gesture, indicated that he was too old, too dried out, to chase a beautiful young chica. But the young woman offered him more incentive with a bump-and-grind pelvic twirl, as blatant and open an invitation as she could give without sticking her tongue in the old man's ear. The old man began to stir. Where there's life, there's hope, and he was still alive.

His steps became livelier and less self-absorbed. He began to dance with her and then seemed to falter. The young woman urged him to find new vitality, to rise to the occasion and live the last hoorah. Now she was more than a mere seductive flirt; there was compassion and generosity in her effort to invite the old man back to the pleasures of life. She looped a red silk scarf around the old man's neck, joining them. The dance became tender and romantic without losing the sensuality of the rumba. The rhythm matched the mood of the words being sung by Amado and the band, a form of traditional Spanish poetry known as *rigina*, consisting of four-line stanzas. (Yambú is sometimes referred to as "*yambú de tiempo España*.")

Now the old man was definitely remembering his younger days. His movements became more fluid and he actively began to chase the young woman, all within the rhythm of the dance. She gave him a "peek" and a "boo," leading him on with a cocked hip and then a radiant smile that promised a long and happy time with her. She let him in close, but he did not thrust, as is done in the guaguancó. A rule of the yambú is no vaccination. The juice of flirtation, not the pride of conquest, is the joy of the dance.

When the dance ended, we all sighed with sentiment and cheered with optimism. The old man and the young woman briefly touched fingertips and went separately back into the crowd.

The band machine-gunned us with a staccato burst of drumming. I wondered how the drummers weren't run over by each other's – and their own – sounds. The rhythmic patterns pounded straight ahead, overlapped, undercut, stood on each other's shoulders, snuggled within the fold of the other drums' beat, and balanced delicately on the liminal highwire between order and chaos. The only thing I could think of for comparison was a ravaging wild river frothing within its banks and yet staying within the banks out of respect for some cosmic rule. All of this was a prelude.

Ramiro knew what was coming but I was unprepared. A muscular young man literally leapt out of the crowd. Ramiro gave a shout, as if he was at a sporting match. The music was a fast 6/8 and the dancer was equally quick on his feet. I didn't know what he was doing, but it appeared to be a combination of modern jazz, experimental ballet, breakdancing, karate, and operatic rumba.

"The columbia," said Ramiro. "It's a solo competitive dance among men to display virtuosity, male prowess, and dancing skills. It's considered the most African of the rumbas. It came out of sugar plantations in rural Matanzas during the slave times. Perhaps only men danced it then because of the lack of women available."

The aim of the dance, according to Ramiro, is perfection of style, bravado, creativity, musicality, and virtuosity of rhythm. The dancer focuses on the high-pitched quinto drum, the most free-form of the rumba drums. He tries to initiate rhythms or answer riffs as if the drum is his dance partner. The columbia is the more abstract of the rumba dances, as the yambú and guaguancó are literal and situational.

After ten minutes, another young male jumped into the competition and the first dancer gave way. The crowd cheered and clapped as if at a bloodless cockfight. Dance as athleticism might be the best way to describe the columbia, although there was no touchdown posturing or clowning, posing as the champ, or boasting to the crowd. Competition as it is known on the playing field or in the boxing ring was absent. The dancers were there to dance, to inspire each other to greater creativity and more daring imagination. No prize was awarded. No one was declared the winner by an applause meter or a panel of judges. The lack of "I'm better than you" enhanced the crowd's enjoyment. The spectators, the dancers, and the musicians were all on the same high.

The rumba I had seen in the United States was a faint echo of the rumba at Hamel Callejón. Rumba first came to North America in the 1920s and 1930s and became a craze there. Then, nearly all Cuban music was lumped under the rubric of rumba. That music was not very involved, rhythmically, and was easily adapted to ballroom dancing, a simplistic style that still largely defines rumba outside of Cuba. To differentiate the anemic dance from the real thing, Cuban musicians in the United States gave rumba an H, as in rhumba, to distinguish it from the real Cuban music.

After the hour-long performance, we went to Amado's house, a 15-minute walk away, so that he could change for the Cubadisco awards ceremony. His house was one of those that fronted directly onto the street in a row of similar small houses. It was not the house I would have expected a major music personality to inhabit. The most prominent features of the small living room were an aquarium and a large model of a fully rigged Spanish galleon. We sat down and talked rumba and politics. Politics is not a shunned topic in Cuba, and when people discuss their government they do not whisper and look furtively over their shoulders for some lurking policeman or informer. During the 1960s, when Castro was in his "Soviet" mode and adopted certain repressive measures, such as the neighborhood-watch committees, which *were* informers, people were more discreet. Rumba has a long history of political involvement, dating back to the slave days. In recent memory, Tio Tom has been a model of rumba political activism.

Tio Tom was born Gonzalo Asencio Hernández on April 5, 1919 in Cayo Hueso, not far from Hamel Callejón. His father, Nicanor, loaded sacks on the dock, while his mother, Carmelia, was a pastry cook who worked in the kitchens of rich people. Tio Tom attended school through third grade and then worked as a bottle cleaner, a magazine vendor, a mason's peon, and a day labourer. He wrote his first rumba at the age of 15 and went on to become well known for his guaguancó and columbia styles of singing, dancing, and drumming. He hit the political big-time, so to speak, with his song protesting against the uncouth behavior of US marines and sailors, whose ships often docked at Havana. On one rancorous night, fun-loving US military men desecrated a statue of Jose Martí, Cuba's beloved martyr and national father. The Cuban government, at that time led by President Carlos Prio, was too servile to demand just punishment for the perpetuators, but ordinary Cubans mounted protests and Tio Tom wrote a guaguancó with a verse that ran, "How is it that these Americans came from abroad/to trample our flag and the statue of our martyr?/All the mystery it holds is in silver and gold/Listen, Mr President. I want your opinion/about the punishment which Cuba demands/against these Americans who have come from abroad/to trample the flag of our Cuban soil." The government read this as questioning the honor of Sénor Presidente and Tio Tom was sentenced to six months and a day in jail for his audacity. However, this didn't deter him from continuing to write anti-imperialist and revolutionary rumbas up through the 1959 Revolution and until his death in 1991.

"There has been a continuity of the political aspects of the rumba," Amado said. "There was a rumbero called the Champion who lived in Compolgia. He created a group called Guaguancó Revolution, which I participated in when I was young. All the lyrics in this group had a political content. He wrote a lot of good compositions with political issues. They were very good songs. He is dead now. Recently, I visited the family to rescue these songs. There are a lot of authors of rumba who write about political issues. That has not been lost."

Amado needed to get to the awards ceremony, so I slipped in one last question: "What is influencing rumba now?"

"A lot of fusion is influencing rumba," Amado replied. "Our group was one of the first to work with fusion, the mixture of bata, Abakuá, and Arara drumming with the rumba. We worked in the *punto cubano*, the country music, music of the *campesino* (farm). Our group is distinct because of this mixture. There will be more fusion. Cuban music is fusion."

Amado went off to be a celebrity and I walked home. (Clave y Guaguancó did not win the Cubadisco award.) On my way, I came across a definite not-hot spot that I had seen many times – the police checking the identity card of a black youth. This was a very common occurrence, and black Cubans were always the targets. When I queried Cubans about this practice, I was told it was only a check to see if the young men were draft dodgers, but I was not convinced. Finally, I asked one of my neighbors, a tall black man. "It's harassment, pure and simple," he said. "If you and I were walking down the street together, the police could stop us. You'd be sent on your way and I'd be taken to the police station. Then they'd let me go. But it would be a loss of time for me. A disruption. A distrust."

On my way home, I stopped for a cool-down break at the Hotel Nacional, a Havana hot spot. The hotel is a national monument and the place for tourists to stay, as it was for American mobsters in the 1930s and 1940s. The back garden is one of the best places in Havana to pass a hot afternoon – the sea breeze blows directly off the ocean and the drinks are cool. Live bands perform there on Sunday afternoons, and this afternoon it was the turn of Yoruba o Andabo, a top rumba group. It must have been my lucky day for rumba.

Another place to see rumba on Sunday afternoons is the Gran Planque. This place hosts a kind of showtime, an odd mix of staged rumba and fashion show. The rumba performers try to recreate how a spontaneous rumba would erupt in the solares, which was like putting on a play about slavery. It wasn't the real thing; it was entertainment and, as such, isolated from its historical context. You didn't know what to believe. Amado summoned it up when he said, "We have to be afraid of the stupidities being made in places like Gran Planque."

10 *Pinar Del Rio*

I took a day trip to Pinar del Rio, the province west of Havana, with my friend Juan D. in his old Mockbuy, a noisy, ugly Russian rattletrap with thin seats and a balky battery. Whenever we stopped, we had to push-start this condemnation of the former Soviet Union system back into action. While driving very fast, Juan D. referred to his family vehicle as "the most dangerous car on the road."

Juan D. has lived with the Revolution for 40 of his 49 years. Like most things in Cuba, he's a mixture of Spanish and African. He has dark skin, a Castilian nose, and lustrous eyes to die for. "My eyes have magic powers," he once confided. "They open hearts – and bedroom doors – even when I don't want them to. My eyes cause me trouble." I misunderstood his Spanish and thought he was referring to his eyesight. "No, my friend. I have perfect eyesight and clear vision. That causes me trouble, also."

He is a seasoned man. He has his opinions. He is an optimistic and a forward-thinking man, a common trait of the Cubans. "D with a dot, not 'de,' but with a dot, like dot com," he clarified when we first met. The "d with a dot" was important to Juan; it symbolized being part of the future, of not being left behind in the world.

We left Havana via the ritzy suburb of Miramar, passing Spanish-style mansions that could be converted to luxury hotels without the need to add bathrooms. We passed the complex where the government party holds meetings, a modern, low-slung complex of linear Frank Lloyd Wright knock-offs linked together so that the decision-makers could go from hotel to meeting room to conference hall without stepping onto the neatly manicured grounds.

We cleared the city and drove southwest on a four-lane carriageway with a good surface. Pinar del Rio is sugar and tobacco country, so a good road is necessary to get the produce to market. The grass median between the lanes was kept trimmed and without weeds. It was decorated with small trees sculpted to look like muffins on sticks, their branches clipped to form circles, and hedges of flaming rhododendron added splashes of color.

Car traffic was light. The most common vehicles were large trucks with beds filled with people instead of stalks of cane. The empty trucks returning to the countryside doubled as buses, picking up people along the roadside, with the driver pocketing a few pesos for his trouble.

We also saw the occasional ox cart trudging along the side of the highway. Ox carts are still commonly used to get to the fields, and they're also used for short trips into town. The carts had a *Don Quixote* look, quaintly romantic in the same way that the 30-year-old jalopies on the road carried the sentiment of wrinkled, faded photographs of another era, now known only by hearsay. The people in the ox carts – vehicles with a single automobile axle and rubber tires – and the people in those sputtering junk-heaps dreamed of a faster, more comfortable vehicle of the modern era.

The land was flat, perfect for the acres upon acres of sugar-cane fields on either side of the highway. Royal palms randomly dotted the landscape, looking like arboreal giraffes wearing outlandish Easter bonnets of lacy feathers. There was also the rare cork palm, a shaggy, endemic relic of the Carboniferous era, found only in Pinar del Rio. When the land was covered by ocean, this living fossil took root on occasionally dry land and has hung on for the past 270 million years.

In the distance on our right – the Atlantic Ocean side – was the dark outline of the Guanicuanico, an ancient mountain chain that runs east and west parallel to the unseen coast. The Rio San Diego halves the mountains into the Sierra del Rosario in the east and the Sierra de los Organos in the west. We took the turn-off into the Sierra del Rosario and headed for the 25,000-hectare (61,773-acre) biosphere reserve called "the rainbow of Cuba" for its natural beauty.

The Spanish first settled in Pinar in 1717 and tobacco farmers

The owner of the tobacco farm

planted in the western valleys. News of their promising success attracted sugar growers, and plantations were established on the plains. Then French coffee growers came and developed *fincas* on the higher slopes. Pinar del Rio was called "the Cinderella province," an ironic term nowadays, as the area has remained one of Cuba's poorest and most backward. The logging excesses of the early Spanish denuded the mountainsides, which in time led to erosion and the collapse of the coffee industry, and eventually the collapse of logging itself. In 1975, the Cuban government began a decade-long effort to reforest the slopes. In 1985, UNESCO declared the region a biosphere to protect the 600 endemic higher and 250 lower plant species. The semi-deciduous and mid-elevation montane pine forest shelters 98 species of bird, including the Cuban trogons, parrots, and the tocororo, Cuba's national bird.

We soon arrived at Soroa, an "eco-retreat" named after the Frenchman Jean-Paul Soroa, who owned a coffee plantation in the valley two centuries ago. In the 1930s, the retreat was a fashionable spa known for its sulfur baths. Now the main attraction is a small, unspectacular (although pretty) waterfall, down to which leads a cement pathway that is often jammed with Cubans and foreign tourists. Returning from the waterfall, I declined the 20-minute hike or the ride on a horse-for-rent to a mountaintop to experience the panoramic view of the countryside. The resort itself, Villas Turitica Soroa, is a short drive from the waterfall. The very pleasant complex of 49 cabins surrounds an Olympic-sized swimming pool.

Perhaps more "eco" is Las Terrazas, a small agricultural village in a narrow valley above Lago San Juan. Founded in 1971, the village of 1,200 is charming, with houses of whitewashed walls, orange doors, and blue shutters. The villagers work either on the land or at La Moka, a hotel operated on ecological principles. As soon as I saw La Moka, hidden from view in a forest of teak, cedar, and mahogany, I wanted to move in. Opened in 1994, it is designed in a contemporary Spanish-colonial style, with a multi-tiered atrium lobby. A lime tree grows in the center of the atrium, its branches reaching outside through the skylight. The rooms have floor-to-ceiling French doors leading to balconies ideal for sitting in the evening to enjoy the quiet.

Touted as Cuba's prime eco-tourism site, the village is largely self-contained, with even its own rodeo ring. At the Centro Ecologico, you can rent boats to go fishing on the lake or hire a guide for birdwatching and nature hikes.

Che Guevara trained his guerrillas for his ill-fated 1965 adventure to replicate the Cuban Revolution in Bolivia on the slopes of the heavily forested, flat-topped mountain La Loma de Tabaurete, which looms over the village. However, the Bolivian peasants did not rally to the cause brought to them by the romantic icon of the Cuban Revolution. Che and his men remained isolated and largely unsupported while the Bolivian Army chased them through the mountain jungles. Che was eventually killed in an ambush.

Instead of staying at La Moka, we headed for the Sierra de los Organos, the mountains less than an hour's drive further west. Our destination was Viñares, in the heart of Cuba's best tobacco country and the jumping-off point for the Viñares Valley National Monument.

The acres of sugar fields – which resemble winter wheat fields on steroids – gave way to small fields of tobacco. Forty-foot-high A-frame *bohios* (curing barns), their shaggy thatched roofs made from Royal palms, replaced the tall chimneys of the sugar factories that puffed out clouds of dark smoke. Fernándo Ortiz observed that sugar has a macho attitude, perhaps symbolized by those phallic smokestacks and the sugar industry's aggressive domination of Cuba's economic life. Tobacco, on the other hand, speculated Ortiz, is gentle and feminine, meant to be sweetly touched and tasted. The curing barns, with their soft, feathery, silver-worn thatch, are the antithesis of the grinding gears and one-ton presses used in the sugar mills.

We stopped at a small tobacco farm to see if they had any of the local product available, rolled as cigars. The farmer, a small man with a finely featured, handsome face and a permanently closed right eye, came out to greet us. A straw hat with a broad, up-curved brim shaded his face from the sun. He carried a plastic bowl under his arm, from which he offered slices of grapefruit and chunks of coconut. I accepted his hospitality.

His brother-in-law, who owned the farm, had recently fallen into a deep depression and cared for nothing, the farmer confided, as if we were close neighbors. It's sad, he said with a sympathetic shake of his head. Conditions in the countryside were enough to drive anyone into a depression. The local tobacco co-op had failed. Since the co-op had replaced privately owned land, the workers really didn't love the land. It wasn't theirs. Instead, it was owned by the absentee State landlord, and the workers were paid only two pesos (about five cents) a day.

"They let weeds grow in the fields," the farmer said, gesturing to the well-tended rows of tobacco. "Here we love our land, but still it's not easy." "*Es no facile*" is an oft-heard phrase in Cuba.

"If someone steals my oxen, I have to pay a fine of 500 pesos," he explained. "That's not fair. The State does that to discourage people from butchering their oxen and selling the meat – which is illegal – and claiming that the ox had been stolen. My oxen died by accident. I had to sell the dead body to the State for 200 pesos. There were 10,000 pesos of meat there. It was my oxen, but I couldn't sell it for its worth. *Es no facile.*"

In the tobacco field, men lifted long poles draped with green tobacco leaves and carried them, one per shoulder, into the curing barn.

The farmer standing in a field of tobacco

Green tobacco leaves are taken to a drying barn for curing

"They earn only 20 pesos a day," said the farmer, gesturing with his chin, "and rice costs four pesos per kilo. The young people understandably don't want to work on the farms, and those who stay don't like to work hard."

He himself was retired, living on 100 pesos (four dollars) a month. Would I like more grapefruit and coconut? He had picked the fruit from the trees behind us. He lifted the lid and discreetly shifted the bowl so I could see the few coins on the tray beneath it. Only then did I understand that he was selling the fruit. He held the bowl out to me, even if I chose to ignore the coins.

I asked the farmer if he had cigars for sale.

"Yes, of course. This is a tobacco farm," he laughed.

On the bar counter of the State-owned restaurant next to the curing barn were neat bundles of hand-rolled cigars. They had no fancy packaging or gold-foil labels. They were not wrapped in a thin sheath of cedar bark, like the expensive cigars in their protective casings. They were plain, simple cigars direct from the curing barn, like sun-ripened tomatoes fresh from the field.

"Here," the farmer showed me proudly. "These are ours." I bought a bundle of eight cigars for five dollars.

The United States government discourages its citizens from purchasing Cuban cigars. This is a quote from a warning sent by the US Treasury Department: "Only persons returning from Cuba after a licensed visit there are permitted to bring Cuban cigars into the United States, provided the value of such cigars does not exceed $100US and the cigars are for that person's personal use and not for resale. All other importations of Cuban cigars are illegal. All offers to buy or sell such cigars in the United States involve cigars that are imported illegally. Contrary to what many people may believe, it is illegal for travelers to bring into the United States Cuban cigars acquired in third countries (such as Canada, England, or Mexico).

"It is also illegal for US persons to buy, sell, trade, or otherwise engage in transactions involving illegally imported Cuban cigars. The penalties for doing so include – in addition to confiscation of the cigars – civil fines of up to $55,000 per violation and, in appropriate cases, criminal prosecution which may result in higher fines and/or imprisonment."

That is a succinct summarization of the US government's effort to intimidate its citizens. As a journalist on a licensed visit, I was allowed to bring back one box of Cuban cigars, as long as it cost under $100. That's the Catch 22. At the cigar factory in Havana, there was not one box that cost under $100, but when I re-entered the United States the customs official waved me through without asking a question or opening my bag. I could have been carrying ten boxes of Cuban cigars. He didn't care, as long as I wasn't importing carloads.

Viñares was a 20-minute drive from the tobacco farm. This town of 10,000 reminded me of those Greek villages favored by backpackers, the first wave of tourists, who find places to hang out cheap while savoring the local flavors. They are "travelers" as opposed to "tourists," a badge they wouldn't be caught dead wearing, but the locals recognize a tourist as a tourist and adjust the prices accordingly. The people of Viñares are the future of Cuba.

Viñares has a rural charm. Shade trees give the town a sleepy atmosphere. The palm trees around the main square, with its pretty 19th-century church and a colonial arcade, lend the appropriate Caribbean touch. The homes are red-tile-roofed houses, many of which advertise rooms for rent. "Chambre for lovers" read one sign, perhaps with an eye for more than the tourist trade. Many of the tourists were Europeans staying in private homes or at the Hotel Horizontes Las Ermitas, a very nice place on a hill one kilometer from town and overlooking the valley.

I was hungry. Juan D. said he knew of a *paladare*, a private house, that served a good lunch. We drove down side streets until he recognized the house and went in to inquire.

"He will serve us fish, rice, beans, salad, and fruit," Juan D. said upon returning, "for ten dollars."

"What do these people take us for? Tourists?" In Havana, I often ate at a linen-tablecloth restaurant that served the same fare for $4.50. "No. We'll find another place."

"The State-owned restaurants will be more expensive," Juan D. said.

"There must be a peso place where the local people eat," I countered.

"I'll go talk to him again," Juan D. offered. He returned in a few minutes. "Seven dollars is the best he can do."

"Not good enough. We'll find another place."

A block away, Juan D. stopped the car and asked a man on the sidewalk if he knew of a paladare. "I'll be glad to serve you," the man replied. This time we were offered the same meal for six dollars. Hunger ruled the moment and I agreed.

"Come to my house in an hour," the man, Pipy, replied and gave directions.

To kill time, we drove a short distance to the Jurassic Park of Cuba, also referred to as a "miniature Yosemite," a grandiose phrase of tourist sloganeering. Hemmed in by mountains, the Viñares Valley does have an unusual landscape. The distinguishing characteristic is the *mogotes* – free-standing, round-topped rock formations that rise to the height of 1,000 feet. These remnants of a limestone plateau that rose from the sea during the Jurassic Era (about 160 million years ago) are the oldest geological formation in Cuba. They do have a prehistoric look, shaggy with bushes, ferns, and that botanical relic the cork palm, a declared national treasure. The mogotes, isolated in the red-dirt tobacco fields, look like wooly mammoths with their backs to the wind. When the mist rises from the valley floor, the landscape has a Chinese-print quality, all spectral mystery and misty illusion on the nature of reality.

We had time to visit the Cuevas del Indio ("Caves of the Indian"), which in reality was one cave in another part of the valley, discovered by a farmer in 1958. The eponymous name comes from Indian remains found near the cave. The Guanahatabey, the initial aboriginal people of Cuba, inhabited this area 4,000 years ago, until the Ciboney Indians – a hunter-gatherer tribe fleeing the Taino Indians moving up from South America – forced the Guanahatabey out. The Carib Indians in turn forced the Taino out as they migrated from what is now Venezuela.

"Indians stayed in the St Thomas' cave, not far from here," Juan D. said. "It's an important cave, archaeologically, and most of it is closed to the public. It's bigger, too, about 43 kilometers long. Local guides will take you in part way, but there are no lights, no tourist paths to follow. The Indians never stayed in this cave, because it leaks and is very wet when the rains come." Juan D. grew up in a small farming town in Pinar del Rio, so this was his home territory.

We paid the entrance fee – three dollars for me and ten pesos for Juan D. – and joined a group of 40 tourists, mostly Germans, entering the cave through a slit in the rock face of a mogote. Inside, a smooth cement pathway took away any sense of adventure. Strong lights fixed high up on the sides revealed pasty-cream limestone walls and massive solidified folds hanging from the 80-foot-high ceiling. We walked for ten minutes and came to an underground river. Two metal boats waited to take us deeper into the cave, their noisy outboards putting a slight stink in the air.

The river extended 13 kilometers back into the cave, but our trip was only three kilometers before the cave narrowed, forcing the boats to turn around. Our guide pointed out a formation overhead that looked like a man smoking a cigar and another in the form of a snake poised to drop on unsuspecting prey below. We followed the river out of the cave to a landing, where local entrepreneurs sold cigars, fresh-squeezed cane juice, and handicrafts. "Lunch should be ready," Juan D. said.

We drove back to town and found the paladare house. A small thatched dining area had been constructed in the back yard, where we were served a fried fish from the local river similar to bream; yucca with garlic; black beans and white rice (called *Moros y Cristianos* – "Moors and Christians"); fried plantains; and a salad of lettuce, tomato, and radish.

On the way back to Havana, Juan D. made a detour into the foothills of the Sierra de los Organos. "I want to visit a friend," he explained. We pulled into the yard of a single-story farmhouse, its white stucco walls stark in the blue twilight. A man came out of the door at Juan D.'s honking, and the two friends enthusiastically pounded each other on the back. We sat on wrought-iron chairs and were served coffee by the wife. Juan D. and his friend chatted rapid-fire, catching up on each other's lives. Then Juan D.'s voice dropped as he asked a question. His friend replied in a muted mumble. Their conversation continued *sotto voce* for another 20 minutes. Then, as if noticing for the first time that the lavender evening had turned into a black night, Juan D. rose and said his goodbyes.

In the car, Juan D. told me his friend's story. After the Revolution, forces opposed to Castro had fought in these mountains. A local militia was raised, and Castro sent army troops to completely surround the mountains, trapping the counter-rebels. It took two years to completely squelch the counter-revolution that was happening in the mountains at the eastern end of island, where Castro had started his Revolution. The friend's parents – both university professors but native to the area – and his older brother were sympathetic to the counter-rebels' cause. "Actively sympathetic," Juan D. emphasized. The parents and the brother were arrested. The parents received 15 years in prison. The brother was sentenced to ten years but escaped to Canada. The friend – a young boy at the time – went to live with his grandparents and, inheriting their farm, never left.

"He's not bitter," Juan D. said. "He's made a good life here. A quiet life." He didn't say anything more for a few kilometers. Then, "Batista put the boss—" (how Cubans often refer to Castro) "—in prison after the attack on the Moncade Barracks, but Castro was pardoned and released after two years, along with other political prisoners."

The attack on the Moncade Barracks in Santiago de Cuba in 1953 was Castro's first military action against the dictator Batista. It was a disaster. Most of Castro's small band of men was killed, along with a few of Batista's soldiers. Those of Castro's men who survived were captured and tortured. Castro was among those captured and was sent to a prison on the Isle of Pines.

"If the blockade is lifted, that will not solve our problems," Juan D. said. "The problem is the system. Do you know that it's written into the Cuban constitution that I, as a Cuban citizen, cannot start or own a factory in my own country? An Italian can come here and start a factory and I have to work for him. What is that?"

In a speech at a special session of the World Trade Organization held in Geneva on May 19, 1998, Castro said that, to that date, the US economic blockade had cost Cuba $60 billion. In a speech four weeks later to the heads of Caribbean governments, he rhetorically asked,

"Hey, who are the main advocates of socialism in Cuba today? The United States is, because they don't want people to invest [in Cuba]."

The Cuban government forms joint partnerships with foreign investors. For example, the Italian who wants to build a shoe factory in Cuba will own 49 per cent of the enterprise and the Cuban government will control 51 per cent. The investor is required to pay the Cuban government a set guaranteed wage for each Cuban worker – say, $15 per day. However, the worker may not receive all that money. The money goes into the national kitty and the government decides the priorities of expenditures according to the needs of the nation, so the worker may receive less than the agreed wage and the remainder of the money will be diverted as the State sees fit – to a hospital, for example.

Juan D. concentrated on his driving, but his jaws were chewing on something. "We have this wonderful free and equal education system. The State will pay fully for a person to become a doctor, but then that person must work for the State for $25 a month for the rest of his or her life. That is a very expensive education for the doctor. Castro doesn't like money. A few years ago, he went on a public rage against money. He said that he never carries money. But he's the President! He doesn't need to carry money! Someone carries it for him. He—" (Juan D. stroked an imaginary beard, another way Cubans refer to their president) "—is deeply suspicious about money and property ownership. He has made the correct analysis about capitalistic exploitation, about how social classes based on money create envy and conflict in a society. He understands how land speculation can force people out of the homes and businesses just so someone else can profit. He's right about the injustices, but he's taken us too far. He has created injustices against the Cuban people.

"You want to know my pop psychology of Our Father [another common phrase referring to Castro]? Castro's father was Spanish. The Spanish hated the North Americans after the Spanish-Cuban-American War. So maybe as a young boy, during his formative years, the young Castro heard from his father the condemnation of the imperialist curs, the Norte Americano bastards. Maybe all his young life he heard about the greedy, power-hungry shitheads who would rather suck on money than on mother's milk. Young children are impressionable. Their subconscious remembers. And when he became an intellectual at university, his mind found all the right reasons to know what his subconscious already told him."

In a speech before CARIFORUM – a special meeting of the Caribbean heads of state and government – on August 24, 1998, Castro said, "Before I read my first Marxist text, by myself I reached the conclusion that [capitalism] was chaotic, absolutely chaotic. That is the reason why I became sort of a utopian communist, someone who begins to imagine a different, more just society. Of course, I knew about justice and injustice, although I did not grow up as a proletarian. I grew up as the son of a landowner."

Then, on February 3, 1999, Castro reminisced about his father in a speech at the University of Venezuela, Caracas: "My father had about 1,000 hectares of land of his own and 10,000 hectares of leased land that he exploited. He was born in Spain and as a young and poor peasant was enrolled [in the army] to fight against the Cubans [in the War of Independence, 1895-98, also known as the Spanish-Cuban-American War]. I think about my father, who perhaps was 16 or 17 when he was drafted over there and sent to Cuba, as things were done in those days, and stationed in a Spanish fortified line. Could my father be accused of fighting on the wrong side? No. In any case, he fought on the right side – he fought with the Spaniards... I consider that they drafted him and he fought on the right side. If he had fought on the Cuban side, he would have been on the wrong side, because that was not his country. He knew nothing about it. He could not even understand what the Cubans were fighting for. He was a conscript.

"Later, he became a landowner. I was born and I lived on a large estate. It did not do me any harm. [Castro's mother was a housemaid made pregnant by her master. His parents married after Castro was born.] I had my first friends there, the poor children of the place, the children of waged workers and modest peasants, all victims of the capitalist system. Later, I went to schools that were more for the elite, but I came out unscathed, luckily. I really mean luckily. I had the fortune of being the son, and not the grandson, of a landowner. If I had been the grandson of a landowner, I would have probably been born and brought up in a city among rich children, in a very high-class neighborhood, and I would have never developed my utopian or Marxist-communist ideas, nor anything similar."

The young Castro was sent to board in the best Jesuit academies. At Belen High School, in Havana, he became a brilliant student, an excellent debater, and a champion athlete in basketball and track. He was also a promising baseball pitcher who later tried out for professional scouts. Their verdict: decent fastball but not good control.

"No one is born a revolutionary, nor a poet, nor a warrior," Castro said in the speech. "It is the circumstances that make an individual or give them the opportunities of being one thing or the other."

Juan D. drove in silence, then said, "He's Our Father. My generation has known no other leader, and he has done good things for us. But he is like a father of a beautiful 15-year-old-daughter who knows the dangers in the world to her. His love for his daughter blinds him so he can't see her own capabilities, her own confidence in surviving in the world. He doesn't trust us. He is unable to let go. Perhaps he's afraid of the empty nest," Juan D. said with a laugh.

11 The Cuban Musical Box

On a full-mooned Friday night in Havana, I joined 70,000 people at La Pirague, a small park between the Hotel Nacional and the Malecón. A street had been closed to create a bigger space there, but still the crowd overflowed onto the Malecón back to the sea wall, shutting down traffic. The event was the Caliente! Festival Internacional de Musica 2001, a four-day celebration of popular Cuban music organized by Swiss entrepreneurs. American jazz pianist Herbie Hancock was the featured guest of honor. Three of the concerts were paid admission, but the outdoor one was free. Free or dirt-cheap cultural events are the norm in Cuba, so everyone, not just those with bucks (*not* pesos), can enjoy the arts.

A young couple standing next to me was, under the guise of dancing, having clothes-on sex. She, doe-eyed and totally dangerous, had her back ironing his shirt buttons. She was working like an industrious maid polishing the family jewels. He, grinning through his goatee, made sure her dustcloth was well oiled. I was into the music, you know, head bopping, shoulders rolling, hips shuffling, but compared to those two hotbloods I was a telephone pole.

The young man encouraged me to roll my shoulders more emphatically, "like you're warming up to hit a home run." I made a suave roll. He shook his head as if I was a kid brother who had fallen off a bicycle. His girlfriend smiled big. The smile was a cage for her laughter, which was threatening to escape. He demonstrated a shoulder roll, a three-in-one undulation. It looked so natural and easy, which is what I thought about a golf swing until I tried to master the complicated mechanics of the simple, smooth motion. I tried to mimic his oil-on-butter move but over-exaggerated, which made me look like a silly tourist trying to join the locals' game. He smiled encouragement and suggested that I try both shoulders together to sort of balance things out. "Like waves on the ocean ro-o-o-lling around the world," he said. I imagined myself on big swells and rolled a few times.

"Now you go up and down," he said.

I looked at him quizzically. One shoulder up, one shoulder down? Yes, that, too, he said, but up and down with the whole body. His girlfriend demonstrated with an incredible shimmy up and down, up and down. Pole-dancing, I told myself. Just think pole-dancing in a topless joint. I tried. Have you ever seen a piece of cardboard try to be crêpe paper rippling in the wind? Raise your arms up, hands high over the head, he said. They both raised their arms. Balance on the balls of the feet, he said, and air fuck.

What?

Like this, he said. The couple was each other's pole on which they shimmied up and down. Could you *do* things like that in public?

"You have to move the hips," he said. I did a hula move. The girl laughed. Yes, he said, up and down, in and out, around and around. Remember that old party trick of rubbing your belly while you pat your head and chew gum? That was as simple as playing dead compared to the young man's hip gyrations. "From the knees," he said. "Knees, hips, and shoulders. They all go together but go differently." I got them to go differently but not together. The girl laughed, not mockingly but just enjoying a good joke. He offered me a hit of his rum. I was a bit more fluid after two swigs, but still, while the couple was graceful and sensuous, I was out of sync and ridiculous, like an over-eager lover stumbling around with one foot tangled up in a pants cuff.

The young man watched for a moment and then offered me a cigar. He meant it as a gesture of inclusion. I took it as a consolation prize.

I thought that the couple was just two lustful whoops grooving outrageously obscenely on rum and music. Then I looked at the couple on the other side of me – they were dancing like dogs in heat. I turned and scanned the mass of people. Hundreds upon hundreds of people were doing what, in many countries of northern clime, would be considered pornographic acts. As I stared – it was like peeking into a bedroom window at a mass orgy – I noticed that the couples were performing actual dance steps: the salsa. No wonder it's the most popular music and dance in Cuba, with an ardent following in New York, London, Paris, Stockholm, and Tokyo. The salsa is salacious, overtly sensual, a sexual come-on, but for the sake of dancing rather than blatant sex – although, by the look on the young woman's face next to me, the dance must feel like foreplay.

The last act of the evening was Juan Formell and his band, Los Van Van, who won a Grammy in 2000 for their album *Llego Van Van* (*"Van Van Is Here"*). Cubans have been dancing to Formell and Los Van Van for nearly as long as they've been working out the steps to socialism. Now 58, Formell has been in the forefront of Cuban popular music for 30 years and is still going strong. He is not an academically trained musician and composer, although he did study guitar and bass; he learned harmony and orchestration from his father. He was part of the Nueva Trova movement and played counterbass in Orquesta Revé, the Havana Libre (formerly the Hilton) Hotel's house band. The orchestra played mostly the traditional *charanga* music, but its leader, Elio Revé, wanted to appeal to the modern dance crowd and asked Formell to compose new music for the old music – that is, to give the traditional a modern sound.

The charanga is considered the "weaker" of the orchestra sounds, heavy on sentimental violins and flutes, compared to the bold and aggressive saxophones and trumpets of jazz bands. Charanga is thought of as a soft, female sound. This is the sound that Revé wanted Formell to strengthen. Formell added into the music the electric guitar and more of the Spanish traditional son sound of the Oriente countryside. The sound changed from music for decorous dancing to more lively, charged music with a vision of the future, a vision that gave Formell the idea of starting his own band. In 1969, he and pianist César "Pupi" Pedroso founded Los Van Van, combining the flutes and violins of the upper-class charanga with the horns and congas of the working-class music. In doing so, they created Cuba's number-one dance band, with a sound somewhere between traditional son and salsa.

Formell kept experimenting, adding trombones and taking out the guitar while keeping the violins of the charanga and adding the organ and synthesizer to accompany the keyboard. He kept the traditional four singers of the charanga style but added Platters-like harmonies, which gained the band a wide audience in the United States. Formell found a way of making a universal music enjoyed by audiences in the United States, Europe, Japan, and South America, while keeping the Cuban flavor.

Out of Formell's experimentation came a new dance rhythm, the songo, created by him and Los Van Van drummer Jose Luis Quintana, known as Changuito. The songo style – a mix of funk, rock, and Cuban percussion, as heard on the album *Te Pone Las Cabeza Mala* – earned Los Van Van comparisons with The Grateful Dead. Two things made the songo different from the salsa: the drumming patterns and the bass-guitar lines. The salsa features the conga; Changuito made the drum kit more prominent by cleverly figuring out how to incorporate patterns usually played on the timbale, patterns that were borrowed from the rumba segunda drum patterns. For the first time, rumba rhythm – usually played on the salsa conga – was played on the trap set.

Formell, a bass-guitar player, devised an innovative style to make songo distinct from salsa and yet maintain the driving salsa beat that makes fools out of old maids. In salsa, the bass guitar plays the traditional ostinato tumbao bass patterns, which reflect African drumming. The bass guitarist and the conga drummer are partners in salsa, so much so that the bass usually plays an acoustic or an electric baby bass for a percussive attack that gives bottom to the conga drums. In songo, the bass player usually plays a Fender electric bass for a more rock 'n' roll range and more independent bass lines from the conga.

Salsa itself is based around the Cuban dance genres of son, guaracha, and rumba, but the name salsa wasn't coined until the late 1960s, and there are several explanations of how the music was given its commercial name. One version claims that the name came from a popular song, 'Echala Salsita,' played by The Septeto Nacional Band in Venezuela in 1966. The song had the chorus "salsa y sabor" ("sauce and savor" – *salsa* means sauce or gravy). Tito Puente said from the stage of the Village Gate on May 21, 1990, "What is salsa? It's tomato sauce. It's spaghetti sauce. In the old days, we had the son montuno, the guaguancó, the guaracha."

Another version of the provenance of the name gives credit for applying the word to the music to Jerry Masucci of Fania Records, who needed a catchy marketing name for the Cuban-style dance music he was promoting to New York Latinos. Yet another version attributes the usage of salsa to Izzy Sanabria, the publisher of *Latin New York* magazine, who is said to have coined the term while emceeing a Fania All-Star concert.

Always tuned to the dancing feet of the youth, Formell's music gained Los Van Van a worldwide following. They toured South America, Japan, Europe, and the United States. On US tours, the band had to avoid Miami because of the antagonistic Cuban exiles and Cuban-Americans who lived there, known as the "Miami Mafia." In 1996, an anti-Castro mob in Miami attacked concertgoers outside a performance by Cuban jazz pianist Gonzalo Rubalcaba. The anti-Castro pressure group was also instrumental in preventing Miami-Dade from hosting a future Pan-American Games. A MIDEM American music-event party was canceled in 1998, under duress, because Cuban musicians were scheduled to play. However, Formell agreed to play a concert date in Miami on October 9, 1999 at the end of a five-week, 26-city US tour. "I think that things have changed and that there are a lot of people here now who are ready to hear music," Formell told *The Miami Herald* a week before the scheduled concert.

The anti-Castro Cubans mounted an attack to stop the concert. DJs on Cuban radio stations, led by La Poderosa and Radio Mambi, urged listeners to deluge City Hall with phone calls protesting the concert. Miami Mayor Joe Carollo and City Commissioner Tomas Regalado appeared on La Poderosa in support of the protest. "It's touching a chord, because this is not a cultural event," Regalado said. "It's a challenge to the capital of the exiled community. It's a political challenge."

Mayor Carollo added, "This is the official communistic band of

Fidel Castro." That assertion came as a surprise to Formell and the band members.

The concert was canceled and then rescheduled for October 11. On that Saturday night, an estimated 3,500-4,000 protesters spat, yelled obscenities, and threw eggs, rocks, and bottles at the concertgoers. Fifty Miami police officers in riot gear arrived to quell the protest.

On stage, Formell told the 2,000 fans, "To us, you represent millions of people. There are more of you who love us than don't love us." Then the band opened with 'Comenzó La Fiesta' ('The Party Has Started').

I called Francisco, Juan Formell's brother and Los Van Van's manager, to try and arranged an interview. "He's recording at the studio at the Nacional Teatro this afternoon. Come on down." I knew that trying to grab a few minutes of a musician's time while in a recording session is like trying to insert your finger into a cement block, but I went to the studio anyway. Francisco met me at the gate. "Not now," he said. "Maybe later. They're really tied up in the music." Then, later, he said, "Not now. Maybe later." Then, still later, he said, "Call me tomorrow." It became a month of tomorrows, and then I ran out of time.

Formell's music is fusion, the essential element of Cuban music. Fusion created Afro-Cuban jazz and Afro-Cuban rock. Fusion is the inspiration of Pablo Menéndez's band, Mezcla, which means "mixture." To show how fusion works in Cuban music, Pablo and his bandmates deconstructed their song 'Ikir Í Addá' while the band was at Pablo's place rehearsing in the cramped, book-lined study he shares with his wife. The mixing board was set up in the living room. They talked about the music between songs.

'Ikir Í Addá' is a Yoruba chant to the orisha Oggun, brother of Chango. Another version, arranged by Frank Delgado, was recorded as 'El Camino Se Hace Con La Fe' ('The Road Is Made With Faith') on Mezcla's *Borders Of Dreams* album. The Yoruba chant was transcribed by Lázaro Ros, the soloist for The Folkloric Ensemble and mastersinger of Yoruba Santeria chants. According to Pablo, he wanted to "make an album where the ancient traditional chants would not be put away as museum pieces but projected into the future as something contemporary and preserved in that way for the young generations." Before recording the song, Mezcla played a festival on Martinique and heard a lot of *zouk*, that island's music. Zouk is a catchy, somewhat repetitious music, not as diverse as Cuban music, but it's a rhythm that stays with you. It stayed with Mezcla's bass guitarist/arranger at the time, Jose Antonio Acosta, who put the zouk rhythm on top of the bata rhythm of Ros' chant.

"We were also listening to a lot of music from Africa," Pablo said. "My guitar patterns, written by Acosta, were taken from west African guitar sounds. Acosta also had me playing some fuzz distortion rock 'n' roll riffs. The keyboards were imitating Caribbean steel drums, and the saxophone was playing the Caribbean flavor heard in calypso. When we finished that arrangement, we were aware that it was a landmark thing we had done in mixing all the different cultural elements – jazz, rock, zouk, Yoruba bata drumming, and influences from southwest African guitar playing. Plus, two-thirds of the way through the song, we did vocal parts taken from the South African style of Ladysmith Black Mambazo."

Then, to add more to the mix, Nueva Trova singer/songwriter Frank Delgado wrote lyrics about the rapprochement of the Cuban government with the Catholic Church. The song was still a chant to the orisha Oggun. The fundamental beat was a basic 4/4 under the faster zouk rhythm. The bata's layers – a complex polyrhythm – were in counterpoint to the zouk rhythm. The kit drummer and the bata drummer worked carefully to be complementary so that their patterns didn't drown out or puddle each other's. The grunge guitar was right out of the Seattle/West Coast movement, while the bass guitar was melodious, doing more than the usual yeoman's task of keeping time, in accordance with the influence of South African bass-guitar work. Riding on top of all this was a sax line with a Caribbean flavor. "The song was one of our biggest hits," Pablo said.

When not in the makeshift home studio, the individual band members sat around Pablo's living room and discussed their musical influences. "Rumba, chacha, guaracha, timba, danzón, folkloric music – all the rhythms of Cuba is in our music," said David

Pimienta, the drummer, "and jazz, rock, reggae, calypso, and other music from the Caribbean. All that goes into the Cuban fusion."

The bass player, Jose Hermida, began his career studying concert guitar before discovering the counterbass. "I began playing rock and blues and later got into Nueva Trova fusion. Now I play salsa, rock, jazz – mainly Latin jazz – sweet funk, rhythm and blues, and gospel. I listen to opera. I am influenced by South African music, because they have another style of expressing the tempo different from we Latin Americans."

Orlando "Cubajazz" Sanchez first studied the clarinet for 13 years and was a classical player. Now he is a composer, arranger, piano player, as well as being Mezcla's tenor-sax player. "Mostly I try to bring the John Coltrane news for the Cuban music," he said. "That is a big heritage in Cuban music – Coltrane, Charlie Parker, others of the great jazz players. The sounds in Mezcla include bossa nova rhythms, Caribbean rhythms, R&B, funky – all the new rhythms. Most important is to try to meet all those combinations, the rhythms, melodies, and styles. I am Cuban, so I have incorporated all those into Cuban rhythms."

Besides his American blues background, Pablo was the lead guitarist in the Cuban Afro-rock band Sintesis from 1978 to 1982. Carlos Alfonso – the founder, musical director, arranger, bass guitarist, and singer for Sintesis – is a near neighbor of Pablo's. I walked the three blocks to talk with Carlos about his original brand of Cuban rock. He lives with his wife, Ele Valdés, and their teenage daughter in a house nicely appointed with art and comfortable, casual Caribbean furniture. Their son, who now records with Sintesis, is past the age of living at home. Ele, who also sings with the band, greeted me at the door and Carlos soon joined us. He is a short, stocky man with pale-yellow hair (dyed) and intense brown eyes set in a small, delicate face.

Sintesis, which was formed 25 years ago, merges ritual Santeria melodies and rhythms and the chants to the orishas with experimental rock, jazz, and other Afro-American forms of music, Carlos explained. His job, as the musical director and arranger, is to keep a fine balance of the forms within the music.

We listened to an album while the coffee was being prepared. Carlos does an excellent job. The power chords of the electric guitar do not blast out, overwhelming the band. The bata, conga, and drum kit can be heard individually, while simultaneously playing together. The jazz piano is not bombastic but rather a light color running through the music. The bass guitar is a strong presence but uses the rhythms of the bata to integrate itself rather than remaining an individual voice. Carlos uses the traditional and the modern to complement each other, rather than running counter and emphasizing the differences in the music styles.

Ele brought in a tray of coffee and the three of us settled in for a chat.

"In North American rock, there was a progression beginning in 1949 that came out of black music to Bill Haley And The Comets in the early '50s, Elvis Presley, the 1960s' hippie rock, acid rock, heavy metal, grunge, to the present. Did such a progression happen in Cuba?" I asked.

"No," Carlos answered. "The main moment for Cuban rock was in the 1970s. It was played underground at private parties. Every neighborhood had its own group, like The Hoodmen, Pacific, Almas Vertiginosas. One famous group was The Kings, and another important group was called The Dadas. There were two main ways of rock then, the followers of the blues and the followers of The Rolling Stones. From there, there was emptiness.

"At first, Cuban rock was a direct imitation of North American rock. The songs, solos, everything was like in the States. We listened to US radio programs like *Hit Parade* and *Midnight Special*. Then came Nueva Trova, like the second phase. More politicized, and with a folk sound like Simon And Garfunkel and Bob Dylan, Nueva Trova became a big movement on a national scale. They were influenced by Western 1970s rock and were very aggressive in their style of singing and playing. Their stage performances were different, more hippie. This was the next step in Cuban rock after the first North American wave.

"Sintesis has always used sounds of all sorts of music. We have used open styles, a mix of jazz with Pink Floyd. I remember the voices of Crosby, Stills, Nash And Young, and they permeated my ears forever. That has been an influence on Sintesis' vocals and instrumentals. The band I most want to record with is Tears For Fears. We don't want to take rock and play it as it is. We are most interested in experimenting with our own sounds."

There is heavy African percussion in Sintesis' music. Carlos uses only Santeria chants and bata drumming. "Abakuá is very mystic, very secret, very select," he explained. "Abakuá is a secret society and I can have trouble with them. They are trouble men. Yoruba is more relaxed, more open, more popular. I'm not a believer, but I respect the spiritual in this music. The music is not based on my beliefs and motives but [in] cultural things. Once, in the countryside, I heard a toque of bata drums and I was astonished with what I was hearing. That remains inside me. I asked why this music calls my attention so strongly."

The guitar and drums are essential elements in rock 'n' roll. Carlos uses them in such a way that the West and Africa meet in harmony. "The bass guitar, with a different accent on the beat, expresses the low accent of the bata," he said. "They are aligned because of the players' knowledge based on Afro-Cuban music and on the feeling, the spiritualism, that comes of it. In this, we have made rock our own."

There is a very serious problem in Cuba for rock 'n' roll musicians and people who like rock 'n' roll, Carlos confided. In the mid 1990s, there was a big wave of salsa music that coincided with Cuba opening to tourism. Everything was focused on salsa, because tourists wanted salsa. Money flowed to the salsa bands. Rock bands lost their best drummers and guitar players to the salsa bands. "They left the electric guitar to play the tres," Carlos lamented. "Rock was eliminated."

"Now we have the Buena Vista Social Club wave," Carlos said. "It's mediocre music. I have to be fair with what I say. There is traditional Cuban music with its values, but this Buena Vista Social Club music was used in hotels, in restaurants. It was never used on the stage. Then the American Ry Cooder came here and put a lot of promotion behind that music. Now we are consuming our own sugar disguised in candies. Our own music has been disguised in this sweet music. It's pitiful, but it's what is happening. This Buena Vista Social Club type of music, saying they found an old musician shining shoes, it's a show. It's a way to deny the reality of present-day Cuba and the issues we face. This old romantic sentiment is a safe way to look at Cuba.

"Because of the success of the old men in Buena Vista Social Club, Cuban musicians don't want to be young. Everybody wants to be 90 years old and play traditional music." Carlos laughed at his joke, but it's no laughing matter for him. "The rock goes back again, loses ground, because the musicians get more money [with] the traditional [music]."

There are two culturally important groups in Cuba, according to Carlos, painters and musicians. "They are two blocks ahead of everyone else," he said. "That's why painters and musicians are culturally important. Music here is not about romance and play and entertainment; our music reflects our problems, our real problems. The Cuban musicians are like journalists. The musicians and the painters criticize social attitudes in the problems we have and embrace the good things we have. He can talk about the queue to get bread, or about the butcher who gives a friend more meat. The butcher is a very important person, because he gives out meat. Food has always been a subject in Cuban music. There is a song that is nothing but reciting the menu of a restaurant, but the twist comes in the last line, when the customer says, 'I want my meat well done and spicy.' Suddenly, the song takes on sexual tones. Cuban music has a lot of that duality, which is why the music can be, and is, a political tool as well as a cultural expression. The musician reflects the situation of the country."

The next day, I met with Juan de Marcos Gonzales, the producer of Buena Vista Social Club's albums and the director of The Afro-Cuban All Stars. We met in the open courtyard beside EGREM Studio, where he was rehearsing for a new album. On the following day, he and The Afro-Cuban All Stars would be flying to Mexico City for a one-night gig.

"I made that project," he said of the *Buena Vista Social Club* album. "I had the idea to make an album bringing in the old guys, the old generation of Cuban musicians, with the punchy big-band sound of the late 1950s in Cuba. They hadn't recorded in a long time. I was living in London at the time, working with Nick Gold, the president of World Circuit Music and a good friend of mine. Nick had a long-time interest in Cuban music. A couple years earlier, he had started working with Sierra Maestra and had licensed from EGREM a Nico Saquito album – which is traditional eastern Cuban music – and an album of Dominjer Mopetalle, a star in the 1940s and '50s of eastern Cuban music. He agreed to make the album with the old guys and at the same time wanted to make a fusion album using African musicians to play the typical sound of the eastern Cuban son. Nick suggested that we call in Ry Cooder to work on that album.

"I came back to Havana with my wife of 21 years, Gliceria Abreu, and we looked for all the old musicians. She was the mom of Buena Vista Social Club, because she took care of all the details. We recorded the first album with the basic musical line-up of Buena Vista Social Club. It was called *Alturas De Lisa* and got a Grammy nomination in 1998. We recorded that with The Afro-Cuban All Stars and all my arrangements. At the Grammys, we agreed to make a second album, but it would be Ibrahim Ferrer's first solo album, so we came back to Havana and looked for musicians. This is the music you see in the film *Buena Vista Social Club*.

"I looked for Eliades Ochoa and Compay Segunda especially for this album. Originally, I was looking for Renaldo Rey and Compay Segunda, because Renaldo is the really, really well-known star. Compay Segunda is very well known right now but was completely unknown before. I found Almarto Portunan on the streets. I told him it would be great if he made this one album, because I didn't have a male voice on the album.

"After we recorded the *Alturas De Lisa* album, Ry arrived to work with the Africans on the planned eastern Cuban music. Unfortunately, the Africans couldn't come, because of visa problems. That's when we recorded the *Buena Vista Social Club* album, on which I was the conductor, arranger, and organizer. At the time of the recording, it was called just "the eastern album." Ry gave his ideas

Juan de Marcos, director of The Afro-Cuban All Stars and producer of the first Buena Vista Social Club albums

on how the album should sound, so he came for the production. One of the really special things of the album is the sound, so it's a very important point that we had Ry. He looked for a sound that I would never have thought of making, like the 1930s, a very dirty sound and very rough, almost no mix. *Buena Vista Social Club* sounds like a recorded rehearsal with nonprofessional mics. That's the sound, and that is very attractive, I think, for the people of the First World. People of the First World are very involved in the very technological psyche, and they need space to relax in. *Buena Vista Social Club* gives that space to relax.

"Here, in Cuba, the album is not that famous, because it's completely normal. It's the music that we have on our streets. You can find 35, 40...I don't know...Buena Vista Social Clubs playing in Havana. But it was something important for Cuban music. It marked the point of [a] return to the position that we had before. Before the

1960s, we were the best sellers of tropical Cuban music in the world. Even in America, we Cubans were quite famous, with people like Machito, Desi Arnaz, Chico O'Farrill, who were performing in New York and writing for films in Hollywood.

"The film was the second thing. The album was done and we had already sold more than a million copies. Ry is very good friends with Wim Wenders, so they came to an understanding to do the film. When we started recording Ibrahim Ferrer's solo album, Wim started filming. We played three concerts with the real Buena Vista Social Club just for the film. I think that the film should be better. Technically, it was excellent, but the message is wrong. Wim Wenders is an existentialist film-maker, so he has a very gray vision of the world. Everything is sad. He's German. They lost a couple of wars, and that's normal, the sadness, for Germans. He used the kind of visual planes and shots and focuses that show a gray and sad Cuba. Cuba is a poor country. We have nothing, but we have the music. We are proud of the music. We are proud to be Cubans. And this is a very happy country, even if we are completely fucked over. But we are happy. That's the problem of the Cubans. We are Latins and half African, so we can make a joke about our problems. It's normal to find a lot of jokes in the streets about our own problems.

"In the film, you can see a very gray Cuba. All the shots are in very bad buildings. It's a massive destructive vision of Cuban reality. Cuba is sunny. In the film, there are several shots of one door green, one door blue – it's the language, very existentialist and surrealist. It's a surrealist vision of the Caribbean. But, at the same time, the film was excellent to promote the album. After the film came out, we sold more albums. But the film does not show the reality of the Cuban society."

Nick Gold, owner and artistic director of World Circuit Music, which produced the *Buena Vista Social Club* album, added details to Juan's account from his office in London: "I did a record with Marcos when he was leading the band Sierra Maestra in the summer of 1994. We got on very well. I asked him if he could expand that band a bit and try to incorporate the style and flavor of eastern Cuban traditional music. During our discussions about the 1950s era of Cuban music, he told me of an idea he had to do a recording using a lot of musicians from the so-called golden age of Cuban music. That those musicians were alive and playing was a bit of a surprise to me.

"Juan said we should record it in Havana, and I was telling him about an idea I had for a long time of doing a collaboration of guitar music from west Africa – Mali, specifically – and the music from eastern Cuba. That project became *Buena Vista Social Club*.

"For several months we went back and forth, looking at repertoire and musicians for both the old-time Cuban musicians record and the collaboration record. We booked a couple weeks at EGREM Studio in Havana and then started having problems getting the Africans to Cuba. They sent their passports by post to get their Cuban visas and they got lost. We [hadn't] lost hope and were talking to other musicians [to see] if they could make it or not.

"I sent Ry Cooder a fax asking if he'd be interested in collaborating on the west African-Cuban project. We had worked together before. He replied with an immediate fax: 'Yes, I'll be there.' I went to Havana and we started working on Marcos' album, which became the first Afro-Cuban All Stars record, *A Toda Cuba Le Gusta*. I fell in love with a lot of the musicians he had brought together, this multi-generational band in celebration of that golden age of Cuban music. He was very interested in the continuation of Cuban music from generation to generation. A lot of the players on the *A Toda Cuba Le Gusta* record we kept for the sessions that resulted in *Buena Vista Social Club*. Most of the rhythm section we kept. I particularly fell in love with Ruben Gonzales and wanted him to stay on.

"When we knew that we didn't have the Africans, what were we going to do? We had another ten days of studio time booked. We had Cuban musicians coming in from different parts of the island. We had repertoire slated that we were going to do with the Malians, and we had a studio full of musicians, too many to work with, and word had spread, so musicians were turning up to see if they could be on the recording as well. There was a fantastic atmosphere amongst the musicians because the first session went so well. Everyone was very excited and energized, especially the older musicians, who hadn't been doing much work, some of them for a considerable amount of time, so they were very up to be in the studio again. Musicians who

Musicians on a break while recording with Juan de Marcos and The Afro-Cuban All Stars at EGREM Studio

hadn't worked together for ten years were together again, so it was quite charged.

"The *Buena Vista* thing went very organically. Marcos conducted a lot of the *Buena Vista* stuff and helped in the shaping of the arrangements. Ry did a lot of work with the sound of how we were recording. He wanted to record the whole ensemble live, so we arranged the musicians [so that they were] physically close to one another and put up ambient microphones, because the sound of the room was so beautiful, and the musicians would [play]. It flowed quite strangely, and we just recorded and recorded. That *Buena Vista Social Club* album won a Grammy in 1998.

"After we recorded The Afro-Cuban All Stars and Buena Vista Social Club, we had two days left in the studio. I asked Ruben Gonzales, the pianist, if he wanted to record, so we knocked off three records in two weeks. Maybe six or seven months after all three records were released, we brought the musicians on tour. Then Ry was working with Wenders on a film and Ry kept playing the *Buena Vista* music to Wenders. Wenders became excited by it. Nothing really happened, and then we had a time when the band was on tour. I thought it was an opportunity to put that band together for concerts, which is difficult, because normally all the musicians were doing their own things and touring. At an Amsterdam show, they were all together, and I wanted to film it. Because we were going back to do another Buena Vista Social Club recording, it all seemed feasible. That's when we thought of doing the film. The second album was Ibrahim Ferrer's first solo album. We were recording that while Wenders was filming the various bits and interviews."

12 Jazz, Cuban Style

Last night, I went to La Zorra y El Cuervo (the Fox and the Crow), a jazz club on La Rampa, to hear Roberto Fonseca, who, at 25, is considered to be one of the best original jazz pianists of his generation. La Zorra y El Cuervo is the most authentic jazz club in Havana. The façade looks like an over-sized British phone booth with "JAZZ" scripted across the front in cool lavender. The club is in a basement, the ceiling is low, and the tables are crowded together. It's an intimate, no-frills place. The musicians walk through the audience to reach the stage area, a section of the floor defined by lights and instruments. The musicians' changing room is the men's rest room. To reach their rest room, women must walk on the edge of the stage area and maneuver past the horn players. When that rest room is not occupied, sax players tune up in it. The best Cuban jazzmen play the club, as well as those just beginning to make their mark. It's a must-stop for US and European jazz musicians when they come to Havana.

Roberto sat at the keyboard with his band, nearly hidden behind a large support column, with his band, Temperamento, stage center. He has a very relaxed style, even when the music is athletic. When I walked in, the sax player was performing aerobics on the scales and swinging from riff to riff with the verve of a trapeze artist. Roberto remained at ease and confident, creating the groove, his notes simultaneously created by music flowing through the groove. His fingers tripped out runs as he picked up the progressions and phrases of the wailing sax. When the sax man took a deep breath for a launch to the moon, Roberto hit a heavy bass chord and smiled hugely, his eyes alight with pleasure, as the sax man climbed onto that solid platform and took flight.

Roberto was satisfied to drift along under the star-sailing sax until the horn man stood aside. Then Roberto strode into his solo. He loves percussion, but he's not bombastic on the keyboard. Even when putting his full weight into the music, he's not a piledriver pounding chords into the audience's head, as if shattering dense cement with his musical brilliance. He has lightness in his touch, an inviting playfulness, even when going full blast. He knows what he's doing and why and how, but that weight of maturity is not allowed to dampen his youthful crackle of energy.

I could hear his scat-singing murmur accompanying the racing of his fingers up and down the keyboard. His playing kept pace in perfect balance with his creative thoughts, never ahead, never behind, always tight in place with the sax in front of him on the stage. The bass guitar stood behind him, and the drum kit and the congas were in his line of sight so that he could see the space in the rhythms to go into, or stay out of, nice and easy at lightning speed. Yet his music was so achingly gentle and so simple that the audience glided along, knowing where the progressions were taking them as surely as a lover knows where a kiss is leading.

After the set, the club's manager, Tony Basanta, invited Roberto to join me. Roberto is a serious musician who has toured North America and Europe, recorded with the jazz legend Frank Emilo and the conga master Tata Guines and, most recently, with Buena Vista Social Club in France, and he also recorded his own album with a Japanese company. He has the slender, supple body of a dancer and a casual sense of style that is as simple and as defining as his music. There's nothing about him that particularly makes him stand out, and yet, as he moved through the crowd to my table, he did stand out. His sense of fun and enjoyment of life gave him a halo of presence. Some might call it star quality.

I asked him what he heard in the phrasing of his music, in the pauses between the notes. "What I hear is like an idea," he answered. "One note, then the other note, is two different ideas. When I play the first note, I think about how I can continue to the second note,

Robert Fonseca, widely regarded as the most original Cuban jazz pianist of his generation

to give continuity to the idea I'm developing. It's a very odd thing. Even I don't know what happens. The pauses allow the listener to catch up and let them fill in those phrases. I try to make the music the most simple it can be so every person gets a sensation that makes him feel well."

"Afro-Cuban jazz is often lumped under the rubric Latin jazz," I observed. "Is there a distinction between the two?"

"Latin jazz is just jazz mixed with Latin music," he said. "Here in Cuba, Latin jazz is fast, more aggressive, [with] more movement. When we make fusion with jazz and traditional Cuban son music, some people call it Latin jazz. Latin jazz is like an accent without the salsa tempo but with jazzy things in the tempo. Latin jazz has Afro-Cuban roots. You can hear it in the rumba that has been joined to jazz. The Afro-Cuban jazz has the rhythms of the bata drums and rhythmic cells that are specifically Afro-Cuban. Musicians can differentiate immediately what is Latin jazz and what is Afro-Cuban jazz. I got the Afro-Cuban from my grandmother, who was a believer in Santeria, and through that I discovered rhythms I never knew. I make my style of music through the knowledge of the ancestors, who brought the orishas. I expect people who listen to know more through the music about this spirituality and culture.

"Without offending the piano, I like percussion very much," he said with a smile. "I like the piano, not only as an instrument of notes but also for its rhythm imitating what the bata drums are doing. The percussion is my leitmotif. With the piano, I can transform the rhythms I listen to in the chorus and in the harmonic sequences. In the rhythms, I listen to Emilito del Monte, son of the famous drum player, because he is a percussionist and knows the bata and all that is related to Afro-Cuban music. He is my right hand and advises me on what we can or cannot do. I also like playing with Elmer Ferrer, who is the hottest electric-guitar player in Cuba. He knows his Afro-Cuban music and makes a lot of authentic Cuban music with jazz. Ruy Lopez-Nussa, our drum player, he is a percussion professor and knows all these things, too."

"You produced the first album of the hip-hop group Obsesión. How did a jazz man get involved in rap?"

Roberto laughed. "I always wanted to be a hip-hop singer, but I've dedicated myself to jazz. The music of hip-hop has a lot of power, a lot of strength. This has a lot to do with the Afro-Cuban music, with the Cuban music, and has a strong connection to jazz. The common point is improvisation. The improvisation of the traditional Cuban music is not different from the improvisation of jazz. That's the influence of blues in Latin music. Blues is the base for improvisation, the truest school of improvisation. The one who knows how to improvise in a good blues can incorporate that into Cuban music. That's why you hear an influence of the blues in Cuban music, especially solos of the melodic instruments in Latin jazz or Afro-Cuban jazz.

"The strength of the Afro-Cuban percussion music is the rhythm, so when we improvise we try to give some rhythm to what we are doing. One of the strongest things in Cuban music is the rhythmic quality. Hip-hop's strength relies on the rhythmic. These are different things, but they have a common point. They are different because they came from different countries, but the language is the same.

"There is not a rap that is plain. That music has picks, a flow, a wave." Roberto's right hand made the undulating motion of an ocean swell. "It's the same in jazz. Jazz has the possibility of entry and of going out, as does rap – like going in and out of the wave but never being out of the water. Cuban music, with its rhythmic basis, gives you the possibility to enter into the rhythm, then get out and enter into it again. I expect hip-hop to become more influential. I expect it will be exploited by Latin jazz and Afro-Cuban jazz."

"How do you come to your original music?"

"How I listen to life in Havana makes my music original. I try to make the music like my life is, and my life is Havana. This is where I was born, where I grew up. It has a lot of Afro-Cuban culture. I listen to the rhythm of normal people's speech and use that in my music. All the things of the streets have made me think the way I'm thinking now, so it is in my music. I try to play the jazz of all that is happening in Cuba. I try to deepen the Cuban. I have my roots, so I don't have to experiment with other things.

"That makes my music different [to] traditional jazz. The life we are living now has a lot of colors...is colorful. Then the chords have colors...[are] colorful. We are in 2001, so it is not the same as 80 years ago. The present is how I'm playing now, using new patterns, but I'm also playing from the ancient African music. I like very much the jungle beat. I mix jazz with Afro-Cuban, son, funky, hip-hop, folkloric themes from Cuba and other countries. I want to create a music that can be assimilated by everybody. That's what I think of my music for the future."

At that point, Tony Basanta came over to give Roberto his five-minute warning before the second set. "I only try to make new music that hasn't been done by anyone," Roberto said. He spoke humbly, so the bold statement wasn't a boast but a mission statement that could be taken as a family motto. Roberto is related to Jesús "Chucho" Valdés, widely regarded as the best jazz pianist in the world, bar none, who married Roberto's mother. *Jazziz* magazine called Chucho "the most complete musician in the world." Roberto grew up in a household where music – particularly classical and jazz piano – was the running conversation.

I repeatedly tried to link up with Chucho. We'd talk on the phone to arrange a slot in his busy schedule. When we finally nailed down a date and time, he won a Grammy with his quartet in 2001. I knew that I'd have to fish fast if I hoped to land him. "What does next week look like for you?" I asked when I called to congratulate him. "A concert in Havana, then Philadelphia, then back here for a day, then to Puerto Rico," he replied. "Try me in a week."

Chucho was a child prodigy on the piano. His father is the legendary jazz pianist Bebo Valdés, who was Chucho's first piano teacher when he was three years old. Bebo left Cuba in 1963 and resettled in Europe while Chucho stayed behind after forming his own jazz trio the year before and electing to remain with the group. In 1967, Chucho and Carlos Emilio created Orquesta Cubana De Musica Moderna, and in 1973 he formed the jazz band Irakere, which means "equatorial forest". The band quickly gained a reputation as the finest Cuban jazz group ever, playing experimental jazz based on Afro-Cuban themes and mixing in folkloric, rumba, funk, and whatever struck their fancy. The band won a Grammy in 1978 with its first US release on Columbia. Irakere remains the premier Cuban jazz band and tours the world, including the United States, although Chucho only occasionally performs with the band, preferring instead his quartet.

When the 1992 US blockade descended on Cuba, Chucho's appearances in the United States became as scarce as rain in a desert. That changed in 1996, however, when trumpeter Roy Hargrove performed with him at the Havana Jazz Festival and invited him to perform with his band as a guest soloist in the United States. The album *Crisol* resulted from that collaboration.

Critics say that Chucho's music builds altars to the orishas and to all things Cuban. His rapid playing catches the polyrhythms of the bata drums. The syncopated phrasing and abundant use of eighth notes is a defining mark in both the African patterns in Santeria drumming and Cuban music – jazz is also plentiful in both. Chucho acknowledges being influenced by American jazz pianists McCoy Tyner and Bill Evans in how he manages the musical language of jazz. There is also a strong presence of classical music underlying Chucho's jazz. In fact, he has considered taking a break from jazz and switching to classical playing. Whatever direction he travels, however, all roads will lead to Cuba. "We Cuban piano players are always thinking of the rhythm base," he is quoted as saying. "We're always thinking of Cuba when we play."

I called Chucho again. His young son answered. "No, he's gone again," the polite boy said. I never did fish fast enough to land him.

After Roberto's last set, I walked home from the club. The lack of tension and aggression on the streets was the chief source of my pleasure on the walks around Havana. It was enormously liberating not to have anxiety attacks about a stranger approaching on a dark street. I felt no need to recoil from other human beings, as I would in other big cities, wary of potential danger. The women I encountered didn't put on the hard-attitude mask of "Don't even think about messing with me or you'll never walk like a man again." Everyone I met on the streets of Havana was relaxed. The threat from fellow citizens was not part of the vibe, unlike in many North American cities, where danger was like traffic, always there. I never experienced a sense of menace on the streets of Havana.

That freedom from tension included not being bombarded by a constant barrage of commercialism. This struck me one afternoon when, at a busy intersection in the heart of Havana, I looked up and saw no billboards, no neon signs snapping at me to *buy! buy!* I was not a moving target for market-snipers. Sex was not being flashed as an unspoken promise if I'd smoke Brand X. The demands of hyper-consumer economics are like a low-tension headache – you don't realize the pain until it goes away. A chief motive of advertising is to make a person dissatisfied. Advertising sows discontentment. It creates wants and desires and then, like a knight in shining armor, presents an anodyne to the discomfort created. I never realized how abusive commercialization and its attendants could be until I was out of whipping range.

When I left the club, I was looking forward to my walk. I knew that I'd be offered opportunities. The opportunities began at the bus stop outside the club, where young ladies offered me cambio services – they'd exchange sex for my dollars. Prostitution is illegal in Cuba; the bus stop was a convenient front where the ladies could pose as if waiting for a bus to avoid being hassled by the ever-present police. Nobody was fooled, including the officers, but the camouflage among legitimate bus passengers gave a better image than a tawdry sex market. The queries were delivered by a soft hiss or direct eye contact. There was no blatant hustle, no provocative strut. The ladies were masters of the soft sell. I turned down the opportunities with a slight shake of the head and a smile. No reason to be rude.

The section of La Rampa I was in – the four blocks from the top of the hill to the Malecón, where the street meets the ocean – is a hot spot. Besides La Zorra y El Cuervo, there are several other clubs and discos where you can dance salsa, merengue, rumba, and liquid robot to electronica. The open-air Café Sofia starts live jazz in the afternoon and stays open 'til late. During the 1940s and '50s, when the US mob ran the Havana casinos, La Rampa was a jumping place full of club-hopping, well-dressed men and women. Now it's more like a showgirl 40 years past her prime but still with a twinkle in her eye. You can enjoy yourself just watching the scene and saying no (or yes) to the hustlers offering girls, cigars, and fake gold rings. There is no hard hustle, no sense of danger, but no class, either.

From the jazz club, this strip of opportunity extends three blocks up the hill to the main intersection at Coppelia. Coppelia is another hot spot, a park devoted to ice cream. It is a mecca, especially for families. There is no entrance fee, but you can spend hours waiting in line. At weekends, from 11am to 11pm, hundreds of people patiently wait in lines that snake around the block, and it's not much better during the week. People are admitted in groups of 20 or so, as space at the tables becomes available. Then, when the guards let you into the park proper, you wait in another line at the center pavilion to be shown to a table. There are no milling crowds, no music, no arcade games. Kids don't run around but instead sit at the tables, models of good behavior. The place is an open-air palace dedicated to the serious intent of eating ice cream. The Coppelia experience is a bit like going to church.

The Cubans love ice cream. Sidewalk stands do a brisk business with all age groups. Cubans are proud of their ice cream for its natural flavors. Frankly, I found it thin in taste and creaminess. I could taste the chemicals in the orange and the dust of cocoa in the chocolate. I did find tiny, tiny bits of fruit in the pineapple but not even the taste of a genuine berry in the strawberry. But a cone was cheap and the ice cream a pleasant treat. I lined up at the stands and waited my turn.

Cubans also love cigarettes and dogs. Castro gave up cigars several years ago, because of the health risk, but his countrymen have not followed him into nicotine abstinence. I don't know if Castro has a dog, but it would be surprising if he doesn't. Dogs are a Cuban passion. Havana is full of apartment-sized canines which their owners take on evening walks without cleaning up after them.

On past Coppelia, other opportunities presented themselves: ice-cream vendors, people selling tightly wrapped paper cones of peanuts or popcorn, outdoor cafés, restaurants, a 24-hour cafeteria. Each person or place was an opportunity to become part of the Havana street scene. I came upon a grand opportunity at Avenida de los Presidentes, a grand boulevard with a wide parkway separating the lanes of traffic. The intersection where 23rd Street meets Avenida de los Presidentes is the late-night hang-out for teenagers. When I walked past, 50 or more were lounging on the ground, the park benches, and the curb under the traffic cop's stand. They looked like disaffected teenagers anywhere: baggy clothes, long and colorful spikes of hair, nose rings, earrings, tattoos, and the repose of slackers. Here was an opportunity to interview socialist slackers. I passed, for I had been thinking of a previous conversation with actor and cultural commentator Alden Knight.

I had invited Alden to the house in order to mine his views on Cuban arts and culture. We were talking about why Cubans understand jazz so well. Who created jazz?, he asked. Jazz was created in New Orleans. And who lived in New Orleans? English, French, Spaniards, and African negroes, many from the Congo, from west Africa, the homeland of the Yoruba and Ewe and Fon and Bantu, the same people who lived in Cuba, the exploited and humiliated. These negroes sang the spirituals, labor songs, soul songs. They created a new form. Why did the Cuban people assimilate the spirit of the music?

"For two reasons," Alden said. "One, our roots are alike to the ones in the United States formed by the native peoples, Europeans, and Africans. The music was improvisation of inner suffering, an inner suffering shared by the slaves and common people in the United States, Cuba, Brazil, and even Europe. Because the racial composition in Cuba was similar to New Orleans, Cubans could assimilate what the music was about in an emotional way. You can express your feelings how you want with jazz. Besides, it was very good music.

"And two, in the age of radio, the music was broadcast from the United States and heard in Cuba. There was a cross-fertilization when Cuban musicians went to New Orleans, to New York, to Los Angeles and San Francisco, and when American musicians traveled to Havana. The musicians already knew each other's language.

"I think," Alden said, "that Cubans give to jazz a sense of permanence and a sense of security. Cubans make progressive jazz that progresses innerly but also in time. It won't go away but continues as a permanent piece of the culture. You can depend on jazz."

Two days later, I got a surprise opportunity from Jose Antonio, my friend and translator and a man who opened doors I didn't know existed. One of those doors opened to Jorge Luis Vales Chicoy.

"Who?" I asked when Jose called and asked if I wanted to interview him.

"Chicoy," Jose replied.

I flipped through my mental Rolodex under C, then under K. "Ah...ah..." I stalled, not wanting to show my ignorance.

"The guitarist who received a Grammy nomination in 1998 for his work with Chucho Valdés, Lázaro Ros, and the group Irakere for the CD *Cantala A Babalu Aye*. And he just won a Cubadisco award [the equivalent of a Grammy] for his instrumental CD *Triangulo*," Jose added helpfully.

"Sure," I said. "Bring him over."

When he arrived, Chicoy greeted me like we were old friends

reunited after many years. He is small in stature and handsome, with dark wavy hair, and he crackles with energy, even when sitting still. This was especially true when we started talking about music. His eyes lit up another three degrees, as if his all-time favorite dessert had just been set in front of him. I asked him about the connection between Cubans and jazz.

"If you listen to the traditional Cuban music, it has a lot of connection to the music of New Orleans in the 19th century," he said. "American music doesn't clash with traditional Cuban music. The chord structures are exactly the same. That is true with the harmonies. The traditional Cuban music is played with percussion and maybe a bass guitar, or two guitars and two vocals. Cuban music is in 4/4 and 2/4, same as the blues and jazz, so Cubans understood musically as soon as they heard the music. In American jazz, we listen to harmonies and improvisations more than the rhythm. That's because we have our own rhythm that is very strong, very intense. We enjoy the American jazz rhythm, but we apply our own rhythm.

"In Cuba, the jazz is played very hot. Very hot. Sometimes we have to lower down the flame that is so hot, so strong. We play jazz like the Americans, but we play it with Cuban rhythms. That's what it needs, the hot rhythm. We play some jazz ballads but with a danzón rhythm. It's a very beautiful combination. It's very still, soft, cool. Chucho and other musicians play the ballads as danzón.

"All jazz is the music you put on when you close the bedroom door. That is especially true in Cuba. Only hot jazz. You have to have hot jazz.

"We apply the folkloric motifs inside the jazz. It's a very rich culture, referring to rhythms, and we have the facility that we can understand the jazz and play it and have it inside our rhythms. The bata drums are very interesting in this, the mingle and mixture of Santeria rhythms with the Cuban jazz. That is very Cuban. For example, in New York, the jazz musicians have made many fusions with the conga drums and kettle drums, but I don't think they have worked with the bata drums. The use of bata is more from Cuba.

"It's interesting that in Cuba we had no schools for jazz. It's like the grass that grows alone. The music schools are very good, but we

Jorge Luis Vales Chicoy, rhythm guitarist of the Grammy-award-winning jazz group Irakere

studied classical music. In our spare time, we played jazz by listening to the records of Charlie Parker, Dexter Gordon, and others.

"I think our music is very accepted by American musicians because they don't feel that we are invading their music but making our own style, our own way, and they appreciate that very much. I also believe that there is a lot of influence of Cuban music, not only in the United States but also everywhere in the world. We try to play with our identity, because it has a lot of future and it's our music. We have Cuban musicians in France, Spain, Italy, England, Canada, everywhere there are Cuban musicians.

"I think that the blockade had some advantages for Cuba, specifically for the music. There was something happening very intense in Cuba and nobody knew about it. Now they begin to see what has happened. First, we learned to appreciate what we have. For example, when a record came into the country, or was produced here, everybody listened. Musicians wrote down each note of the record and passed their notes on. In the United States, some people don't see what they have. Also, in Cuba, due to the blockade, there was no trade in music. Our music was only in the artistic sense. There was no business, no commercial music. And still today, the music is being made with an artistic sense and not with a commercial sense.

"There is a danger of changing, because of the tourist economy. There will be commercial music, but there will also be a lot of music with a very strong artistic base. I think that the ideas of the Revolution are very strong, but the music has always been strong and will continue to be strong. It's something of the country, this being strong.

"And our system with State support doesn't favor commercialization. Musicians get a State salary. We don't need part-time jobs. Maybe you cannot get rich, but you have time to practice and create. A rich man controls his time. Our richness is the time to create. A Cuban band – for example, Los Van Van, NG La Banda, Irakere, any band – plays very tight arrangements. Outside musicians are astonished how tight we play. In a Cuban band, you can hear the bata, the conga, and the drum kit distinctly, individually, but they are like only one instrument. The reason is that our bands have time to rehearse. In the United States, the musicians cannot rehearse like we do, because they have to rush about finding work. There is no time, and the musicians are not paid to rehearse. This results in very good musicians that don't need to rehearse, but they never achieve to play so tight, so close to each other, like if they rehearsed all the time together."

Chicoy said all this in nearly one breath. When he paused, I slipped in a question: "What's it like to play in a famous band like Irakere? What's the inside scoop? What is Chucho Valdés, the leader, really like?"

Chicoy laughed. "You work for a tabloid, yes? Playing in Irakere is like a school. I have all the freedom to create and see how the people around me are creating. It's not a static band. Chucho gives everybody a lot of freedom. Playing with Irakere is very exciting, an adventure, like going down a fast river with everyone doing their part and having the discipline to play the arrangement with everyone else. In any one arrangement, there is 50 per cent written and 50 per cent free. The arrangements are very well written, and you have the possibility to create at the same time. I think that Cuban musicians have more freedom because of the clave, that strong, simple beat. If you don't have this inside your body, you cannot play. Our music is on tempo, the first beat. American music is behind the beat. Our music is very syncopated.

"I play the rhythm guitar in Irakere, which is a very big and hot band. I have to play with strength, because of the saxophones and trumpets and Chucho on the piano and the bata drums and conga drums. You see why the guitar has to be powerful! If you listen to Chucho's quartet, he plays a big piano, but with Irakere Chucho integrates into the band. That is a mark of a Cuban band. We play as a whole band rather than for the solo. That's one characteristic of Cuban jazz. You can listen to American jazz, where the brightest is in the improvisations [and] the theme is just a pretext. That is not so with a Cuban band."

La Zorra y El Cuervo is not the only hot spot to showcase jazz in Havana. The other favorite spot is Jazz Café on the third floor of the Galeries de Paseo, a modernistic-looking curve of green glass across Paseo Avenue from the Cohiba Hotel at the Malecón. There is no sign outside advertising the club. You don't even know it's there until you follow the curving stairs past the well-stocked grocery store on the second floor and come to the door at the top of the stairs. The place is slicker than La Zorra y El Cuervo, with a black-marble bar and comfortable upholstered chairs. The room is also twice the size of La Zorra y El Cuervo. There is no cover charge. (La Zorra y El Cuervo charges $5.) A full dinner menu is offered, whereas La Zorra y El Cuervo serves only sandwiches. The music usually doesn't get going until 11.30pm, but the room is crowded by 10.30. You should arrive early to get a table, for the stage area cannot be seen from the bar.

Across the street is another hot spot, the Habana Café, attached to the five-star Cohiba Hotel. From the outside, it appears to be a swank nightclub, but inside it's Las Vegas on the college circuit, more fun than sophistication. A yellow 1950s Chevy convertible just inside the door sets the tone. Hanging over the main floor is a real, full-sized, prop-driven Cub airplane, minus the landing gear, as if it never intended to land, which may be a subtle message to the customers. A red Harley Davidson motorcycle decked in shiny chrome stands on a pedestal. Across the room is a 1950s Oldsmobile whose lights blink on and off to the sound of a beeping horn and a revving motor to announce various acts, which range from singing waiters to acrobats to stage-show routines to disco music and live pop bands. On the walls are *faux* old signs advertising Gillette, Coca Cola, and Firestone tires, a montage of photos meant to give the feel of Clark Gable's Hollywood, a fishing net over colored lights…you get the idea.

The Café Cantanta, in the basement of the Nacional Teatro, is a hot dance spot. A long red canopy covers the stairs leading down into it. The entrance fee is $20, the highest I encountered in Havana, which helps subsidize the much cheaper tickets of the plays and musical events in the theater upstairs. The word "hot" has several connotations in the connection of Café Cantanta – hot as in hot salsa, hip-hop and other music; hot as in "How hot do you want it, baby?" When I arrived, a crowd of people waited around the entrance, mostly young women. One asked if I'd pay her way in. "Why?" I asked. She cursed me roundly, which didn't seem a good reason to shell out $20. Inside, they were like fleas on a dog, and I was the dog. The working girls worked hard to part me from my cash. They didn't even take turns. Three or four made their pitch of sweet companionship simultaneously. Once I made it clear that the music was my love, things settled down, except on the dancefloor. Red hot. Steamy hot. That's one hot place to dance.

13 Cuban Reggae

"I don't understand why the Rastas believe that Haile Selassie is God," Raul Rodriguez admitted.

His admission took me aback. "Raul," I said, leaning in close so that no one could overhear us, "should you be saying that? Think of your fans." Raul is the founder and leader of Cuba's only reggae band, Manana Reggae. He is a firm believer in the musical message of reggae, so how can he doubt a main tenet of the reggae philosophy?

I had fortuitously stumbled across Manana Reggae (*manana* meaning "with feeling" in Yoruba) in the previous week at an out-of-the-way theater where they were performing with a couple of Ricky Martin knock-off Cuban hip-hop groups. The pre-teen girls squealed along with the hip-hop, but the entire audience erupted by the time Manana Reggae hit their fourth chord. The music literally lifted people out of their seats and sent them dancing in the aisles. They moved differently from the audiences I had seen in Jamaica dancing to reggae. Jamaicans danced smooth and cool, a studied, self-conscious suavity – except when they were bouncing up and down out of their minds with ecstasy. The Cubans danced reggae salsa, adding extra shakes and rolls and shimmies to the Jamaican bounce. They danced as if they were laughing out loud. There was fun in their music, a lightness and liveliness I had found missing in Jamaican reggae. I laughed out loud with pure relief that I was not going to be lectured by the music, a tendency of Jamaican reggae. What was it that made the sound and feeling of Cuban reggae discernibly different from Jamaican reggae? That's what I wanted to

179

talk about with Raul, but he threw this who-is-this-God screamer right at the heart of reggae.

"Can you explain about Haile Selassie?" he asked.

I tiptoed into this theological minefield. Well, I began with my outsider's rational analysis, you see, there are a couple ways of looking at this. The Rastas needed a role model, a powerful, unbowed black man who had not been broken under white domination. Haile Selassie was the black emperor of Ethiopia. Ethiopia was one of two African nations that had never been colonized, the other being Liberia. Haile Selassie traced his lineage back to the biblical King Solomon, so the Rastas chose the leader of an ancient African kingdom that had survived in the white world. Haile Selassie was a useful symbol on which the Rastas could build a case for their own legitimacy and demands for respect.

The Jamaican Rastas were angry over the colonization of Jamaica, which resulted in the deculturalization and humiliation of black people there. They were angry with the black elite in Jamaica, who perpetuated the colonial model for their own power and profit at the expense of other Jamaicans, including the Rastas. The Rastas appointed themselves as saviors of all oppressed people, and they needed a Savior figure at the head of their crusade. And then, there are many, many Rastas who sincerely believe that the man Haile Selassie is in fact the living God on Earth – not in a symbolic or metaphoric sense but in fact. If a carpenter's son can be God, why not an African emperor?

"Rastafari is not necessary information in Cuba," Raul replied. "I have learned about Rastafari and Haile Selassie, but we don't want to be involved in that philosophy. We don't want to touch political themes in which we can be compromised. Our political philosophy is our music."

This, I discovered while talking with Raul, was one of many differences between Jamaican reggae and Cuban reggae, both musically and philosophically. Raul once wore dreadlocks, but he cut them off. Why? I asked. Dreads are one of the powerful symbols of the Rastas and reggae. Dreadlocks are a political symbol that sets Rastas apart from the society whose values they defy. Dreadlocks

Paul Rodriguez (r), founder and musical director of Cuban reggae group Manana Reggae with Isaac Cruz, the band's pianist

have spiritual symbolism. The locks are a psychic antenna, a mystical link to the earthforce that connects Rastas with their god and his power. The shaking of the locks, or tossing them back and forth over the head, as Marley did on stage and Burning Spear still does, is thought to release spiritual energy to bring about the destruction of Babylon.

"With respect to the Rasta philosophy," Raul said, "it's not necessary to wear dreadlocks to make reggae. You have to wear them in your heart. Dreadlocks are a symbol. The music vibrates in each musician. Without dreads, you can still make good reggae. Reggae had a look, like Bob Marley with his dreads, but other musicians, even The Beatles, made reggae without dreads."

Well, what about Babylon? Rastas label everything that is oppressive, or supports oppression, as Babylon. Any economic, political, religious, or educational institution that supports these attitudes and values are manifestations of Babylon. Any countries or peoples who have benefited from colonialism or international capitalism are part of Babylon. For the Rastas, Babylon embodies the cultural ethos of the forces that work against the people of God. "Surely, Raul, you who live in a country that has been under attack from the greatest Babylon of all, according to the Rastas, the United States – surely you have adopted reggae's opposition to Babylon?"

"The Rasta concept of Babylon is not an important concept here," Raul said in simple dismissal.

Well, what about repatriation back to Africa? Jamaican Rastas look to Africa as their true home, either in reality or in their hearts. Many insist on being given a plane ticket to Africa and clothes and money and land. Others say that physically returning to live in Africa is not the issue. They say that they return to Africa every day in their hearts, and that it's not necessary to drag their fridge or car with them. But repatriation is an important theme in Jamaican reggae.

"Repatriation to Africa is not part of the theme of Cuban reggae," Raul responded. "We do not have this psychology. I was born with the Cuban Revolution. It has been taught to me since I was a child. Cuba is our homeland, so we don't think about returning to Africa."

In Jamaica, reggae is seen as an evangelical music meant to spread the beliefs and values of Rastafari. Mortimo Planno, Jamaica's esteemed intuitive philosopher, appointed Marley to carry the message of Rastafari to the world through reggae. Reggae preaches about Jah (God).

"Preaching is not part of Cuban reggae," replied Raul. "We don't do that. Our message is a wider message. We don't play our music only to the believer but to everyone, no matter that they don't believe. In our music, we want people to feel self-respect and to reflect. We focus on themes of love and what people feel. Our goal is to have people open their eyes. I say in one of my songs, 'The light is in our eyes and we are unable to see it.' This is similar to what Marley did with his themes. Marley sang about peace and love and called for struggle.

"There is a different situation in the world from when Bob Marley did his songs in the 1960s. Then and now are different epochs. In the United States, for example, the songs of the black churches – gospel – don't have the same meaning as in the past. The same thing is happening in reggae: we take the musical base of reggae and elaborate on it in the way that matches with this time. Bob Marley made the music to be fighting for the rights of the negroes, who felt oppressed. The music was meant to encourage that fight. Music is one of the stronger arts, so that is why Marley used reggae for the struggle. Reggae nowadays is a struggle for the improvement of the human being, for any person to have a better life. Manana Reggae wants to call to the conscience of everyone to have a better life. This is the fight for improvement of the human being. In that, we sing about spirituality, against drugs, against war – even little wars, like quarrels in families, the son against the father."

If the ideological foundation of Jamaican reggae and Cuban reggae is different, what about the music?

"There is a big difference between Jamaican reggae and Cuban reggae," Raul said. "Jamaican reggae has its characteristics as heard in Bob Marley and The Wailers. Reggae made in Cuba has Cuban accents, although the base of reggae is maintained, so we respect the style while making the style our own."

Part of that style is the mood of the music. Behind the Jamaican *no-problem-mon* smile is a simmering anger rooted in the country's colonial slave past and its post-colonial legacy. At the risk of tarring them all with the same brush, Jamaicans are an oppressed people under their sunny dispositions. The Cubans, who also have a slave history (30 per cent of the Cuban population is of African descent), do not live under a dark cloud of suppressed anger. Jamaican reggae is bouncy and, in that, optimistic, but deep in the chords is a sullen aggression that gives the music its compelling heartbeat. Cuban reggae is a more genuine laughter.

Raul told me an insightful reason for this. "The Spanish were a different kind of slavemaster than the British," he said. "The British tried to break the spirit of their slaves. They took away their drums, crushed their culture, forbade their religious practices, and tried to tear out the very soul of the people. That's way Jamaican reggae is resistance music, a fighting music, a music about redemption and salvation, for the same reasons blues were born in the United States. The British slavemasters' attitudes and methods gave their slaves the blues, but in Cuba the Spanish slave-owners were not so totally oppressive. They allowed the drums, the religious practices, and the festivals of their slaves. Africans – the Moors – occupied Spain for 800 years, so perhaps that is why the Spaniards had an affinity [with] Africans. Spain and Africa are neighbors, so they are not so much strangers to each other. We Cubans are basically not angry about anything, and that's heard in our music."

As Raul explained it, Cuban reggae is more complicated than Jamaican reggae. The rhythmic patterns are more complicated, because they incorporate many elements of the Cuban music, which in itself is complex. The rhythm of reggae is very simple in the binary compass. For example, the Nyabinghi drum in Jamaican reggae is the heartbeat – one-two, one-two, very steady – while the Cuban bata drum is polyrhythmic, with multiple layers of sounds coming out of one drum. In the Cuban style, the reggae has a different accent in the conga. There is another harmony in the voices and a marked harmony in the bass guitar. The horns are played in a son style.

"We make a fusion sound," said Raul. "We mix son, funk, and jazz with the reggae. This gives a very specific sound while maintaining the roots, like the counterpoint that is characteristic of reggae. Another main characteristic of reggae is the syncopated rhythm, [where], in Jamaican reggae, the weak tempo is stressed. We respect those patterns but add to them the theory of Cuban music. The fusion in Cuban reggae makes the music more accelerated, more charismatic.

"The Cuban characteristics give reggae a happier sound, more lively. The Cuban elements enrich the music. This gives the music a gay character while maintaining the basis of the music."

Raul told me that Manana Reggae is searching for its own originality, its own sound, by mixing Afro-Cuban music with reggae. "We have to adapt reggae to our own situation and mix it with our own Cuban music. In Afro-Cuban music, there are groups like Sintesis that mix rock to make their own sound. There are others that mix jazz with Afro-Cuban music to get their sound. Reggae uses the Nyabinghi drum, which has African roots. Yoruba, in Santeria, uses the bata drum, which has African roots. The Nyabinghi is a religious drum. So is the bata. Maybe we can mix Yoruba into reggae. But if you use the bata in that way, it would be very aggressive. The bata is very explosive. Then the Nyabinghi [wouldn't] be the fundamental part of this type of reggae. So we have to be careful, because we want to maintain the roots of reggae in our music.

"But it's very interesting to use more bata. We are exploring incorporating the bata, which has a faster rhythm than the Nyabinghi. That would be a valid enrichment that has worth. Music is nothing more than the combination of sounds and tempo. It would be a great ambition to incorporate bata, but we should sit and think about it. If we start in that direction, we cannot quit in the middle, because it is too difficult."

A characteristic of Jamaican dancehall reggae is computer-driven rhythm. The computer replaced studio musicians in part because of economics and in part because of creative stagnation. Record producers in Kingston found it cheaper to use computer-based sound loops. Different artists could use the same loop, or slight variations, over and over again on their songs. This led to the criticism that much of current Jamaican reggae sounds the same and that the sound isn't very interesting. The music is eating itself, critics claim (including roots-reggae musicians), and leaving the audience hungry.

"I don't like computer-created sounds," Raul told me. "I like the live sound. It's more valuable to watch or listen to live music instead of listening to computerized sounds. To see a musician making a great effort to have an outstanding performance that is of value gives greater enrichment than watching a computer. Here, because musicians receive a State salary, we don't have the same economic problem as in Jamaica; the entire band shares the work we do, which is why we obtain the quality. The computers are highly sophisticated, but our work has been conceived for musicians to play. Everybody works with great love, without thinking of economic problems.

"We are not against technological progress – that can make the work easier – but it's livelier with musicians working the instruments. It's not the same to play with a computer that substitutes or produces the guitars or drums. It's better to work with live musicians, because it is a little colder to work with computers."

Manana Reggae has a small but enthusiastic following – the fan base is growing, even during a salsa boom, a noteworthy feat – but reggae is definitely out of mainstream Cuban music, so it's not on most Cubans' musical radar. Puzzling out how to increase the market is a matter of survival that preoccupies Raul: "In Cuba, it is difficult for any group to grow a market for themselves. The Cuban music business is much more controlled than in other places. There is not the wild free market like you have in the States. There is much competition for studio time, so it is difficult to get recorded. The financing is difficult. We have to do self-promotion. There are no PR firms here like in the United States. The enterprises that manage the groups try to promote their musicians, but they really don't know how to do it. That's why the bigger Cuban groups sign with foreign promoters. The Cuban music business has lots of problems."

He paused, as if deciding whether or not to be depressed about the state of the Cuban music business. Then he brightened and said, "You know the best way to deal with the music? Listen to it. That's all I want people to do, listen to our music. This Sunday, we're playing at a peña. Come party with us. It's on 23rd, between B and C at four o'clock."

So, on Sunday afternoon, I went looking for the party. I expected to find the bands playing in the park on the corner of 23rd and B, but it was empty and quiet. I asked at the food stand across the street, but the man shrugged. I wandered down the street trying to sniff out party vibes, or least hear music vibes, but I found no clues. A man stood in the doorway of a three-story house with a Restaurant Amor sign out front.

"I'm looking for a peña around here. Do you know about one?" I asked him.

"The Peña Cordinación con Elda Corrillo?" he replied and pointed to the roof of the building. "This is Elda's House."

That's how the peña is commonly known: Elda's House. The

peña, as I found out, is held on the first Sunday of every month and is a benefit for a children's cancer hospital. Like other peñas, it isn't advertized.

Three other people arrived, and together we entered the building and found the back stairs. There was no indication that the building was occupied, even by the restaurant. On the second floor, a row of windows looked directly into a well-furnished living room, perhaps Elda's. A twisting, narrow stairway led upward. At the top, I eased through a people-clog in the doorway and stepped out onto a roof packed with an audience. Part of the roof had been covered and folding chairs had been set out, leaving a performing space. A crooner resembling Chubby Checker with a Chuck Berry pompadour was crooning before the audience, dressed for a Las Vegas show.

Raul waved from the back of the roof from his place in the standing-room-only section. He enthusiastically shook my hand and introduced me to his friend and some-time bandmate Javier Bode. I was too distracted by the splendid overview of Havana to pay proper attention. "Excuse me?"

"I'm with the band Yerbabuena," Javier repeated. "We're playing today, too." Yerbabuena proved to be the shocker of the day.

Peña Cordinación con Elda Corrillo is definitely a hot spot not to be missed. The acts there that day ranged from a stand-up comedian to a rumba dance troupe to a traditional septeto band to a breakdancing act, as well as Manana Reggae and Yerbabuena. All of the acts were of professional caliber, and the comedian was well known from television. The four hours of entertainment for only a contribution to the children's cancer hospital was one of the best deals I found in Havana.

The comedian had people falling out of their chairs with laughter. Sometimes a line would elicit a gasp and hands-to-the-mouth disbelief from the audience. They'd look at each other with wide eyes that said, "Can you believe he *said* that?" and they would roar at his thinly disguised political jabs and acid observations, comments that he couldn't have made on television. (He asked me not to reveal his name here, just to be on the safe side. His act was

The band Yerbabuena. L-r: Javier Bode (lead vocals), Jane Pérez Lopez-Quintana (piano), Damian Jane Lantigues (bass guitar), and Migues Rafa Inglesias (lead guitar)

no secret, he said, but why wave a red flag unnecessarily?) He did a skit that poked fun at how things get done in Cuba – or don't get done. The skit began in fits and starts as he stopped, backtracked, forgot what he was doing, and started again. His timing was impeccable as the skit gained momentum, then stalled again, then stumbled forward but never really quite got started or carried on in a definitive direction. Outwardly, he was a bumbling old man simply trying to get from A to B, but the audience howled in recognition at the broader political commentary.

The afternoon's acts accurately reflected the diversity currently running through Cuban society: the rumba dancers in folkloric costumes came directly out of the African Cuba; the traditional septeto band playing classic son was the Spanish voice embedded in the Cuban culture; the rapping/breakdancing act was the current street scene; Manana Reggae was Caribbean brotherhood; and Yerbabuena was exemplary of the newest sound of a hip, hot, intelligent, blasting band that takes all the best of Cuban music and remixes the lot into a sound that snags the imagination and sets the feet dancing. The band – Javier Bode, Miguel Rafa Inglesias, Janet Pérez Lopez-Quintana, and Damian Jane Lantigues – is the new Cuban fusion of rock 'n' roll, traditional Cuban, reggae, ballads, funk, jazz, and Caribbean rhythms. They put all of this into a distinctive sound with such creative variety that you wanted to hear the next song just to see what they'd come up with.

Later, I arranged to meet with Javier and Miguel at Abdala Studio, regarded as one of the finest recording studios in the world, where the master mix of the band's first album was being prepared. Abdala Studio is an understated, one-story complex of white buildings on a residential street in Miramar, Havana's upscale suburb. Inside, Javier and Miguel showed me the recording studios with proprietary pride. The state-of-the-art mixing boards were British. The executive leather chairs for the engineers were Italian. The three studios were spacious, with large windows separating the recording and the engineering areas.

Javier, Miguel, and I settled into the cafeteria, where a European soccer match was on the television. Javier and Miguel both wear ponytails and are full-time musicians. Javier is married with two children, one four years old and the other five months. He graduated from the School of Language, but his first (and only) job has been as the singer/songwriter for the band. Miguel, meanwhile, is the lead guitarist and director of the band. I asked them to explain how the Cuban music industry works for them as musicians.

"To be a paid musician, a professional, you must belong to a State-run enterprise," Javier said. "If you don't belong to an enterprise and the police catch you playing on the street or in a restaurant, you can get a fine, and the restaurant will also be fined."

To become a member of an enterprise, a musician must audition before a jury, which may include both musicians and nonmusicians, such as a musicologist and, perhaps, a political appointee of a cultural committee. The enterprises, which have a managerial function, are divided into categories of music: traditional, folkloric, jazz, country, etc. The musician auditions for the enterprise of his or her musical area. "If they like your music and find your music proper for Cuban culture and that you play to the Cuban standards of professional musicians, you are accepted," Javier said.

What happens if you're competent but they don't like your music, or it's too radical – like Cecil Taylor on the piano – or too non-Cuban?

"They don't deny you entrance," Miguel answered. "They can say, 'We think that your music is good, but it's not proper for this enterprise, so try to find another enterprise.'"

Once accepted by an enterprise, a musician receives a salary, like any other worker. The money comes from the central government. "We don't have to a drive a taxi or have a second job," Javier said. "We have enough to live on. Music is considered work, a way of working in Cuba."

"But the salary is not steady," interjected Miguel. "It depends on the work we do. We don't get a check each week. Every band is given an evaluation and the salary is dependent on the evaluation. If you are evaluated A [ie a top-level band], then the salary is good enough. But we're not talking great salaries here. It's the same situation for artists as it is for doctors and engineers, who are also State employees."

Unless you are an internationally known artist, or perhaps famous within Cuba, this is how the system works: someone wants to put on a concert; they contact the enterprise or enterprises that represent the type of musicians wanted for the concert, be it traditional, salsa, jazz, or a combination; the enterprise checks its *plantilla* (the list of its musicians) to see who is available and then contacts the musicians. It's the enterprise that makes the contract, rather than the musician.

"The institution giving the concert doesn't say to the artist, 'I'm going to pay you 20,000 pesos for this,'" Javier said. "The artist never negotiates directly for the contract. The enterprise does that and takes a cut of 42.7 per cent of the money, and the rest goes to the musicians. Out of their share, the band must pay for the cost of transportation, a soundman, assistants, whatever. What remains is divided among the musicians. An outdoor venue with lots of people brings in more money. A small club or party or union function is not very profitable. Well-known musicians get a better deal – they can arrange for a cut of the door – but for the ordinary working musician or starting musician, it is a hard road."

"A musician's life in Cuba is like the musician's life everyplace," Miguel added. "Rehearsals, studies, getting ready for concerts, rehearsals, studies, getting ready for concerts, fighting all the time to get more money."

"We also have a representative," Javier said. "An agent. He tries to find work for us. As soon as he gets some work, he goes to our enterprise and tells the enterprise where we are going to work. The agent gets the contract from the enterprise. Then the agent takes the contract to the place that wants to hire us."

To make the pesos stretch, the band had to economize. At the beginning, they didn't have a keyboard player, because they didn't have a keyboard, and so Miguel made his guitar mimic the timbre of the keyboard. "Not as a sound, but as a rhythm, as the intention of the Cuban music," Miguel clarified, "as in the intention of the tres, a high-pitched sound that is special and different. To economize, we didn't make so huge with the brass, keyboard, and piano. The harmony of the guitar lets you enhance what you want."

"But we have rich, complex rhythms," added Javier. "We are influenced by Caribbean and African music and by rock 'n' roll, but we don't want to be a rock 'n' roll band. There are many, many rock 'n' roll bands in Havana, but they are underground, because it is not our music. If you play pure rock 'n' roll in Cuba, you won't find a market. People – the audience – don't like it so much. People like to dance to Cuban rhythms with the congas and such. If you want to play rock 'n' roll, it's up to you, but do it as a hobby. Take Sintesis, the best Cuban rock 'n' roll band – they have used a fusion of Afro rhythms with Caribbean rhythms to make their own rock 'n' roll. They are very intelligent, because they fit everywhere. They go to New York and they fit. They go to Africa and they fit. They play in Cuba and they fit. They became famous because they were intelligent."

Finding a way of achieving a toehold in the music business is a central matter of survival for Yerbabuena, as it is for bands everywhere in the world, but musicians dealing with the Cuban music industry have a special situation – the socialist system imposes conditions on record companies that are not found in the capitalist system. Marketing in Cuba is in the Dark Ages compared to aggressive commercial methods, which may be a disadvantage to musicians but spares the general society from abusive intrusions by profiteers who consider it their God-given right to hijack your telephone line or litter your email with their sales pitches. The distribution system is constrained. Also, musicians living in Cuba are barred from making money in the world's richest music market: the United States.

That evening, after the discussion with Yerbabuena, I walked to the park to visit John Lennon. He knew all about breaking into the music business, the vulgarities of dealing with record companies, and the balancing act between art and commerce. A tour group surrounded him, laying flowers in his lap and taking photos. I sat on a nearby bench and thought back to a discussion I'd had long ago with Allen Ginsberg. Allen and I had known each other for years, although I wasn't really part of his circle, nor he of mine. Nevertheless, we'd run into each other periodically and enjoyed some interesting conversations. One day, we got talking about art and commerce. Both of us were really broke and Allen was worried about how to get his teeth fixed. But you're a famous poet, Allen, I said. How can you be broke?

Being a famous poet has nothing to do with being rich, Allen replied. Art is an activity completely independent of commerce. The basic activity, the basic insight, the basic energy that goes into art has to do more with inquisitiveness, curiosity, exploration, and a kind of gaiety and glee in composing feelings and doing whatever you want to do. The whole point is *vision*, the vision of unity and humor that is well and beyond any financial consideration, beyond life and death. If money is the basis of art, if it can affect art, then it's not a very deep art. Art is not commercial. Art is art. Commerce is commerce. An artist is lucky and fortunate if his work has commercial value, but commerce is not the criterion for its genesis. The criterion is the exuberance of expression. The dwelling on the commercial scene is a problem that comes to artists who haven't had a primo vision and therefore haven't gotten beyond the personal (or the complaining) stage. The reason why someone is an artist is that they get out of the commercial trap by realizing that it is only a trap. Real art is beyond value. Subjectively, it may be invaluable, but it is beyond objective value. If the art is on that level, then that is where it gets really interesting.

Many of the Cuban musicians I had spoken with – Edesio Alejandro, Carlos Alfonso, Roberto Fonseca, the rappers – had realized the trap of commerce, but they, too, like nearly everyone, cannot be free of commerce. In that, Cuba itself is in the same boat as its artists – how can it be *in* commerce but not *of* commerce? Cuba and its partners, the artists, are still working out the intricate steps of that dance.

14 *The Music Blockade*

One afternoon, while walking through Cayo Hueso, I heard the clear, sharp, single note of a trumpet. I thought that perhaps I hadn't heard right. Perhaps I'd heard a startlingly melodic car horn. But then I heard a trill so precise, so sweet, that there could have been no mistake. Somewhere close by was a hell of a good horn player. I rounded a corner and saw 20 people standing in the street outside a house. Those in front leaned through the two windows while those behind, in the third and fourth ranks, stood on tiptoes to see over their shoulders. As many people as possible had crowded into the doorway. Then, like a thousand butterflies, notes of music poured out of the house and over the heads of the people and floated down the street, like monarchs on migration.

I edged close enough to see the musicians inside. They sat on straight chairs in a semi-circle facing a man who appeared to be their leader. The trumpet player was a young man of unflappable style. He hit his cues as surely as a master blacksmith pounds the exact spot needed to shape hot iron into delicate beauty. The tres player on his right provided a light rhythmic line, the bright notes riding above the bass guitar. The rhythm guitar, maracas, and bongo drums kept the rhythm running full tilt on its tiptoes so that, when it hit the listener, all of the heavy cares and woes that might encrust the spirit were shattered and light replaced the darkness of worry.

The group was an old-style septeto playing a traditional song, but there was nothing of an ancient feel about their sound. More people joined the crowd. A policeman wandered up, trying not to look too interested, as if that might diminish his authority, but he couldn't help himself, and became part of the crowd. A heavy-set man with a white beard began to rotate his hips. The woman next to him shook her shoulders. Their feet began to shuffle. A twitch rippled through the crowd, now about 30-people strong. If the policeman had any thoughts about crowd control, they were empty thoughts, for, although he didn't smile, he danced.

In a septeto group, the solo trumpet player is the musical leader who makes or breaks the band. He is the voice, the golden bird that must lyrically soar between 19th-century brass-band cornet and modern jazz. The tres player is the piano of the group, keeping the grounding harmonic rhythm, like the left hand of ragtime, and a twinkling melody of the right hand traipsing across the higher keys. It's the combination of the brassy horn and strings that gives the septeto its crisp yet subtle sound. Septeto Nacional, the most famous of the Cuban septeto groups of the 1930s, played mostly sones and boleros, their music falling between the *guajiro* string groups and the brassier *conjuntos*. The group practicing in the house rode that same groove, but there was something fresh and new in their sound.

After 20 minutes, the musicians packed up. I waited outside for the man in the white shirt, who appeared to be the leader, and invited him for a drink at the corner café. He introduced himself as Alejandro Suarez, who founded this band, Sierra Maestra, in 1976 while a student at the University of Havana. "We leave to Australia next week on tour, then to Europe to play a string of festivals," he explained over a can of Cristal beer, "then a 17-city tour of the United States, if our visas are approved. Last year, we were in Cuba only four months. We are a bit tired." He lit a cigarette. "We are not as young as we were."

Yes, he said, the group plays only traditional music influenced by bands of the 1920s, but with new harmonics. "We have influences from funk, pop, and rock mixed with the old music. Cuban music is very flexible. Perhaps that is why it's so popular around the world. Traditional Cuban music is very popular. In Germany, our last tour was sold out three months in advance. And tickets cost $50! In France, they like Cuban music better than jazz. In Holland, they like jazz and Cuban. There is a lot of the same in both musics. In

Japan...whoa, Japan! Cuban music is very big, very popular in Japan. In 1998, we made a film in France, *Salsa*, and it was released in Japan. When we played Japan, people packed our shows. I cannot explain this. I think people are getting bored of the electronic sound, the noisy. Cuban music has rich melody. That's why people are looking to Cuban music."

Along with Buena Vista Social Club and The Afro-Cuban All Stars, Sierra Maestra was one of the three pioneer groups that reintroduced Cuban music outside of Cuba.

"I've played in the United States in 1996 and '98," Alejandro said. "Boston, Chicago, Los Angeles, Santa Monica, San Francisco, Seattle... I can't remember all the places. People of all ages came to our concerts, Latinos and Anglos, and they liked us very much. We went there to promote the band and the music. The United States is a very strong market, the prime music market in the world, so it's important to get a name there. By US law, Cuban musicians can't receive money in the United States. It's a stupid law. Friends in the States made arrangements for us to play at universities and cultural clubs and some small clubs. We were just working for expenses and to promote the music. And managers in the United States take advantage of Cuban groups because they know of our problem. The managers try to give us as little as possible. But we, our group, have written into the contract that we must stay in four-star hotels, minimum."

He paused to finish his beer. "I almost hope we don't get the visas to the United States this time, although there shouldn't be a problem. We can afford to go there only once or twice to promote the music, because we can't make money there. The United States is important, but it's not the only market. We record on New World Music in London, so Europe knows us well. What happens in the US market depends on the political relations between the United States and Cuba. I don't know what will happen there."

He stubbed out his cigarette and answered one last question: "The future of Cuban music on the international stage? Now there is a rediscovery, a wide opening, but the music will not boom, [will] not remain on the top of popularity, but it will remain strong and steady. You will hear Cuban music for a long time."

Alejandro Suarez, the founder and director of Sierra Maestra, one of the three bands responsible for introducing Cuban music to an audience outside Cuba

For years, the US government has made it difficult for Cuban musicians to tour in the States. During the Ronald Reagan and George Bush Sr administrations, between 1980 and 1992, Cuban musicians and artists were routinely denied visas to the United States. Then the folkloric rumba ensemble Los Múnequitos De Matanzas was invited to participate in a cultural program. They were granted a visa. Perhaps they were seen as benign. In Cuba, comic strips are called *múnequitos*. A folk dance group that named itself The Comic Strips From Matanzas – how serious is that? (In the 1950s, there was a famous song in Cuba about comic strips, hence the group's name.) Actually, the ensemble was then, and continues to be, one of the best rumba groups in Cuba, if not the best.

Los Múnequitos De Matanzas' US tour was a huge success. In the wake of popular acclaim, the cultural freeze imposed on Cuban artists performing in the United States began to thaw. The first band invited to conduct a major tour in the United States was Pablo Menéndez's Mezcla. However, four days before they were to depart Cuba for the United States, the State Department revoked their visas.

"I was an American citizen with an American passport, so they couldn't stop me from entering the United States," Pablo told me, recounting the incident. "Our piano player, Rebeca Mauleon, one of the most well-known authorities on salsa piano playing, lived in San Francisco, so she was already in the States. So two of us were in the States, but the five Cuban band members were shut out. We started to raise hell. After a lot of pressure on members of the US Congress to get in three folkloric performers we wanted for the tour, they were given visas, but the band members were still denied. Rebeca asked some San Francisco musicians to help out. We put together a group and did the tour. During the tour, we showed videos on a huge screen of the Cuban band playing in Cuba, so in that way they were with us.

"For a lot of people in the United States, it was a revelation to see us on stage. We were well fed. We wore nice clothes. The band was a mixture of ages, races, and hairstyles, so we weren't some monolithic government-approved clones. Most Americans didn't and still don't have the slightest idea of what was and is really going on in Cuba. For us, it was an incredible experience. There are many very strong cultural influences from the United States on Cuba, especially in music. A lot of our musical heroes are musicians from the United States, so to get the recognition and respect that we got on that tour, to see that people respect Cuban musicians, that helped to inspire a sense of national pride that is very much part of being Cuban."

In the meantime, the cultural organizations that had invited Mezcla and Pastors For Peace, which for years had been battling the US government over Cuban issues, took the case to court. Pastors For Peace, based in New York, had much experience in such matters. They started the Friendshipment program, which took old computers and office supplies from the United States to elderly care homes in Havana. The US government would stop the shipments on the Canadian or Mexican borders, whichever Pastors For Peace was trying to cross. Customs officials even seized an old school bus intended to transport Cuban old folk to hospitals.

The case went to the Superior Court of Northern California. The government's only legal basis for denying the visas was a presidential proclamation by President Reagan, who then had not been president for twelve years. Presidential proclamations are not law. The US Congress, led by Senator Jesse Helms and Congressman Richard Burton, moved to close the loophole. The resulting Helms-Burton Act gave all presidential proclamations on Cuba – dating back to President Eisenhower, who initiated the first Cuban embargo in 1960 – the force of law.

"So now there is a legal standing to deny visas to Cuban artists," Pablo continued. "But the Helms-Burton Act has a provision called 'Track Two,' which says, in essence, that the Congress wants Cuban artists and musicians to visit the United States and see how wonderful US capitalism is and go back to Cuba, become dissidents, and overthrow the Castro government. That is a very childish notion, because Cuban artists travel around the world. When I speak to musicians in the United States, I've usually been to more countries than they have. We've seen capitalism in other places, like Denmark and Switzerland, and those places look a lot more attractive than the Bronx or east Los Angeles."

One of the musicians who came to the aid of Mezcla was Carlos Santana. He issued statements to the press decrying the ridiculousness of denying visas to Cuban musicians.

"Carlos was amazing," Pablo said. "In certain ways, we are mirror images. He was born in northern Mexico. His family was a fan of old-timey Cuban music, so he listened to a lot of that when he was young. As a teenager, he went to Tijuana and started playing rock 'n' roll and then the blues. I was born six years after Carlos, into a blues family. My mother, a folk/jazz/blues singer, was singing in 1958 and into the 1960s in Chicago. Her back-up band was Memphis Slim and Willie Dixon. I played in her band as a boy, so I always had a lot of blues around me when I was young. Carlos called Mezcla 'the cleanest, freshest water I have ever tasted.' The mix of our cultural roots are very similar, so when we played together, without any rehearsal, it was as if we had been playing together all our lives."

In recent years, Cuban musicians and artists have had an easier time of getting US visas, but they still don't receive royalties on their music sold in the United States or played on US radio. Getting airplay on mainstream radio stations in the United States is difficult. "If you are a musician based in Cuba, you will not, in general, get airplay in the United States," confirmed Charlie dos Santos, the vice president of A&R for Havana Caliente Records, based in New York. (Havana Caliente sponsored Los Van Van's first US tour in 1997.) "The Cuban songs played on the radio in the States are usually sung by a Puerto Rican, or a Colombian, or an American. You will not hear from a Cuban artist, especially one who resides in Cuba. There are a couple who, like Celia Cruz, sort of denounced the Cuban government and have lived in the United States for years who get airplay, but there is a boycott against Cuban musicians who live in Cuba. You have to talk to the people in charge of the radio stations to get an answer to why that is. It's like the blacklist in the 1950s. In some ways, it's subtler. You hear things. Nobody wants to step up and say that they are boycotting, but you get radio stations in Miami that say, 'We're afraid to play this because of bomb threats.' The existing salsa radio market has completely shut out Cuban artists, mostly for political reasons. This has happened in the hot spots that control the trends, like New York and Miami.

"There is a trend for more Cuban-based musicians coming to the United States to perform, but that is not happening within the Latin market. They are being promoted within the world-music market. Cuban musicians have the sense of taking their culture into the world. They're starting to see a lot more potential. I'm hoping that Cuban music doesn't turn out to be a fad. This next year will decide how much it's worth to keep investing in artists down there...or not."

It is an unavoidable truism that the majority of the most powerful and influential entertainment distribution companies are headquartered in the United States. It is very difficult for a musician to gain worldwide fame or success without the distribution support of those companies. And the US market is the big pot of gold. If you're a big success in the States, you'll be a big success everywhere, musicians told me over and over again. That's the brass ring to riches and fame. It's very difficult for Cuban musicians living in Cuba to get the necessary promotion and entry into the higher level of showbusiness without these big distribution companies.

Given the political situation, which has effectively frozen Cuban-based musicians out of the US market, at least on any significant scale, the musicians and Cuban record producers have a problem – a problem that Gloria Ochoa and Cari Diaz, producers for Bis Music in Havana, are trying to solve.

Gloria Ochoa is a 20-year veteran of the Cuban music business. She was a radio-program director for many years before she joined Bis Music. Cari Diaz was also in radio when she risked her career in a meeting with the Ministry of Culture and Fidel Castro. Cari does not look like a firebrand; she is small in stature, with long black hair, and on first meeting her she seems reserved and quiet. In her case, however, appearances are deceptive. When she stood up in that meeting, she delivered a blistering criticism of the Cuban music industry, ticking off the poor business practices, mismanagement, inefficiencies, and petty rivalries that riddled the industry. Castro and his minister listened attentively. When Cari sat down, there was the expectant silence of waiting for the big boot to fall. Then Castro and the minister agreed with nearly everything she had said. She was rewarded with a new car and was hired at Bis Music. In 2001, she won a 2001 Cubadisco award for her production of the CD *La Rumba So Yo*.

I met Gloria and Cari at Bis Music's offices, a converted house in a residential area of Miramar. Gloria is tall with short hair and has a very quiet, studious manner, but when she smiles she reveals herself to be a person of wit and warmth. Meanwhile, Cari's boldness and decisiveness were not hidden under a bushel; when she had something to say, she jumped right in and made her point.

"We in the Cuban record industry must find alternative ways of surviving," Gloria said, "or our fate might be like what happens to any independent producer in any part of the world. They have less possibilities of surviving when facing the big companies. But nowadays, things have changed, and the big companies are coming to Cuba in order to negotiate with Cuban companies."

The success of Cuban bands such as Cubanismo, Buena Vista Social Club, The Afro-Cuban All Stars, Irakere, Juan Formell, Los Van Van, NG La Banda, and Orishas caught the attention of major distributors. Those and other bands have opened a commercial niche in the world micro-market for Cuban music. There is a growing market for Cuban music, ranging from the 1950s' sound to the contemporary.

"This indicates that there is a big future for us," Cari said. "The technology of communications, such as the Internet, has allowed the world access to information that has been limited by the US blockade. In that sense, part of the blockade has been lifted. The blockade does not allow the American businessman to do business with Cuba. It is an unfair and unjust situation that limits the development of trade in a free way. It's harmful not only to Cuba but also to the big American companies. Big companies from France, Spain, and Mexico are doing business here, but not those from the United States. Not only is Cuba affected, but the American companies that want to work with Cuba are affected by these stupid laws."

"These policies of limitation affect not only economics," Gloria said, "but also the lack of information to the world about Cuba and its cultural values. Many people in the world don't know what's happening in Cuba. For example, Buena Vista Social Club – those musicians were the biggest stars in Cuban musical history. They were stars in this country for many years, 30 to 40 years, before the rest of the world heard about them. Cuban musicians were known first through their relationships with European record companies. Before Buena Vista Social Club, there was Cubanismo. They were known through an English company. So the big international record companies have been the best collaborators we've had. Without them, it would have been impossible to achieve the place Cuban music has in the world market. They deserve all our respect.

"The political situation with the United States limited the access of Cuban talent to the world. That's what happened. But some Americans have been very helpful, like Jimmy Maslom, director of the record label Ahi Ná Má; Ned Sublette of Obadisc; Peter Watroos and John Pareles of *The New York Times*; Judy Kantor, who writes for *The New Miami Times*; Rachel Faro; and John Fausty."

Bis Music is an auto-financed company – that is, it functions as a private business but is within the government system. Gloria described the system to me. The State doesn't own a share of Bis Music as it does with some other businesses, like tourist hotels or the Panataxi company. Bis Music sets its own budget, hires and fires as it sees fit, plans its own strategy to make profit, and is expected to make a profit. However, Bis Music is "inscribed" in the Ministry of Culture.

"We, as a company, have to finance our expenses and, from our profits, provide funds to the development of the culture in the country," Gloria said. "In other countries, these cultural projects are financed by foundations, for example, but in Cuba they are assumed by the Ministry of Culture, with funding provided by companies like ours that are profitable. The funds pay for teachers, masterclasses, and training courses, sending people abroad to study, financing the art schools where everything is free for the students. That is one reason we have so many well-trained musicians and people who listen to the musicians.

"The way Cuba works is different from the way capitalistic systems work. In Cuba, it's very important that financing works for the social systems. All the Cuban enterprises in different fields provide financing to support that area. The cultural companies, like ourselves, provide to the branch of culture. A heavy-equipment enterprise provides to the industrial sector. A transportation enterprise provides funds to the transportation sector. The cultural enterprises have [a] responsibility to collaborate with the Cuban State to finance all these activities. As this is a socialist system, there is a need for providing funds, due to the special situation. In some way, the State has to guarantee the support they give to the development of culture."

The amount of money that an enterprise contributes to the State's coffers depends on the profits of the enterprise. "According to what we foresee the profits to be, we determine how much goes to the Ministry of Culture," Gloria told me. "All the enterprises study their budget for the next year, and the funds they will give is determined by project growth. The percentage is worked out between the enterprise and the ministry."

Some cultural enterprises – most notably the major recording studio EGREM – are auto-financed businesses that aren't expected to make profits. EGREM has the special charge of producing all types of cultural products – folkloric music, current popular music, music for children, classical music, oral histories, literature, poetry, and various forms of international music. The government doesn't allow EGREM to go bankrupt.

So how does Bis Music make a profit? By producing artists that sell, just like any other record company in the world. And how do they find talent? Gloria and Cari do what every record executive does: they read trade publications, such as *Tropical International* and *Salsa Cubana*; they go to shows and concerts and listen out for new talent; they continue to nourish and expand their network of musicians; they listen to piles of tapes and records sent to them; they keep up with the hit-lists; they try to get their artists airplay on the radio; and they get their clients' videos on television. Production of music videos only began in Cuba about four years ago, but they already have high production values and are as good as anything on MTV.

However, Cuban record companies don't devise strategies to produce hits or create stars through marketing. There are no life-sized cardboard cut-outs of musicians in record-store windows, no slick posters. In fact, it's difficult to find record stores at all. There is one record store in central Havana, across the street from Coppelia, the ice-cream park near the Havana Libre Hotel. I found another true record store in Miramar. I suppose there are others, but nothing obvious, and certainly no mega-record stores. This matter is an issue of economics. A $15 CD is a luxury item for the average Cuban. If Cubans buy music, they buy cassettes that sell for two to four dollars. Many musicians have a clause in their contracts requiring that a certain number of cassettes of their music be produced.

"We go to any part of the island to find wonderful talent," Cari explained. "We select what we are interested in working with, sign the artist, and work with them, just like any other company in the world. As producers, we look for music that shows all the creative possibilities of our artists. We look for the elements that can be commercial in the market. In Cuban music, there are lots of genres and styles that have potential to be commercialized. We try to produce quality music because it's a heritage of our country. We try to preserve our historical and musical heritage and to develop it. Among all these possibilities, we can work on danceable, popular music – hip-hop, fusion, rock."

Distribution, distribution, distribution in the music industry is equivalent to location, location, location in real estate. Bis Music distributes through Artex, which has 270 outlets islandwide, the largest network in Cuba. Artex also produces the CDs themselves. EGREM also has a distribution network which, according to Gloria, cannot compare to the capacity of Artex, which has exclusive rights to handle Bis Music product. There are also foreign distribution companies with distribution outlets, such as Caribbean Production, LusAfrica, and TUMI Records.

"It's fundamental for any Cuban artist to start in Cuba," Gloria told me. "There is not a more selective and difficult audience to conquer than the Cuban audience. The Cuban audience knows about any kind of music. It's difficult to be a star in Cuba. If you are a star in Cuba, you can be a star anywhere, and everyone differentiates a Cuban from Miami and a Cuban from Cuba. We think that real Cuban music comes from the musicians living in the country, because the social and cultural transformations that the Cuban people have made have influenced the making and feeling of the music. The artist assumes the reality of his or her environment. The musician lives and creates from that experience. The Cuban music from Cuba has a particular way of sounding and of what it says. That's why Cuban record companies look for their artists in Cuba."

Nick Gold, owner of World Circuit Music, shares Gloria's optimism, but also sounds a cautionary note on the near future of Cuban music in the world market. "Cuban music has massively flown up in popularity," he confirmed from his London office. "Where you went into a shop before, there would be three or four records of Cuban music. Now there are racks and racks of Cuban stuff. But I don't know if Cuban music is going to become even more of a presence on the world music scene. People – especially the media – like things to be trends and then go away. Some journalists and critics are becoming possibly bored with Cuban music. They have been inundated with it. It's quite sad. There is so much coming out of that tiny island, it has almost reached saturation levels. But the stuff that is going to be coming out, things we are working on now, is very, very different from the Buena Vista Social Club sound. There is really a lot of creativity going on."

15 Helio's Music Lesson

Helio Orovio met Allen Ginsberg in a Havana jail. "I had been at a party and drinking and got into an argument, and that became a fight, so the police came," Helio told me as we sat under the shade trees on the patio of the Writers' Union (UNEAC, the Union de Escritores y Artistas de Cuba) at 17th and H, a favorite hang-out for Helio and other writers and musicians. It was Wednesday afternoon, time for the weekly peña, which is one of the true hot spots of Havana. We had arrived early to get a table with a fine line of sight of the performing area. "I was in the holding cell when a policemen brought in Ginsberg and three Cuban writers. The police didn't know who he was, but I did. I told the cops to put him in the cell with me."

Helio is an esteemed musicologist, poet, and journalist who publishes articles on Cuban music in US and European publications. He wrote the first *Dictionary Of Cuban Music*, and when we talked he was writing a television series about the history of rumba. He is regarded as a maven on Cuban music from an historical point of view. He has amusing black-and-white eyebrows and a fuzz of sparse white hair on a nearly bald head and a playful sense of humor. You know when a good line is coming by his face, which lights up, his lips puckishly twisting with pleasure. He loves to gossip and goes from party to party to meet his friends, as he is well known in art circles.

"Ginsberg had been smoking marijuana on the street corner outside Coppelia. There are always long lines outside the Coppelia, and there is Ginsberg offering a joint to policemen. 'You should try it,' Ginsberg told them. 'It's good for you.' They hustled him directly to jail."

Ginsberg had been invited to Cuba to judge a poetry contest, to give classes on American poetry at the Writers' Union, and to deliver a Walt Whitman lecture at the University School of Letters. He had become involved in Cuban affairs in September 1960, when he met Castro during the Presidente's New York visit to address the United Nations. In his book *Ginsberg, A Biography*, Barry Miles writes, "There was a press conference, and Allen astonished the gathering by saying, 'Marijuana is revolutionary, but the imperialists have invented all kinds of stories about it just so no one will smoke it and rebel. What does the Cuban Revolution think about marijuana?' The Cubans were surprised by the question, since it was not something the revolutionaries had any kind of position on. There had been clandestine farmers in the Sierra Maestra for whom marijuana was second only to coffee as a cash crop. At first, Castro had turned a blind eye to them, but then he began to crack down. At the time of the press conference, marijuana was illegal in Cuba, just as it had been before the Revolution. [It remains illegal to this day.] With so much work to be done, the Cubans clearly didn't relish the thought of people sitting around stoned."

Helio and Ginsberg were both released that night. "We smoked a joint in a park," Helio said. "During the late '60s, many of the American revolutionaries came to Cuba and I met them all – Eldridge Cleaver, Angela Davis, Stokely Carmichael – [and] every Black Panther who arrived. They were very interested in the ideals of the Revolution and how we were making the ideals a reality."

Helio paused to freshen his rum glass. Ginsberg was deported a few days after they met, he told me, picking up the story – not so much for the marijuana but for a lot of things he had said, especially about the persecution of gays, or what he believed was persecution. Ginsberg didn't understand very much about the Revolution and its problems. He saw issues through his North American perceptions, which often didn't apply to the Cuban situation. He verbally stepped on toes. He said that Castro's brother, Raul, was a homosexual, and that he, Ginsberg, had had a sexual fantasy about Che Guevara. Ginsberg may have just been repeating rumors about Raul Castro, but it was a very sensitive subject. A series of *faux pas* resulted in soldiers escorting him to the airport, where he was placed on a plane bound for Prague.

During the time of his adventure with Ginsberg, Helio was finishing his *Dictionary Of Cuban Music*, the first such reference work to be written. The compilation was an arduous task. He worked alone, without support, which made even the seemingly simple task of verifying a musician's birthdate time consuming. Many of the musicians came from small towns, and the records were spotty or non-existent. He wrote on the backs of old television scripts because of a severe paper shortage.

"I'd drive in from home, about an hour outside Havana, and wait until the Writers' Union closed," Helio said. "Then I'd ask one of the personnel if I could borrow a typewriter. I'd work until I couldn't stay awake. I did it as homage to the musicians who would otherwise be forgotten. It was a mission for me, something I had to do."

There had always been music on the island, Helio pointed out, even back in prehistoric times. The Arawak, who arrived from northern South America in around AD 1100, fashioned drums and tambourines from the trumpet tree. The skins of aquatic animals, such as the manatee, were used for drumheads. Woodwind instruments were carved out of tree limbs and animal bones.

The Spanish arrived in 1492 and described indigenous dances as *los ariétos*, meaning "Indian or indigenous song and dance." The purposes of the dances were to raise spirits, bring success, and please the gods. The dances were based on an oral tradition of chorus and group dances, in which 500 to 1,000 men and women participated. A leader, called a *tequina*, would begin by walking, jumping, hopping, stamping, turning, and doing leg lifts. Soon, everyone would follow, imitating his steps. At times, dancers held hands or locked elbows as they danced in procession; at other times they danced individually. The dance was very structured. Dancers proceeded and then retreated a set number of steps. The dance ended when the dancers were utterly exhausted and couldn't continue, which might take four or five hours or all day and night.

Cuba's traditional musical history, however, began when the conquering Spanish colonized the island, between 1510 and 1517.

By the end of the 17th century, most of the indigenous population of Cuba had been wiped out by disease, hard labor, and brutality. The Spanish then began importing slave labor from west Africa. The slave trade in the Americas lasted nearly 400 years before it staggered into abolition in the late 1880s. During that time, several million Africans of diverse ethnic origins and cultures were transported to the New World, and they changed forever the music, culture, society, and psychological make-up of the region. The Yoruba (from Nigeria), the Bantu (from Congo and Angola), the Ewe-Fon and the Fanti-Asanti (from Dahomey, now Benin), and the Malé or Mandinga (from Sudan) were crucial to the musical development of the New World. Their cultural influences are still heard in modern jazz, rap, and popular dance music, including call-and-response antiphonal singing; polymer, such as duple and triple meters played simultaneously; and polyrhythms, which include syncopation and the superimposition of different parts, yet always with a pulse that tends to divide patterns into two or four beats.

In Cuba, the influence of Yoruba is primary in the western and northwestern regions, such as Havana and Matanzas; Kongo-Angolan is in central and eastern regions; Arará is in the northwestern and eastern regions; and Abakuá is mostly in the northwest. This is why the musical traditions of western and eastern Cuba are so distinctly different today. African drumming, chanting, and dancing – as well as Santeria – occurs predominantly in the western and northern parts of the island, especially on the Havana-Matanzas axis. Little African-based music or Santeria influences are found in eastern Cuba, where the music is Spanish based, with Santiago de Cuba as the hub for son and other forms of traditional country music.

Cuba experienced a huge increase in slave and sugar-cane production after the Haitian slave rebellion in 1791-1802. That revolt directly contributed styles of music that became the foundation of modern Cuban music. The French planters fleeing Haiti brought with them the *contredanse*, a dance derived from the French court dance of the homeland. It immediately became a dance craze within the Spanish and French planter class. (The composition 'San Pascual Bailón' dates from 1803.)

In Haiti, the Afro-Haitians had added a syncopation called the *cinquillo* (a fast, five-beat throb) to the contredanse, which in Cuba took on the Spanish accent and became *contradanza*. This rhythm, very similar to the Argentinean tango, is basic to today's Puerto Rican music and the Dominican and Haitian *merengue*. Black musicians further syncopated the beat of the *ritmo de tango*. In 1856, a contradanza called 'Tu Madre Es Conga' ('Your Mother Is Congolese') introduced the held first note, an effect identical to Afro-Cuban songs.

The present-day *habanera* Cuban style of music and dance is the immediate descendant of the contradanza. The habanera's *ritmo de tango* was virtually identical to the cakewalk rhythm. Both are versions of a rhythmic motif common in wide ranges of Afro-American music.

However, while the plantation slavemasters were dancing, they were also trembling in their boots. The increase in the slave population caused fear of insurrection. Plantation owners tried to deculturize the slave population. They attempted to strip the people of their identities, cohesion, and dignity in order to secure a workforce entirely dependent on the white planter class. The slave-owners mixed the different African peoples – who often did not understand each other's language, customs, or belief systems – in order to prevent revolts from fomenting. In the long term, this led to the cross-fertilization of music and cultural practices and eventually to the slave rebellions.

One result of the planters' policy was the *cabildos*, homogeneous African ethnic groups that operated as mutual-aid societies or lodges. Eventually, cabildos consolidated multiple African ethnic groups and solidified African culture in Cuba. The cabildos played an important part in rebuilding and maintaining African ethnic identities in a new, transatlantic context. They also conserved several African languages, ritual practices, belief systems, dances, songs, chants, instruments, and instrument-making techniques.

Cabildos were formed by slaves and free blacks who, as owners of property and slaves themselves, constituted the black elite. Each cabildo was associated with a particular African nation. In Havana, each cabildo usually had a large kitchen; a yard, where the animals used in the rituals were kept; and an orisha or santo room, where all the religious activities took place. The Africans adopted the overlord's religion as a screen behind which to hide and protect the belief systems brought from Africa. Cabildos were formally devoted to the Catholic cult of saints, but they provided the framework within which worship of the Catholic saints could be combined with the worship of African deities or orishas. This also contributed to the existing music of Cuba, as seen in bata drumming and the chants of Santeria and Abakuá.

The dichotomy that exists in Cuba today between the Spanish and the African, the white and the black, co-existed in the cabildos, and, as in Cuba today, that dichotomy achieved a self-serving balance. The hegemonic Christianity of the saints sought to make the Africans accept as the will of God their position at the bottom of the society, but in African belief systems – as seen in Santeria – the universe is controlled by mysterious powers that an individual can manipulate in his or her favor. African religious systems make no distinction between the supernatural world and the natural world. African religious thought strongly influenced slaves to take action against their owners. Rituals carried out in the cabildos encouraged resistance against the Spanish overclass.

By the mid 1800s, the rate of slave suicide increased, as did rebellions. The most notable uprisings took place in 1825 and 1843 in Matanzas. The largest and best-organized slave revolt took place in early March 1844. It was called La Escalera ("The Ladder") because those arrested in the following political repression were tied to ladders and repeatedly whipped until they died. Four thousand people were tried by military tribunal. Ninety-eight were condemned to death, about 600 were sentenced to prison, and more than 400 were deported. The revolt had been organized and carried out through the tribal organizations and dance groups of the plantations.

Between 1850 and 1870, the importation of slaves increased dramatically. From 1868, some 476,288 slaves entered Cuba, the majority Congolese and Yoruba, especially women. This was the result, in part, of internal conflicts within Yorubaland. In the 1700s, the Kingdom of Oyo had been a major supplier of slaves from the territories it controlled with a powerful cavalry, but in the mid 1800s the kingdom fell due to internal conflicts that arose between the king and the hereditary nobility, conflicts encouraged and abetted by the Moslems and the British to further their own slave-trade profits.

Among the slaves transported to Cuba were the Ifá (Yoruba priests and priestesses). In Africa, the Ifá were the carriers of the arts and sciences and were considered the intellectuals of the society. They provided important leadership in carrying on religious rituals and music essential to maintaining the link between human beings and the gods. The black elite in Havana assisted them in buying their freedom and contributed to their support. The Ifá, and the Yorubas in general, imbued an aesthetic into the developing slave culture. In Yoruba, *ona* ("art") cannot be defined outside the context of the processes of creation and the purpose of creating. Art captures the *ewa*, the "beauty," that is the essential quality of the subject, whether this is a physical object in a sculpture or the ineffability expressed in music.

The Abakuá Society, which was established in 1836 in Regla, across the bay from Havana, has also left a mark on Cuban society and music. Abakuá (also referred to as Calabali) originated in the "leopard societies" of the Abákpá, Efor, and Éfik peoples of the Cross (Odán) River in southeastern Nigeria, in what was once known as El Calabar. The word Abakuá has its genesis in the tribal name Abákpá. The Abakuá were fiercely anti-colonial and anti-slavery. The Abakuá Society was founded as a mutual-aid society, and part of that aid was used to buy slaves their freedom. The Abakuá members became the backbone of the port-workers' society and are still a strong union force on the waterfront. They were influential in the development of rumba as it evolved on the docks of Regla and Matanzas.

Abakuá is a closed, male-only society. Members take an oath of loyalty to the society's sacred objects, esoteric knowledge, and the duties of the society. The saying "Friendship is one thing and the Abakuá another" succinctly states the principle that the society comes first, even before friendship, if circumstances dictate that a choice must be made.

Abakuá ceremonies are based on performances of liturgical drumming, dancing, and chanting. Abakuá dancing re-enacts stories of mysterious beings that communicate through postures, gestures, movement motifs, and the intangible expressiveness of the *ireme diablito* ("spirit masks"). The *fundamento* – the sacred law and moral authority in all aspects of the society – is the core principle of Abakuá teachings. Fundamentos are objects in which supernatural forces are concentrated. Ultimately, the fundamentos represent the supreme divinity, Abasí, the source of all existence. The fundamento central to all ritual action is the bongo ékue, the sacred drum through which the voice of God is heard.

The Abakuá esoteric language used exclusively for ceremonial purposes has found its way into secular music, to the strenuous objections of Abakuá traditionalists. In the 1920s, Ignacio Píñero, a member of the Abakuá, composed 'En La Alto Sociedad,' which includes Abakuá phases, and was barred from becoming a dignitary in his Abakuá group. However, this didn't stop Píñero from continuing to record and write Abakuá chants for commercial recordings. When he sang, "In the colonial days, the days of the *sese eribó*," Benny Moré (1919-63) was referring to one of the Abakuá fundamentos, the sese eribó drum, used to initiate new members. In his classic mambo 'Bábarabartíri,' Moré makes coded reference to Abakuá.

Contemporary rumba/folkloric groups such as Los Múnequitos De Matanzas and Grupo AfroCuba play Abakuá ceremonial music, and many members of those bands are Abakuá members. Popular singer Isaac Delgado had a top hit in Cuba in 2001 and uses Abakuá references in his music.

Every Cuban musical genre, past and present, is rooted in these African sources, combined with Spanish musical forms. The danzón, which became the national dance craze in the late 1800s, is a good example. The danzón is the progeny of the French contredanse. The first danzón, 'Las Alturas De Simpson,' was presented in Matanzas by Miguel Failde, a great cornet player in a popular *orquesta típica* (a cornet band supported by clarinets and trombones, with timpani predominant in the percussion). He added subtle African rhythms to the European base, along with the call-and-response montuno section. This created a balance between the formal ballroom gyrations of the contredanse and syncopated African rhythm. The result was a simulacrum of ragtime. The danzón spawned the danza, donzóncha, and danzónette, couple dances popular with the upper classes at their private clubs and societies.

From the 1870s to around 1916, danzóns were usually played outdoors in the town square by orquestas tipicas. The same danzóns were played indoors by groups known as *charangas Frencescas* (French orchestras), or *charangas* for short. The charangas were composed of violins backed by flute lead, and the timpani were replaced by the smaller timbales.

The mambo and chachacha were created directly from danzón. In 1938, Orestes "Cachao" Lopez, a cellist in the charanga group of the great flautist Antonio Arcáno, composed a new rhythmic danzón that he called *mambo*. In the Bantu/Kongo language, *mambo* means "to chant, to sing, to dance, or to express through the voice." The conga and bongo were added to the charanga's flute-and-violin sound. To this new rhythm, Antonio Aracáno added elements of the son, which resulted in more swing and riff-based rhythm. This became very popular with the black and working-class Cubans. The danzón, once reserved for the elite class, soon evolved into the proletarian mambo. Perez Prado took the new music to Mexico in the late 1940s with his big band, where it became very popular, while the Cuban bandleader Machito introduced the music in New York with his big band.

The chachacha evolved from the mambo. Enrique Jorrin, a violin player with Orquesta America, is credited with creating the chachacha in the 1950s. He said that the name was suggested by the scraping sound of the dancers' feet.

This evolution of Cuban music went on to affect North American music. In the 1850s and 1860s, Louisianan composer Louis Moreau Gottschalk (1829-69) made extensive use of Cuban elements. In the past, he had studied in Paris, and was friends with Chopin. He first went to Cuba in 1834, settled in New Orleans in 1855, and then returned to Cuba in 1857. Cuban music was part of the cultural mix in New Orleans and one of the ingredients of black music very early on. When Cuban slaves were emancipated in 1866, many of the able-bodied men signed on as stokers on the steamships plying the Caribbean routes. They commonly abandoned ship at the first port, which was often New Orleans. There they picked up on American ragtime, blues, and early jazz, and in turn added their music to the stew.

Jesse Pickett, one of the semi-legendary generation of late-19th-century black musicians, used habanera rhythm in his 1880s composition 'The Dream.' The piece eventually became part of the jazz repertoire, losing its original Latin base in the process. Pickett, who played with Eubie Blake, used 'The Dream' to teach Blake to play ragtime. He gave it two parts: first fast, then slow drag with blues. That was a kind of reversal of the Cuban contradanza's common two-part form. The blending with blues is typical of the way in which Latin ingredients have always melted into US music.

In 1895, John Philip Sousa's operetta *El Captain* had notionally Latin themes, and Victor Herbert included a piece called 'Cuban Song' in his 1897 musical comedy *The Idol's Eye*. This marked the beginning of a Broadway flirtation with Latin themes that was to last 50 years.

Jelly Roll Morton claimed that the "Spanish tinge" was the essential ingredient that differentiated jazz from ragtime. "In fact," he said, "if you can't manage to put tinges of Spanish in your tunes, you will never be able to get the right seasoning – I call it – for jazz."

The real impact of 20th-century Cuban music – which was huge – came from popular composers like Moises Simons, composer of *The Peanut Vendor*, and other composers who straddled both conservative and popular music. The recording of *The Peanut Vendor* was important because, for the first time on record, it combined serious and experimental jazz writing with an authentic Latin rhythm section.

The crossover between black and Cuban music increased as more black US musicians came into contact with Cuban music. In 1900, WC Handy and his band traveled to Cuba. He was particularly enamored with the small bands he found playing in the back streets. "These fascinated me because they were playing a strange native air, new and interesting to me," he wrote of the experience. "More than 30 years later, I heard that rhythm again. By then, it had gained respectability in New York and had acquired a name: the rumba."

Ernesto Lecuona and his rumba band, The Lecuona Cuban Boys, recorded rumba for Columbia in the 1930s. Lecuona's main influence on US Latin music was through the huge popularity of compositions like 'Siboney,' 'Maria La O,' and 'Para Vigo Me Voy (Say Si Si).' The habanera, the son, and the romantic work of Lecuona *et al* fed directly into mainstream American popular music.

Towards the end of the 1930s, a new type of Cuban band called *conjuntos* became popular, based on the black carnival parade groups. The conjuntos groups consisted of trumpets, voices, and conga and, like the early New Orleans jazz groups, added piano and bass when they played indoors. The raucous conjunto sound was at first no more popular in polite society than New Orleans jazz was in its early days.

Arsenio Rodriguez, an Afro-Cuban percussionist and a master of the tres, was the most important name in the development of the conjunto. He was born in Matanzas Province in 1911. As a youth, he was blinded by a mule kick, and therefore as a musician was nicknamed "El Ciego Maravillosa" ("The Marvelous Blind Man"). He came to New York in the 1950s for an operation to cure his blindness. The operation failed, but he never returned to Cuba.

Rodriguez's lyrics reflected the concerns of black Cubans of Congolese descent. His sympathy for the cause of the international black struggle is expressed in 'Aqui Como Alla' and 'Vaya Pál Monte.' Several of his songs make reference to Afro-Cuban music and rituals – 'Chango Panchanga' is based on a Yoruba chant used in Santeria, while 'Yambú En Serenata' has many elements of the slow yambú rumba.

In 1945, Woody Herman recorded 'Bijou,' subtitled 'Rhumba À La Jazz,' while – according to Marshall Stearn's *The Story Of Jazz* – Johnny Mandel first developed the Latin-jazz blues tune 'Barados,' later recorded by, and credited to, Charlie Parker.

Parker also recorded with the Cuban bandleader Frank "Machito" Grillo, a singer/maraca player who came from Cuba to

New York in 1937. His band, Machito's Afro-Cubans, was a pivotal group in the coming of age of Latin jazz. With Machito, Parker recorded the song 'Mano Mangue,' which continues to be a successful Latin jazz song. Herbie Mann also made a number of recordings with Machito.

Mongo Santamaria became a major contributor of American jazz in the late 1940s and 1950s. When Chico O'Farrill left Cuba to live in New York, the composer, trumpet player, and arranger introduced more elements of Cuban music into jazz and New York music.

On the West Coast, in Los Angeles and San Francisco, Cubans were influencing American counterparts such as George Shearing. They made a fusion of music with the elements of folkloric Cuban music mixed with cool jazz.

The "Cubop" of the late 1940s and the 1950s was simply part of an ongoing fusion process. It sprang from the new bebop movement, which at the time seemed a total break from the jazz past, with its emphasis on harmonic improvisation and the apparent abandonment of melody. In Cubop, Latin and jazz elements were more equally balanced than they were in previous music. The genre had three creative leaders: Stan Kenton, Dizzy Gillespie, and Machito.

By 1947, Kenton was committed to adopting Latin music as part of the developing style that he called "progressive jazz." In mid January 1947, he recorded 'Machito,' which represented the transition between light Afro-Cuban jazz and Cubop. Then, on December 6, 1947, he recorded his new arrangement of *The Peanut Vendor*, complete with a four-trumpet passage full of then-evolutionary discords.

Dizzy Gillespie succeeded in blending bebop – then the creative cutting edge of jazz – with the purest Afro-Cuban percussion and singing and pushed Latin fusion beyond the "fun" image and into serious jazz. By February 1948, with Cuban drummer Chano Pozo, Gillespie had composed 'Afro-Cuban Suite' and 'Manteca,' the latter of which became a jazz standard in Gillespie's band's repertoire. Both songs integrated Abakuá ceremonial music and chants with jazz harmonies. Pozo, born Luciano Pozo y Gonzales, was a member of the Abakuá society, and wrote several Latin jazz standards, including

'Tin Tin Deo.' Meanwhile, Bo Diddley, who had enormous influence on British rock, used Latin sounds and the maracas since forming a street trio in 1949.

Rhythm and blues was also strongly influenced by Cuban music. The piano playing of Antoine "Fats" Domino – the jazz musician of 'Blueberry Hill' fame and who came out of New Orleans – has a marked Latin tinge. Domino acquired much of his style from an older New Orleans pianist, Roy "Professor Longhair" Byrd, who described his playing as "a mixture of rumba, mambo, and calypso." His Latinized New Orleans piano rhythms became part of mainstream rock 'n' roll during the 1950s.

Chuck Willis' 'CC Rider' was based on the rumba-inflected patterns that Fats Domino made popular. In 1954, Ruth Brown's 'Mambo Baby' reached first place on the R&B charts. LaVern Baker's major hit 'Tweedle Dee' got a lift from a riff that was essentially a simple, on-beat clave pattern. Meanwhile, Ray Charles' song 'What'd I Say' also had rumba patterns, further evidence of the Latin influence on US black music in the 1960s.

During the 1990s, Cuban-tinged jazz and popular dance music was heard increasingly in mainstream world music. Even when it wasn't obvious, the Cuban style of music seeped into the background through the work of people like Luis Conte, a percussionist who has played with the Who's Who of popular music – Phil Collins, Madonna, James Taylor, Steve Winwood, and Ray Charles, to name a few. He has also recorded four of his own albums, the latest being *Cuban Dreams*. Conte left Cuba when he was 15 for the United States, where he now lives.

"When I play the conga drum, the technique is of a Cuban drummer, even if the music is not Cuban," he told me during a brief conversation when I caught up with him on a recent James Taylor tour. "American pop music like that by Puerto Rican singers Ricky Martin and Marc Anthony has roots in Cuban music, although it's not real Cuban music. And now salsa has become more accepted by Central American people. I was in Mexico City and went to a couple smokin' Cuban clubs packed with Cuban musicians living in Mexico. But to get into the mainstream hit music, the Cubans have to sing in English. That's the first thing that has to happen. Hit songs that last long have beautiful lyrics, plus music."

The rum bottle on our table was nearly empty by the time Helio got through his cursory summary of Cuban music. Emptying the last of the bottle, he said, "Timba – which has a lot of rumba, a lot of jazz, a little rock, a little funky, and a little rap – is the latest form that Cuban dance music has adopted up to this moment. The timba was in the late 1980s and the early 1990s what salsa was in the United States in the 1970s and early '80s and what chachacha was during the 1950s. As popular music, this line can be traced back to the mambo in the 1940s to the 1950s; rumba in the 1940s and '50s; danzónette and bolero in the 1930s; habanero son in the 1920s; and danzón in the 1910s. The fashion of timba will pass, because it's not a mother music.

"I think that the next hit of Cuban popular music will come from the line of the romantic boleros," he concluded. "That is part of the roots, and everything returns to the roots, eventually."

The deep-blue plastic tables on the patio around Helio and me had filled with people who knew that the peña was the best-value entertainment in Havana. The story goes that the UNEAC building is an old mansion that once belonged to a banker who committed suicide in a second-story bedroom after his bank had been nationalized and he was left with only $2 million. Lots of stories go around the tables at UNEAC when writers, poets, musicians, artists, and composers gather there on Wednesday afternoons. The mood is very convivial, with lots of backslapping, shouted greetings, and displaying of latest publicity stills or brochures for openings of art exhibitions. This particular showcase peña, held every other Wednesday, is hosted by Ambia, a television personality, hence the name Peña Ambia.

Ambia moved through the crowd to the open space in front of the steps leading to the wraparound porch. He is a squat, thick-bodied man with a shaven head who always wears a flowing African shirt and a Caribbean straw hat for the peña. He roamed about with a mic talking to friends, bantering with the crowd, and being the emcee as he introduced the first act.

A smooth crooner sang two ballads. The guy's voice was like butter spread in front of a bedroom door – when you listened to him you slid right into seduction. Next came an elegant young woman in a white, skin-tight dress with a voice and style that could pack any New York lounge. A woman in the audience took the mic from Ambia and gave a dramatic reading of a poem. Then a matronly woman with close-cropped hair and retro 1950s eyeglass frames sang a wonderful rendition of a song popular in the 1940s.

An Abakuá ensemble from Mantanzas then performed a rumba in Yoruba that is sung at the opening of an Abakuá ceremony and is meant to open a person's heart and consciousness. The singer (the *mórwa*) was backed by three drums: a conga; the banká, which is a flat piece of metal struck with a hardwood stick; and a gourd shaker covered with cowrie shells. The singer set up a call-and-response pattern that, after 15 minutes, became hypnotic with its chanted cadences. The driving rhythm of the band shook people from their tables and onto their feet. The music was deafening, the rum was flowing, people were shaking their whole bootie and then some, and Helio toasted me with a new bottle of rum. I spent nearly every Wednesday afternoon thereafter under the shade trees on the patio at UNEAC.

16 Son Of Santiago De Cuba

In 1604, the pirate Gilberto Giron kidnapped Bishop Juan de las Cabezas Altamirana. A black slave, Salvador Goloman, joined the search for the bishop. He tracked down the pirate, killed him, and rescued the bishop. The people in the town of Manzanillo celebrated the bishop's safe return with guitars and drums. This was supposedly the birth of son, which became the centerpiece of Cuban music. Of course, Manzanillo is the hometown of Benny Moré, Cuba's greatest performer of son, so maybe there is something to the story.

Manzanillo is in eastern Cuba, the Oriente, where all the troublemakers supposedly come from. Hatuey, Cuba's "first rebel," the Indian chief who led an uprising against the Spanish, started his revolt in the Oriente. The War of Independence against Spain started in the Oriente, and was led by generals from the region. Cuba's legendary hero of the independence, the "bandit" Manuel Garcia – a political Robin Hood – roamed the Oriente in the 1880s, extorting money from wealthy landowners, often by kidnapping them and bartering for their freedom. The money funded the patriots' war against Spain. He crowned himself "king of the countryside" and taunted the Spanish governors with letters to Havana newspapers extolling his successes against their army. The Oriente is also the home province of Fidel Castro and the place where he and his men started the revolution that overthrew the dictator Batista.

The Oriente was Cuba's version of the Wild West and is still regarded as the wildest part of the island. The mountains of the Oriente contain Cuba's largest national parks and wilderness preserves. The region is distinctly different from the western end of the island in that the people have their own distinct dialect, music, and pride. The people there – especially the inhabitants of Santiago de Cuba – speak in a singsong lilt, as if they can't get music out of their voices. My excuse to visit the Oriente was La Festival de la Trova ("the Festival of Ballads"), held every mid March in Santiago de Cuba, Cuba's second city. I decided to take the overnight train from Havana to attend the festival 750 miles away on the opposite end of the island, and there began the adventure.

Train tickets are sold at train stations. I needed a train ticket. I went to the train station. Logic is a reliable guide, except in an illogical situation. After bumbling around in the main station, waiting in various lines only to be told that I was in the wrong line, I was directed to leave the station. Once outside, I was to turn and face the station. Then I was to walk along the right-hand side of the station to a gate marked "LADIS." At this point, I was beginning to feel that I was the butt of a cruel joke. My informant told me that, if I wished, the famous Casa de los Vino was just beyond the gate. He gave me a friendly pat on the shoulder and sent me on my way.

I went outside the station and followed the directions. After walking a block, I once again suspected that the zigzag of Latin rationality was mocking the straight-and-narrow logic of my Cartesian mind. Then, following the curve of the street, I saw the word "LADIS" in big letters above an iron gate. Beyond the gate was a roof without walls. Under the roof sat a young woman at a wooden table. On the table was taped a warning: "BUY TRAIN TICKET HERE AND NO WHERE ELSE." This was the special gate for the express train to Santiago de Cuba. I presented my passport (document checks are de rigueur for foreigners and Cubans alike when traveling within the country) and handed over $42 for a one-way ticket.

The train was scheduled to leave at 7.30. By 7.00, I and 20 other travelers occupied the iron benches in the small garden that served as a waiting room. There were only a few Cubans among the American, Japanese, French, and German backpackers. One old fellow caught my attention. He was clearly in his 70s, skeletal in frame but bright eyed and joyful in face. With him were two beautiful young Cuban women dressed in Spandex pants and tops that left the midriff bare, which must be the national costume, given how many Cuban women – regardless of age, shape, or size – wear the outfit. Cuban women wear clothes as a fan dancer wears feathers – as a tease. At first, I thought that the young women might be relatives come to see grandad off, but the obvious affection shown was not familial. Nor was he a rich lech with two trophies, since they were about to endure a twelve-hour train ride rather than take a one-hour flight. When I reach this man's age, I thought, I want to be like him. I watched carefully for clues on how to achieve a happy dotage. He smiled and laughed a lot. He appeared kind and caring. He was frisky with his humor. He carried his own bag when we were summoned to board the train. He might have been just plain damn lucky.

A long string of unlighted cars had been pushed onto the track next to the platform. To place complete faith in the model "I think, therefore I am" is to be gullible. The paradigm "What is isn't" has equal validity. A man with a flashlight escorted us out onto the platform. One by one, we pulled ourselves up the high step of a car, heavy backpacks swinging awkwardly, only to be told to dismount on the other side. Our guide urged us to go "*mas rapido* – quickly!" across the tracks, as if a speeding train was expected at any moment. We scurried around another set of cars nearly filled with people stowing their luggage and settling in. Our shepherd directed us past the first-class coaches to the second-class cars and gestured, as if showing sheep the way into a corral.

The conductor – a hefty woman with a fine-featured, pretty face – checked our tickets and allowed us to board. When I entered the car, my first thought was, How did all these people get on the train? Only a few seats remained unoccupied. They must have boarded from the main station while I'd been sent on a treasure hunt ending at the beginning. I had an urge to check my back for a sign saying, "Kick Me." I found my assigned seat and stowed my bag on the overhead rack.

The seat was red vinyl and, on first testing, not uncomfortable. However, the reclining mechanism proved balky. I pulled the lever and pushed hard against the seat to force it back. Nothing. I slammed myself into the seat back, which did not move one whit. I stood and jerked the reluctant seat back and forth. People were watching me being defeated by an inanimate object. I tried to finesse the lever mechanism with a light touch while applying gentle pressure on the seat. I tried a surprise attack by going behind the seat and suddenly grabbing it. I tried feigned resignation, sitting down with a heavy sigh while surreptitiously balancing my weight and shoving hard back against the seat. Nothing. A man in front of me, whose seat was fully reclined, motioned me to stand. He raised the reclining lever, placed a hand on the back of the seat, and, after a moment of concentration, as if preparing to break boards with a karate chop, dropped the seat back.

I had expected the atmosphere to be Latin – loud music, people shouting and gesturing (that is, having a normal conversation) – but the car was subdued and orderly. The lack of at least one blaring radio surprised me. Cubans need music the way that fish need water. In all my time in Cuba, I never did find a café or a restaurant that did not feature music as part of the main course. In the communal taxis, if music wasn't playing at conversation-stopping levels, the passengers querulously asked the driver what was the matter. Refusing to believe, as the driver claimed, that the radio was broken, they would twist the knobs in their own verification test. I was rarely out of earshot of music coming from homes as I walked the streets. On one memorable evening, everyone on a six-block stretch was tuned to the same classical music show on the television, providing a continuous soundtrack to my meandering.

I had seen Cubans go ballistic Latin – throat veins bulging from shouting, hands and arms windmilling in the most threatening manner toward the person being addressed – but that was usually when discussing baseball. Otherwise, Cubans were poised and openly friendly, never pushy or embarrassingly exuberant – except when dancing. If there is music, Cubans cannot abstain from dancing any more than a butterfly can swim.

I had seen Cubans try to restrain themselves, as at a rumba concert at Havana's beautifully restored Teatro Amadeo Roldan, a theater that encourages symphonic decorum. The audience sat as if in church, giving due respect to culture. By the time the band hit the third song, a few shoulders began to twitch. Then a few hands flew up in the air, waving to the intricate polyrhythms. Bodies half rose out of their seats and then dropped back. People glanced at their neighbors with conspiratorial smiles, then spontaneously erupted in flat-out dancing.

If praise is deserved, then give it in full exhalation, and that's what the audience did. They were in the aisles, crowding the stage, filling every space with wild dance – old ladies in their Sunday best, proper matrons in conservative dresses, gentlemen in dress shirts (men hardly ever wear coats and ties in Cuba), teenage girls in slinky and tight, their dates in casual cool, little girls in frilly dresses – all were up and raising the temperature of the place.

But, in the railroad car, my fellow passengers pulled out jackets and sweaters, or wrapped themselves in towels to ward off the chill of the air conditioning. The solid, heavy rumble (*not* a clickety-clack) of the train as it passed through the black countryside had a soporific effect. Before drifting off to sleep, I thought of the conversation about son and Cuban country music that I'd had with Barbaro "Barbarito" Torres, who is perhaps best known as a member of Buena Vista Social Club. He has also recorded with The Afro-Cuban All Stars and now tours with his own group, Barbaro Torres And His Cuban Gang. Their most recent CD is entitled *Havana Café*.

Barbaro's musical roots are in son and campesino (farmers') songs. He was born in Matanzas in 1957 and grew up in "that land of many poets and lute players," he told me as we sat in his living room with his wife and musical manager, Sonia Perez Cassola, who is also a musicologist. They live with their teenage son on the upper floor of a pink, two-story house, which appeared to be under restoration. In the living room were the trappings of an internationally successful musician: a Sony CD/tape player, a 36-inch Sony television, a PlayStation (presumably for his son), modern black *faux*-leather chairs and sofa, and a laptop computer. It was a nice place, nothing fancy, with a balcony overlooking the crowns of shade trees.

Barbaro taught himself the guitar and lute when he was eleven years old and turned pro at the age of 14. In his early career, he was stereotyped as a country player of son and was a regular on the folkloric weekly television show *Palmes y Canes*, which featured country music and dancing, but he wanted to break out of the mold so as not to be confined by the traditional structure of son and country music. "Traditional music has served as a bridge to the current music," he told me. "It was music largely forgotten, but it led to the breakout of Cuban music, as seen with Buena Vista Social Club. I tried to make an evolution in country music."

He put zip into his playing style and began to incorporate contemporary rhythms and influences into his country music. "I was called 'the Cuban Chuck Berry,'" he said. *"The New York Times* called me 'the Jimi Hendrix of Cuban music.' I dance while I'm playing, like Chuck Berry. In the case of Jimi Hendrix, I played behind my head, behind my back, under my leg, played the guitar upside-down, as Hendrix did with his guitar. I did this without having seen the videos of Chuck Berry or Jimi Hendrix. I wanted people to see the country music differently."

A main trunk of Cuban traditional music is son, although son is not the primary root of Cuban music. That honor goes to *quiribá*, from which evolved *nengón*, from which developed son. Son is considered to be the first popular genre of Cuban music to use a drum played with the bare hands. Salsa is a branch of son, as is the salsa dance, borrowed from son, guaracha and rumba. Son was also the basis of the 1930s rumba craze in the United States.

The music originated in rural Oriente, where old songs from Spain combined with African call-and-response choruses and the African characteristic of the melody having no rhythmic connection with the underlying percussion. The farmers who created son invented a new instrument, the tres, which remains the main stringed instrument of traditional Cuban country music today. The tres reputedly developed from the west African *kalimba* finger-piano, rather than the more obvious Spanish lute or guitar. It was invented as a substitute for the piano, which the farmers could not afford to buy or haul around the mountains to their parties, and serves the same percussive role as the piano. It has six strings grouped in three pairs, with the two top strings tuned an octave apart, one high and one low. On the traditional tres, this tuning was on the bottom two strings.

"The son is very satirical and full of double meanings and humor," Barbaro told me, "much like the character of our rural people. It has always been used to make social and political comments, like guaracha. The style of son – the improvising and decima – lends itself to that role. Often, there are two singers who challenge each other to come up with a better improvisation, and these contests can go on for hours, so they talk about everything: the price of food, their neighbor's infidelity, the crops, the bumbling government, the beautiful woman. In son, there are two ways of improvising: one using quartets – that is, four lines – and the other using decima, using ten-line rhymes. Both forms come from Spanish poetry. In the improvisation, son has a lot in common with hip-hop."

"Besides improvisation, the themes used are very important as a link between son and hip-hop," injected Barbaro's wife, Sonia, a musicologist. "Both forms talk about the culture, life, love, social issues, what is happening to all the people. So, in that, hip-hop is a continuation of a tradition in Cuban music. There are sones for different regions of Cuba. The most famous are from the Oriente. Matanzas and Camaguey have son, and the most important are from the Pinar del Rio province."

Sonia then began to hit her musicological stride. "You can say that, if Cuba was not unified, there would be two musics – that of the Oriente and that of the Occident, which is what we call western Cuba. Like the music of Haiti is different from the music of the Dominican Republic, although both countries share the same island. But the music of the Oriente became the music of the Occident and that of the Occident became part of the Oriente's music. They were unified through the radio and became a national music."

Barbaro said that he listens to American country and western music and blues, and that there is a difference between Cuban country music and US country music. Cuban country music is not only about heartbreak and lovers and sadness, as is the tendency in American country and western; Cuban music has more of an edge, a bite.

"I like very much the blues," Barbaro said. "I listen to Charlie Musselwhite in particular. There is a chance I will record with him and BB King and Bonnie Raitt. There are elements of Western country music and blues in Cuban music. The rhythmic pattern of the blues, the basic 4/4 beat, is in much of our rural music. In the son is a lot of blues, but we don't play the music pure, like it was inherited from other countries; we take the basis of that music and we transform it into our way of making music. That's why Cuban

Barbaro Torres of Buena Vista Social Club, "the Jimi Hendrix of the Cuban lute."
His wife, Sonia Perez Cassola, is a musicologist and her husband's musical manager

music will come out more and more on the international stage. In my opinion, the Cuban music and the American music are the most important influences on world music, followed by Brazil. Those are the three strongest centers of popular music."

Barbaro teaches at the National Institute of Art, and his approach to country music has created a new interest in country music among young musicians: "My students are most interested in the way of playing, the technique in which I play the farmers' music, the country music. I like bringing out other patterns in the music. I broke new ground for the lute, and younger people started looking at it differently. There was a little taboo, because the lute was only thought of as for country music, but because of my ideas I play it in a contemporary way, so more students are interested. In their music education, the students incorporate classical music into roots folkloric music and popular music. They make fusion. You can have classical influences in the phrasing of the horns in a dance band, for example. This incorporation of the classical and folkloric and traditional and popular is very characteristic of Cuban music."

Neyvis Pínera is a music student who has taken up country music. She's a member of Son Como Son, who recorded the album *El Aquaque Caiga, Yo Me La Tomo*, and she is one of only six female tres players in Cuba. "The tres was never taught to women," she said, "because it is regarded as a man's affair. It's very characteristic of the instrument that it needs the strength of a man, because it's a very strong instrument. You have to study a lot – especially the Cuban rhythms – to play it. For a woman to play the tres, she must fall in love with the instrument. When I began to study the tres, I realized the great possibilities of the instrument, not only to play Cuban music but tango, Latin-American music, jazz, and samba. It can be used in every genre, without limitation. I've tried to introduce tres into the Latin-American music and also the classical music I'm interested in.

"It's almost incredible that the players back in those older times – who did not study music – made such good music. It was music they did for fun. It's incredible how good it is, especially the duo Los Compadres, or the trio Matamores, or Níco Saquito, and, more recently, in the 1980s, Manguaré, when Pacho Amat was playing with them."

I must have fallen asleep, for I blinked awake at dawn's first light. Other passengers stirred, stretched, unwrapped themselves, and made the morning run to the toilet. When I pushed open the toilet's door, the foul odor nearly shoved me back into the corridor. The floor was wet and sticky with urine as the train's swaying misdirected men's attempt to hit the hole that emptied directly onto the tracks. It was an experience to make you hold your breath.

At the penultimate stop, 20 kilometers before Santiago de Cuba, my seatmate warned me about pickpockets who often got on the train there. When we disembarked at Santiago de Cuba, he and another man protectively bracketed me so that I wouldn't be an easy target. However, as we walked out of the station, we were all targets of a large crowd shouting offers of rooms for rent and taxis for hire. For a moment, I imagined that I was a movie star and they were fans making fools out of themselves for my attention. I waved and smiled and they redoubled their hard-sell antics. I moved down the line just out of reach of hands thrusting cards at me and attempting to grab me.

A plump, round-faced girl nodded and smiled. I nodded back. "My mother sent me," she said. She was the youngest daughter of Dr Maria de la Cruz Figueroa, from whom I had arranged, through friends, to rent a room. "Did you have a pleasant trip?" she inquired as she escorted me through the bedlam.

Dr Maria, a widow with three daughters, the youngest still a teenager, is a specialist of internal medicine at the local polyclinic. She was on a year's sabbatical because of a stressed heart. Her small, crowded house had an extra room and a bath built on the roof, which became my festival headquarters. Dr Maria was round, overweight, and had bad teeth and immense personal warmth. After ten minutes with her, I felt as though we had been the dearest of friends our entire lives. As we sat chatting in the front room, a young man in a T-shirt and shorts wandered in.

"This is my son-in-law, Ever Alvarez Cadrera," Dr Maria said. "He was up until four this morning. He plays in the group Septeto de Buena Fe and is very busy during the festival. He can tell you why son here in Santiago is different from the son in Havana."

"Santiago de Cuba is the heartland of traditional music," Ever began, sitting down on the couch, "and son is a root of that music. The son was born in Santiago de Cuba and is more traditional here than in Havana. From my point of view, the son of Santiago is more pure, more authentic, than the son in Havana. In Havana, the son became more salsa, which is different from the son in orchestration and sonority. All the musicians from Santiago, when they want to make salsa, they go to a salsa group in Havana. They don't make it here.

"But in Havana or in Santiago de Cuba, the son talks about the reality for the people. From the triumph of the Revolution to our day, many lyrics from son reflect the realities and the changes that have come since the Revolution. Many of the lyrics talk of the Revolution. In the music of the '60s and '70s, there were songs and composers who reflected in their lyrics their support and approval [of] the Revolution. In this, the music served as a confirmation of the reformation of the political position. There are also songs since the Revolution that reflect the realities of our society.

"I see a similarity with son to the country music in the United States. But in the United States, the country music is music from the country. Here, it's not so in this way. There is another type of country music here, the campesino music. The son you will hear here in Santiago is not exactly like the son in the country, but in the festival you will hear the son that is made in the country."

As we spoke, Ever's wife, Dr Maria's eldest daughter, prepared breakfast, the best food I ate while in Cuba. Afterwards, I walked to the festival site on Calle Heredia, the city's cultural main street, named after the poet Jose Heredia (1803-39), the first Cuban poet to champion independence. A large plaque marks his house, inscribed with one of his poems. Three blocks of the street contains all of the venues for music during the festival – the Museum de Musico, the Writers' Union, the library, and the Casa de Trova, where the tradition of the trova began when Virgilio Pala opened a small café on the site 120 years earlier. Pala liked the music so much that he offered musicians free food and drink to play. Word spread – as it would, amongst musicians – and the café became the center of the trova.

Pala didn't make any money, but the café became such a beloved local institution that it wasn't allowed to go out of business, even when he died. In 1995, the little café, with its wooden swinging doors and paneling, was renovated. An interior patio was added. The light airiness destroyed the dark moody atmosphere. The place now has the feel of an historical heritage site, rather than that of a dive where music was more important than appearance.

I wandered down the street to the Parque Céspedes, the tourist hang-out in the city, and took a table on the veranda of the Hotel Casa Grande overlooking the plaza. Graham Greene's character Wormold in *Our Man In Havana* stayed at the Casa Grande, as did Greene himself. I thought that, if I sat there and cast my mind into the mold of Graham Greene's imagination, I'd soak up writerly inspiration. I wasn't the only one with literary aspirations, judging by the number of tourists sitting at the small, marble-topped tables, sipping coffee and scribbling in notebooks or on postcards or tapping on laptop computers. The veranda's colonial-style balustrade, with thick balusters topped by a four-inch-thick slab of pearly marble, was a convenient footrest and a barrier behind which we visitors watched the locals in the plaza without risk of actually being approached and perhaps asked for something, like dollars or the time of day.

I surveyed the plaza from my perch. The south side of the square is completely taken over by the Santa Ifigenia Basilica Metropolitana, with its twin towers. Originally begun in 1528, the cathedral sits above a row of shops beneath its forecourt, the landlord of shops and souls. On the west side is the former home of Cuba's first colonizer, Diego Velásquez, whose remains rest in the cathedral. It is purportedly the oldest house in Cuba, dating back to 1516. Its most prominent feature is the wooden Moorish window grille that runs the length of its façade, from which proper Spanish ladies could watch the street scene without being seen. On the square's north side is the site of the original Spanish headquarters, made of wood and palm thatch and occupied by the first colonial governor, Hernándo Cortés. Fidel Castro gave his victory speech from the balcony of the present building on January 2, 1959, after Batista fled the country on the previous night.

In the center of the square are palm and shade trees and benches for people to sit. A young boy pushed his friend in a wheelchair around the interior of the square. They seemed to be playing, two good pals fooling around, amusing themselves. How nice, I thought, getting that liberal warm fuzzy feeling. The young boy approached a tourist sitting on a bench and obviously asked for money. He was ignored. He persisted. He got a cold shoulder for his trouble. He gave up. Curious, I went and talked to the boys.

The boy in the wheelchair was suffering from more serious disorders than just malfunctioning legs. His bloated body was scrunched crookedly in the wheelchair. His hands were those of a stroke victim, frozen into claws. His head lolled down, so in order to look at someone he had to roll his head onto one shoulder and tilt his eyes up. Then I could see that his mouth hung partially open.

"What's your name?" I asked the mobile boy.

"Jose. And this is my mother." Startled, I looked closer. The thick dark hair was cut in a bob. The skin was female. She rolled her head back to look at me and smiled.

"My son is a good boy," she said.

According to Jose, who was twelve years old, he had dropped out of school to care for his mother. They made their living begging in the plaza. He seemed bashful, telling me their story, and particularly mournful at the school part. "You're a worthy man, Jose," I said, and handed him several dollars.

When I left the square, a man approached me. "Give me a dollar."

"Why?"

"Why not?"

"Why?"

"My mother is dead." The man was in his 60s.

"So sorry. But now you don't have to spend money for her food, so you have more money."

He continued to argue with me about why I should give him money, following me down the street, demanding, not asking, that I put money – US dollars, not pesos – in his extended hand. When I continued to refuse, he said, "You'll be remembered," as if calling a curse down on me. Several times during my stay in Santiago de Cuba young boys boldly demanded money from me, something I did not encounter in other parts of Cuba.

As I walked back down Calle Heredia, I came upon three street musicians entertaining a crowd of children. The guitar player wore a green felt ten-gallon hat and a well-worn suit coat with a rhinestone sheriff's badge pinned on the lapel. The maraca player had no teeth and the look of a bumpkin straight out of the hills. The conga player arced his eyebrows, which made his tender eyes appear to miraculously double in size as they balanced on the upturned points of his wide smile. "I'm Benny Billy and this is the Benny Billy International Show," said the guitar player. He was a handsome man with a baritone/tenor voice that perfectly mimicked Benny Moré. He sang lovely ballads, his voice rich and full, while accompanying himself on a three-stringed guitar. "I made it special," he explained. "I wanted to sound different."

Benny was a showman who hooked you with his voice and amused you with his tricks. He pulled out his wallet and flipped it open. It burst into flames. "*En candela!*" he exclaimed, a Cuban expression meaning "a flame," itself a colloquialism that means "I'm broke." The kids and adults watching burst into laughter. Benny took out a well-thumbed deck of cards and fooled the kids with sleight-of-hand tricks.

"Give me five dollars for my next trick," he told me. I handed him a ten-peso note. "No, dollars," he said. "This is an international act."

He took my bill, folded it inside a piece of paper, folded the paper, and *presto!* The five-dollar note had disappeared. He folded the paper again and *presto!* The bill reappeared. "For my band?" Benny asked and pocketed the bill at my nod.

It took nearly 40 years for the traditional music of the Oriente, such as the son, to travel to Havana. The son arrived in the capital just prior to 1920, carried largely by the musicians of the Permenente, as the Cuban Army was then known. The trio Matamoro, who could sound like an entire orchestra, made son popular in Havana. When son made it to the salons of Havana, the trumpet was added to the tres, claves, and maracas of the original son ensemble, creating the septeto style, which set the foundations for the conjuntos and orquestas heard today. Ignacio Pínero and his Septeto Nacional put a hot trumpet to the central clave rhythm and the son was on its way to becoming an urban dance. The septeto trumpet style combined elements of 19th-century cornet, the music of the Iberian bull rings, and early New Orleans jazz. Jesús Alemany, the trumpet player and leader of Cubanismo, exemplifies this style today.

In Havana son met rumba and the music got another boost in popularity. The piano, bongos, and marimbula were then added, and son became the most popular dance in Cuba. Some music mavens argue that son is Cuba's national dance, while others make a case for rumba or the conga. When son first came to Havana, it was social outclass music, confined to the dancehalls and rooming houses of the colored workers. The "white" class and "cultured negroes" did not dance the son or the rumba, as they were for the "lower status," but as the music became more complex and the rhythms more infectious, even the racists and the snobs couldn't resist. The bands, which consisted mostly of black musicians, were invited to play at private parties of the overclass. Until son arrived, white society danced the

Benny Billy's band is the last of a tradition of trova bands that played in the streets of Santiago de Cuba

foxtrot, the two-step, and other North American dances to jazz played by white orchestras. Son played an instrumental role in breaking down racial barriers and cultural pretensions, a legacy that lives on in present-day Cuba. The colored classes were consigned to the economic, social, and political margins in Cuba until the music of the working people – the people of the land – opened a channel for the black man to become more than a day labourer.

In the late 1930s, son took on another dimension when the solo trumpet was augmented by the second trumpet and then a third trumpet and piano. This style, pioneered by Arsenio "The Marvelous Blind Man" Rodriguez, was called *son conjunto*. During the 1950s, Benny Moré, "the Sonero Major," updated the music once more with contemporary elements from jazz, mambo, and chachacha.

Benny Billy stuck to ballads as he crooned to his street audience. "He is exactly like Benny Moré," one man said appreciatively. "He could have been famous. He had offers, but he chose to stay here."

In the heyday of trova, the streets of Santiago de Cuba were full of street musicians, but only Benny Billy and his band remain. The people of Santiago de Cuba recognize the treasure they have in Benny Billy. He is a well-known and much-loved tradition – an entertainer, a talented musician, and not nearly the fool that he implies. Neither is he a poor itinerant street performer, the impression that he conveys. I found out from Dr Maria that he owns a nice house in town and does well for himself.

Later that evening, I returned to Calle Heredia for the party. A stage had been erected at one end, where Eliades Ochoa was to perform. He is best known outside of Cuba as a member of Buena Vista Social Club, but he has been a star within Cuba for 30 years. He was sponsoring this year's festival – that is, he paid all the costs. His sister, Maria Ochoa, a well-known performer of campesino music, performs in and around Santiago de Cuba. She was playing that night, too, at a place outside the city.

The origins of campesino music are in Spanish chants. The *tonada*, the *punto cubano*, and the *punto guajiro* are the names given to the songs of the country men. They are sung in the octosyllable metric that is used in the decima rhyme of Spanish poetry. Other styles are the "controversy" and the "forced foot." The son tradition began when a farmer threw an open-air party, or *quateques*. The punto cubano (sung in chorus), the guajiro, and the son montuno were an essential part of the entertainment provided by the partygoers.

Calle Heredia had the flavor of New Orleans' French Quarter. Spanish balconies of wood and wrought iron protruded over the narrow street, which was jammed with a thousand people. The women were dressed in their party best, fashions ranging from Barely Concealed to Cuban Moderate. The Barely Concealed style was thin pieces of clinging material artfully draped over a virtually naked body. The Cuban Moderate style was skin-tight sheaths in neon colors. The music may have been traditional, but there were no Spanish dresses with full skirts in the crowd.

The men were as colorful as moles, but it's always like that. The only fashion statements were clean cowboys hats, which were the Sunday version of the daily workwear on the ranches in the surrounding countryside. A small, thin man, aged by weather and hard ranch work, worked his way through the crowd. He wore an outsized, broad-brimmed cowboy hat. His well-worn white shirt, buttoned at the neck, was his nod to formal wear. His baggy green pants hung off his skinny hips. He carried a battered guitar case with the natural ease of a gunslinger twirling a six-shooter. Here is the spirit of the festival, I thought. This festival was begun by people like him for people like him. I followed him.

He wandered from venue to venue, listening to the musicians for a few minutes and then moving on. Around him, everyone but the children was openly drinking a lot of rum straight from the bottle. The more sophisticated ones poured a of couple fingers in a cup with perhaps a splash of soda. The people of Santiago de Cuba are dismissed by the people in Havana as hicks, but they don't seem to care. They consider themselves to be the real people of the land, fierce defenders of freedom and the creators of the original Cuban music. The real traditional music was born here in Santiago. The trova was born in Santiago. The real son is from Santiago. Those *Havanarnos*, with their noses in the air – what do they know? We have son. They have salsa. Salsa is a minor variation of son. What more is there to say?

Oddly, the party lacked a sense of gaiety, despite the music and the rum. Perhaps the people saved the big whoop for their carnival in the summer, when they wore brightly painted masks and danced the conga through the streets. Perhaps the youngbloods found the Festival de Trova a bit of an anachronism. But what was the old cowboy looking for? Other *campáneros*? Were the musicians too slick for him in their matching outfits, which were no more than color-coordinated shirts and pants? Was he looking for Benny Billy? When the old cowboy had heard every group playing, he walked away from the festival. Perhaps he had heard it all before. Perhaps none of his friends were here, and without his friends there was no *quateques*, the open-air party.

At midnight, I, too, walked away from the festival. The music was sounding all the same. No one was dancing in the street. People were just standing and drinking. The whole thing felt like a small-town street carnival where people played the carnie games but were essentially spectators. Besides, I had planned a full day of sightseeing for the next day before leaving for Baracoa. I needed a good night's sleep in Dr Maria's rooftop room.

17 Quiribá And Baracoa

In the morning, I walked up San Juan Hill, looking for the mythical footsteps of Teddy Roosevelt. It was a hot and sticky Sunday morning, and by the time I reached the modest hill on the outskirts of town I was hot and sticky. Imagine fighting in such humidity, struggling up a quarter-mile slope raked at a 45-degree angle while soldiers at the top shoot to kill you. Why did Americans come here to fight in Cuba's Second War of Independence, especially when the US government didn't want an independent Cuba?

Spain seemed too weak to maintain control of Cuba, a prize that both Britain and France had tried to snatch away. The United States didn't want those two powerful, imperialistically ambitious nations as near neighbors. Besides, US governments had coveted Cuba.

In 1783, John Adams, later the second president of the United States, indicated that Cuba was a natural extension of the United States.

In 1808, President Thomas Jefferson made a bid to purchase Cuba from Spain and was rebuffed.

In 1825, John Quincy Adams, Secretary of State under President James Monroe and the sixth president of the United States, insisted that the "law of nature" indicated that Cuba would one day "gravitate only to the North American Union."

In 1848, President James Polk offered Spain $100 million for Cuba. President Franklin Pierce upped the offer to $130 million, and his successor, James Buchanan, twice again made the same offer. Spain wasn't selling.

In 1868, Cuban guerrilla fighters revolted against Spain in the First War of Independence. They were on the verge of victory and then the movement collapsed. The 1878 Pact of Zanjón gave the rebels amnesty and kept Cuba under Spanish rule.

In 1895, the poet, journalist, spiritual fountainhead, and national leader Jose Martí led the Second War of Independence. He was killed in battle on May 19 of that year, but the war continued. Martí remains the most popular man in Cuba today, followed by Che Guevara. Busts of Martí are seen everywhere; Che is on T-shirts, and a 40-foot modernistic sketch of his face adorns the façade of a building facing Havana's Plaza de la Revolution. Castro has forbidden any personality cult centered on himself. There are no pictures of him and no statues on public display.

In 1898, President William McKinley attempted to end the Second War of Independence by offering to buy Cuba, but again Spain refused. Then the battleship USS *Maine* was sent to Havana harbor on the pretext of protecting American citizens. The ship was mysteriously blown up, and the United States declared war on Spain on April 25, 1898, citing "manifest destiny," as promulgated by the 1823 Monroe Doctrine, as justification to invade Spanish-held Cuba for "our peace and security."

On July 1, 1898, Teddy Roosevelt and his Rough Riders joined Cuban soldiers for the charge up San Juan Hill. Their victory turned the tide of war and Spain surrendered on July 17. The Stars and Stripes was raised, not the Cuban flag, after this "splendid little war." The US military demanded that the Cubans surrender their weapons, and the US Army occupied Cuba until 1902.

On top of San Juan Hill, I walked from memorial to memorial erected for the Cuban and American war dead while listening to children's laughter coming from the Ferris wheel in the amusement park below.

Moncada Barracks is the other famous battlefield within Santiago de Cuba's city limits. The barracks housed troops of the dictator Batista when 26-year-old Fidel Castro led an ill-fated attack on July 26, 1953. It was a Keystone Kops operation from the beginning and ended in disaster. Most of the rebels, including Castro, were captured. Sixty-four of the captured men were tortured and assassinated. Photographs of their bodies were smuggled out of the city in the bra of a pro-Castro journalist and their publication won sympathy for the rebels. Castro was sentenced to 15 years in prison on the Isle of Pines (now Isla de la Juventud, or "Isle of Youth") but released in a general amnesty after two years in jail.

Castro might have had a personal grudge against Batista as well as an idealistic bone to pick. In 1952, Castro was planning to run for a seat in the Cuban Congress and had a good chance of success. In the early-morning hours of March 10, 1952, only weeks before the presidential elections, Batista staged a *coup d'état* to overthrow Carlos Prio, the democratically elected president, whose regime was riddled with corruption. Batista's coup ruined Castro's hopes for being elected to Congress. Cynical commentators snipe that Castro sacrificed his men in the ill-conceived and miserably executed Moncada Barracks attack in order to make a name for himself, that he wanted to separate himself from the crowd calling for Batista's overthrow and that any attention-grabber would serve his purpose. After the attack, and after Castro's brilliant speech in defense of his actions, he was acknowledged as a front-runner in the race for Batista's seat.

From San Juan Hill, I took a botala to the barracks. The botala was a quarter-ton truck with benches along the side and down the center of the bed and covered with a canvas top. The official capacity, printed next to the door at the rear of the truck, was 25 passengers. I counted 43 people crammed in and more hanging off the back, held secure by people inside so that they didn't fall off.

The Moncada Barracks, a complex of mustard-colored buildings that covers a city block, is now a school. What was once the parade ground is now soccer and baseball fields. No historical plaque or heroic statue marks the site. The only reminders of the battle that started the Cuban Revolution are the pockmarks of heavy-caliber machine-gun bullets at one end of one building.

In my tour of the city, I found no monuments to the War of 1912, which was also centered in the immediate area around Santiago de Cuba. The successful War of Independence was, in large part, instigated by, led by, and fought by Cubans of African ancestry. After the war, the traditional power elite of Spanish landowners assumed that their pre-war position of privilege would continue – that is, that they would control the politics and economics of the new country, an assumption not shared by their black brethren-in-arms. Accurately judging the political winds, the blacks organized their own political party, elected members of the new Congress, started a newspaper, and in general acted out their entitlement.

The inevitable conflicts stewed and brewed, and what was essentially a political power struggle erupted in a race war. In 1912, only 24 years after the emancipation of the Cuban slaves, over 6,000 Afro-Cubans were killed by their fellow Cubans in an armed conflict. Cuban documentary film-maker Gloria Rolando made a film about this crime, entitled *Roots Of The Heart*. I had met Gloria in Havana at a showing of the film. Afterwards, we had a talk on racism and discrimination in Cuba, which, for Gloria, a strong feminist, includes prejudices against women.

"People will tell you that there is no racism in Cuba," Gloria said. "'Look how well we are mixed,' they point out. There is no hatred between blacks and whites as there appears to be in the United States." Racism in Cuba is not overt, Gloria agreed, but is the more insidious silent racism of complicity. "The racism is primarily economic racism," she said. "Blacks are doctors, teachers, professionals with jobs tied to the peso economy of government pay. The government strongly enacts anti-racism policies, but the mental subconscious, or consciousness, of the slavery attitudes persist in some people. Jobs with access to the dollar economy are primarily for the whites."

Here's another Cuban joke. A woman goes to a psychiatrist and says, "Doctor, I need help with my husband."

"What's the problem?" inquires the doctor.

"My husband is a neurosurgeon. Every night he has terrible dreams. He thrashes around and wakes both of us up. Life is getting unbearable on so little sleep."

"What are the dreams about?" asked the doctor.

"He dreams that he is a bellboy at a tourist hotel," replied the wife.

"Oh," said the psychiatrist. "He's having dreams of grandeur."

Implicit racism and explicit political commentary are embedded in the joke. A bellboy at a tourist hotel has access to the dollar economy through tips. Such jobs generally go to lighter-complexioned Cubans, although that is not a hard-and-fast rule.

Gloria related the case of a friend: "If a black person applies for the job of an interpreter at a tourist hotel and speaks English, German, and French, the person will be told, 'Sorry, we need someone who speaks Italian' – that happened to a daughter of a friend of mine – and the job will go to a less-qualified white. There cannot be blatant denial of a job based on color in Cuba – the manager can be fired for that – but there are variants of the-apartment-has-been-rented discrimination."

The explicit political commentary is that a bellboy at a tourist hotel can earn more in tips in a week than a neurosurgeon is paid in a month by the government. This imbalance is seen as a result of government socialistic policy that forces certain professionals into service for the public good without just compensation. One consequence of the economic disparity is the barring of all Cubans from certain five-star tourist hotels, such as Havana's Hotel Inglaterra.

"This is to prevent envy," I was told. "The farmers can afford to stay in such hotels, because they make good money selling food in the markets, which is allowed on a free-market basis, but professional people cannot afford such hotels, because they are on a low, fixed government salary. So Castro decided that no Cuban can stay at such hotels. That is his attempt to level the playing field."

Gloria finds the role of Cuban women analogous to that of the neurosurgeon. "Women are measured at different levels in Cuba – the professional level and the ordinary life of the woman," she said. "The woman as a professional – a doctor or scientist or teacher – her economic role has been recognized by the government. All doctors, regardless of gender, are paid the same. And there is a high percentage of female professionals, perhaps higher than males. But there is a dynamic between the professional woman and the woman who also works in the home. She must care for the children, buy the food, prepare the food, keep the household running. Cuban men expect this of women. At the same time, she must continue to economically contribute to the family, so she has two jobs.

"I don't think there is a feminist movement in Cuba like it is

Gloria Rolando, a documentary film-maker and a keen commentator on the roles of women in Revolutionary Cuba

interpreted in the United States. What is discussed here is the role of women in this society. The conception of our society, even the official opinion, is the right to work together and to recognize what has been done. When something good has been done, even by a woman, it should be recognized. The contribution of women in the arts has been outstanding in music, dance, and painting. There is a group of Cuban women painters who are very important. In the past, there was only one all-female orchestra, but now there are ten women orchestras. There are famous female pop groups, like Azúcar."

Women have always been important subjects in Cuban music. The journalist and author Lino Betancourt Molina made an analysis of how women are seen in Cuban songs. Historically, Cuban composers focus on two female physical features, the eyes and the mouth. In Cuban music, women, in part or whole, have been, and continue to be, objects of veneration, worship, praise, seduction, or the bitch that breaks the man's heart, behaves badly, and runs around with other men – a typical country and western scenario.

"In these cases," Lino said on the afternoon I visited him at his apartment overlooking the Malecón, "the composer takes the opportunity to insult women. Fortunately, these are the fewer songs. Almost always, the songs are romantic love songs. This is precisely true of the trova. The trova players Maro Corona and Miguel Companioni each have more than 100 songs dedicated to women, most of them love songs, loving fantasies, or serenades in a praising way. These romantic, sentimental images of women have not changed much over the years. The Nueva Trova singers/songwriters presented women more realistically as the militia woman, the scientific woman, the woman at home."

The other tourist site of note at Santiago de Cuba is the Basilica del Cobre, "the Cuban Lourdes," situated 25 kilometers from the city. As I approached the town of Cobre, people along the road held out beautiful floral arrangements of sunflowers, roses, gladioli, and other flowers meant as offerings at the church. They were so artistically arranged that I bought one for its beauty alone. As I passed through the town, riding in an open clamshell taxi – a motor scooter with a partially enclosed rear seat for two passengers – hustlers offered bits of copper ore. When I refused, they threw the small chunks onto my lap, hoping I'd throw money back. I threw the ore back. One man threw his shiny silver-and-black souvenir back to me, saying, 'Keep it for luck.' How can you dis such hustlers?

Cobre was the center of copper mining during the Spanish colonial era of the 1500s. The mines, the oldest in Latin America, played out long ago out and are now closed. When I arrived at the basilica, on a hilltop on the edge of town, my driver, a cheerful woman, parked in the shade of a small tree in the lot behind the basilica. The pit of an abandoned mine scarred the opposite hillside. The entrance to see the most revered religious relic in Cuba, the Virgin de la Caridad del Cobre, is from the parking lot, not through the front doors of the imposing basilica.

When I entered, I saw not the holy relic but a huge display of *milagros* ("miracles") given as offerings of thanks. The first milagros to catch my eye were tiny tin cut-outs of hands, arms, and legs bunched together on loops of wire, like keys on a ring. Other milagros included tiny carved wooden crutches, a wooden car, a doll, pictures of small children hopefully recovering from life-threatening diseases, bottles containing sheets of paper inscribed with messages of thanks, epaulettes from military uniforms, and a Cuban flag from the veterans of the War of Independence. A special case contained signed baseballs, a folded jersey from the Cuban Cubs, a soccer ball, and sports trophies in thanks for a victory – or praying for one.

But I couldn't find the Virgin. The lady at the information desk directed me upstairs. I found the Virgin on her private altar at the top of the curving marble stairs surrounded by banks of flowers. People sat in the pews in front of the altar or knelt in prayer.

The statue dates back to the 16th century and is encased in a protective glass box on a silver pedestal, reminiscent of a tennis victory cup. A gown of gold brocade covers the surprisingly small figure. A halo of *faux* diamonds and gold filigree forms a semi-circle around the head, which is the size of a one-year-old child's fist.

According to legend, the statue was found toward the end of the 16th century by three fishermen caught in a violent storm out in the open on the Bay of Nipe, near Cobre. The terrified fishermen prayed to God for safe passage. Then they spotted something floating on the waves and pulled it into their swamped boat. It was a small piece of carved wood, perhaps 20 inches tall, describing the legend, "I am the Virgin de la Caridad." In Spanish, *caridad* means charity, as in "love your neighbor as you love yourself," and so the Virgin del Cobre is also known as the Virgin of Charity. Unfortunately, the legend masks the real artist, who is now forgotten.

Ethnologists speculate that the Virgin might be linked to Chola Anguenge, a powerful ancestral spirit brought to Cobre by the Congolese slaves who worked in the copper mines and who hid their deity from the Catholic Spanish under the skirt of the Virgin.

In 1952, Ernest Hemingway placed his Nobel prize for Literature medal in the Virgin's shrine. On May 6, 1988, two men stole the medallion. They and the medal were found several days later. The medal is now in the safe keeping of the Archbishop of Santiago.

My tourist duties over, I returned to Santiago de Cuba to catch the next bus to Baracoa, a five-hour ride over the mountains of the last Cuban wilderness. I had a choice of two buses to take, the Viazul or the Russian truck/bus.

The Viazul is the pleasant way to get around Cuba. The European tour buses have comfortable seats, televisions for watching videos, air-conditioning, and a smooth ride. The Russian truck/bus is the going-native way of traveling, a monster capable of conquering any muddy mountain road to remote villages, outfitted with benches in the bed, which looked like a two-tractor shed with canvas siding. You entered from the rear, but there was an escape hatch on the left front. The Viazul cost $15 for a one-way ticket; the Russian truck/bus cost $10 for a one-way ticket. I queued up with the Australians, Germans, British, Norwegians, and Swiss for the Viazul.

The road out of Santiago de Cuba goes east through rolling farmland of sugar plantations and tobacco farms originally established by the French settlers who had fled the slave revolts on Haiti. Many revolutionary war memorials were along this road, which runs through the Baconao Biosphere Reserve. The reserve officially begins at San Juan Hill and extends 40 kilometers to the border with Guantánamo province. It's a good place for hiking and biking, I was told, and especially rewarding for birdwatchers. The Sierra de la Gran Piedra forms the backbone of the reserve and also of the Gran Piedra National Park. Fidel Castro and 18 other survivors of the Moncada Barracks attack fled into these mountains, where they hid out for a week before being captured by a Rural Guard contingent.

We made a quick stop at the bus terminal in Guantánamo, a sprawling and not very attractive city. The song 'Guantanamera,' made famous by Woody Guthrie, is about the women of Guantánamo. (Actually, the song is based on the action of a radio soap opera that was sung at the end and beginning of each segment as a plot summary.) Guantánamo is also the site of a US naval base. During the 1950s, the sailors supported a thriving prostitution business, and many of these Guantanameras supported Castro. They charged their sailor clients twice, once with cash and again with bullets, grenades, or weapons, which they passed on to Castro's men. The base itself is out of sight of the city, sitting at the mouth of the large bay.

Past Guantánamo, the road follows the coastline before climbing into the mountains of Punta de Maisi, the easternmost point of the island. Parts of these mountains have never been explored and are protected within the Cuchilla del Toa Biosphere Reserve, the last refuge of the endangered ivory-billed woodpecker. The Rio Toa, the largest and wildest free river in Cuba, runs down these mountains, which at one time isolated Punta de Maisi from the rest of Cuba. It wasn't until after the Revolution that the only road – the well-paved, two-lane highway known as La Farola, on which the bus twisted through repeated turns – was built over the mountains to Baracoa.

Baracoa is an Indian word meaning "highlands." The Tainos Indians arrived there from South America about a century before Columbus, and approximately 350 Taino descendants still live in the area around the village of Caridad de los Indios, the only region in Cuba where they survive. Columbus supposedly first set foot on the New World, near Baracoa. The town, founded in 1510, is the oldest in the New World and was Cuba's first capital. I expected a quaint colonial town, picturesquely shabby, with Old World charm. I had to let the charm of Baracoa grow on me, however, for it wasn't readily apparent.

Baracoa is deceptive. Take the beach as an example. The long arc of gray sand is totally left to its own devices. Seaweed and land-litter remain until they are washed out to sea. There are no beach chairs, umbrellas, refreshment stands, or hotels, because the beach is on a flood plain. Every May, the time of seasonal heavy rain, the beach is more like a swamp. The beach itself is perfect, though – no crowds, no commercialization of the natural state, no trinket hustlers. At the far end, where the Rio la Miel (Honey River) emerges, is a lovely shade tree and swimming hole. People looking for the postcard-perfect groomed beach with creature comforts would turn up their noses at this beach, which is another reason why it's perfect. Baracoa is known for its savory honey, sweet water, and cocoa. A cup of thick, rich cocoa is part of its inhabitants' daily breakfast.

The town appears small. That's because the population of 80,000 is spread out around the bay. It also appears that not much is happening when, in fact, there is a building boom in progress to keep up with the influx of tourists. There are three brick factories working to meet local demand. Homeowners are adding second-story guest rooms as fast as they can put them up. There are 250 rooms in private homes available, despite the government's heavy taxes of $100US per month for each room rented. (The tax is meant to discourage private enterprise and direct the tourist dollars into the government-owned hotels.) The nicest resort in town is an army enterprise, owned and operated by uniforms.

Baracoa seems to have no sense of its long history. The town comprises primarily one- or two-story houses and buildings of no architectural significance. The only real historical building is the Cathedral Nuestra Sénora de la Asunción, dating from 1805. (An earlier church on the site was destroyed by pirates in 1652.) The squat, gray, ugly, towerless church is in disrepair. Its claim to fame is the Cruz de la Parra in a glass case next to the altar. The 28-inch wooden cross was allegedly left on the beach by Columbus in 1492. Carbon dating has proven the wood to be about 500 years old and of a variety of native hardwood of the seagrape family that grows abundantly around Baracoa.

In the small plaza opposite the church is a statue in honor of Hatuey, Cuba's first rebel. Hatuey was an Indian chieftain who fought the Spaniards on the island of Hispaniola (now divided between Haiti and the Dominican Republic) and fled to Cuba after his people were defeated. When the Spanish tried to settle Baracoa, Hatuey led guerrilla warfare against them from the mountains. On February 2, 1512, the Spanish captured Hatuey and condemned him to burn at the stake. As he stood on a pile of faggots, a Spanish priest offered to baptize him, promising that he would then go to Heaven. Hatuey reputedly asked whether Spaniards also went to Heaven. Yes, answered the priest, to which Hatuey replied that he didn't want to go to the place where there were "such cruel and wicked people as the Christians." Besides, added the chief, heaven is where my wife is, so my heaven is here upon this Earth. Then the Spanish burned him to death.

The other historical curiosity in the town is the Hotel Rusa. The three-story, mustard-colored hotel was built by Madalena Menasses Romenaskaya, a member of one of the richest families in Czarist Russia who survived the October Revolution, Lenin's promise to wipe out the ruling aristocracy and replace them with a worker's state. She, her husband, and her mother moved to France. Mima, as Madalena was known, and her husband made a living as a dance team touring Europe, and in the mid 1920s she moved to Havana. (The husband disappears from the story at this point.) Ten years later, she moved to Baracoa, then a very isolated town accessible only by sea, where she founded several small businesses there and built the Hotel Miramar in 1957, later renamed the Hotel Rusa in her honor. She was an active contributor to the Revolution until her death in 1978. Fidel, his brother Raul, and Che Guevara have been guests at the hotel, as has Cuba's national poet, Nicolas Guillen.

Baracoa appears as lively as a sleepy dog on a hot afternoon, and during hot afternoons the town is somnolent, but on Friday and Saturday nights the townspeople move into the streets and party. It's like a town barbecue. People set their tables and chairs in the streets, put out the food and rum, and dance to the live music that is performed at five of the town's clubs. The Casa de Trova, across the street from the church, has the best traditional country and son music. On the opposite corner is the Disco 485, where "the Russian" plays. He is a local musician named Edvardo who wears long dark locks, a brooding look, and *faux*-Cassock boots with tassels.

It was at the Casa de Trova that I heard about Teresa Roché and quiribá. Teresa, a professor of dance who lives in Baracoa, made a discovery – along with Maria Colon, a professor of music – that has rewritten the history of early Cuban music. The academically accepted progression of the development of Cuban music forms went from nengón to changui to son. Roché and Colon found a precedent to all of those forms, the quiribá, at a pig roast.

"The quiribá is perhaps the oldest root of Cuban music," Teresa said when we met at her house in Baracoa. "The quiribá is a Spanish music, quite simple country music from the farmers. There had been references to it in a rural song called 'El Quirito,' but everyone thought it had died out. One day, in 1982, I attended a pig roast at Jamal, a small farming town down the coast from here, and the quiribá was being played and danced."

Quiribá and nengón are closely linked, according to Teresa: "They are the primary son, not a variant, as we had supposed. I can say that the quiribá and nengón are the origin of son. This means that salsa comes from quiribá. All non-African Cuban music spread from quiribá. The music has no spirit of the rumba. Maria and I have presented our findings to musicologists at the university, and they have been very encouraging about our findings. The local families Palmero-Romero and Romero-Palmero have kept the quiribá alive here. This confirms that the birth of son was in Baracoa."

The quiribá is the simplest music, with a narrative line, verse, and chorus and basic rhythmic cells. The nengón is played in quartets and decimas. Both forms are improvised, and the chorus of each is sometimes repeated continually. The outgrowths of these forms, son and campesino music, have a faster tempo.

The early instruments for quiribá were bass, guitar, and drums. The bass was made from the bowels of the *jutía*, a typical Cuban animal as big as a rat. Teresa showed me a drawing of how the bass worked. A long string of cured jutía gut was tied to a branch and stretched at a low angle to a hole dug in the ground that served as an echo chamber. The drums, which resembled the bongos, were played on the right leg rather than between the knees, as with present-day bongos. The body of the guitar was made from a palm trunk. The strings were bowels of the jutía and covered with wax, "something like floor polish," Teresa said. "This instrument pre-dated the tres."

The nengón and the quiribá have very traditional functions in rural life. The nengón is a running musical narrative that people make up on the spot during a party. The subject can be anything, but, like the son and guaracha, the lyrics are often satirical or ironic and poke fun at people's pretensions and foibles. The performers – the farmers – like to make controversy, and the songs are a challenge to see who can outdo the other. The nengón can last for an entire three-day party, with people taking turns, adding their verses and insults, while the quiribá was played to signal that the party was over, or would be continued at another house, and could go on for three days itself, or at least long enough for the next host to go home, slaughter a pig, lay in beer and rum, and get the farm chores done.

Every year, in March, Teresa organizes a celebration in Baracoa for the nengón and the quiribá. "In this town, we discovered the tradition of quiribá," she told me. "Now all the parties in Baracoa finish with the quiribá. There are many traditional groups in Baracoa now playing the quiribá and nengón. We have tried to revive the festivals of the quiribá as they were in the past. We have a pig roast in the country way, on a spit; rum in barrels; tubers; and other country food. And we dance the old music."

The nengón dance is danced in a circle and has the mood of a community social dance. The dancers shuffle "like smashing coffee beans," according to Teresa. "The quiribá dance is more lively, more free. It is a couples dance, with twirling in the square-dance style. The women have an independent role. I have interviewed people in their 70s and 80s who have danced the quiribá, so we know it."

Teresa invited me to stay for the next quiribá celebration in Baracoa. Unfortunately, it was a year away, so I reluctantly returned to Havana.

18 Tourism, The Musical

The traveling put me in a tourist mood. When I returned to Havana, I took another Viazul bus for the three-hour ride to Varadero, a premier beach resort and the symbolic stage for Cuba's ongoing economic and cultural dance.

Traveling in Cuba always brought surprises. At the bus station in Havana, I found the special office to purchase the ten-dollar one-way ticket to Varadero and was told to wait, but I wanted to go to the gate and get in line for an upfront window seat. No, wait here, the clerk said without explanation. Soon, the waiting room was filled with passengers, mostly Europeans, waiting for further instructions. Everyone kept checking the television monitor that showed the departure times for buses, like the screens in airports. Our bus destination flashed on the screen. People reached for their backpacks. The clerk continued with her paperwork. We fidgeted, the first twitch of taking matters in our own hands, as is the custom of people from countries where aggression is the way to get things done. I have a T-shirt emblazoned with the motto "Individual Rules."

At the precise moment that our bus was to leave, the lady clerk rose from her desk and motioned for us to follow. We filed out of the waiting room, which she locked behind her, and trailed after her, as dutiful as baby ducks, through the terminal to the gate, which she unlocked. We stepped out to the empty bus-parking slot. The clerk disappeared and returned with a baggage clerk, who handed out claim checks as the bus rolled in. I had the sense that the whole procedure had been carefully choreographed.

Once under way, the conductor, in his neat uniform of white shirt and black pants, announced our destination in Spanish and again in endearing and hard-fought English. Then he came around with a tray of boiled sweets. As we cleared the city limits, he put on a video, an American action thriller titled *Overkill*, a perfect metaphor for the economic choic253es and cultural dangers looming over Cuba's horizon.

Mixed economy is the name of the game for the Cuban government. Pure socialism has proven impractical, so capitalist entrepreneurs are being invited to invest in Cuba on a 51/49 split, with the Cuban government being the majority shareholder in the enterprise. That is how the tourist hotels at Varadero are built. The government sees the tourist industry as a cash cow, but there is concern about being hoisted on the cow's horns if care is not taken. The social impact of increased tourism is a hot topic in Cuba among government officials, black youths, workers, artists, and intellectuals. The arguments are:

The tourism trade will bring jobs and cashflow;

The tourist trade will make Cubans a nation of maids and cause a schism between people with access to the dollars and those left behind stuck in the peso economy;

The tourism trade will erode social values. The sex tourists – particularly Spanish and Italian men, who arrive by the planeload – are despised and loathed, but they are a main source of dollars to women otherwise frozen out of that economy, or who choose the path of easy access;

There is a worry that tourists will introduce a drug culture to the island. Marijuana is grown in the Sierra Maestra mountains in the Oriente, but at present drugs are a minuscule problem in Cuba. I was offered girls, cigars, and gold rings on the street, but never drugs;

Musicians are concerned that the tourist demands will encourage only lounge music and staged rumba shows that will rob the music and dance of their intrinsic cultural worth.

"Cuban music has that pressure already," says hip-hop producer Pablo Herrera. "It has been polluted and infiltrated by commercialism, which [is] poisoning our culture. For example, salsa

"Our Country Or Death!" Patriotic billboards such as this can often be seen along the roadsides in Cuba

has been pretty much driven by what corporate powers want to express or want us to use as an expression of ourselves."

Is the Cuban music culture strong enough not to be overwhelmed, or severely compromised, by outside influences?

"I think that the moment is here, or coming soon, of testing ourselves as to our endurance as a power," Pablo said. "If you go to war, you're definitely going to be wounded, either physically or mentally. War is war, let's make no mistake. You'll always receive some kind of trauma. That's just life experience. That's how you implement yourself. That's how you better yourself. It's impossible to go into something and come out pristine. You're always going to be penetrated by things. The cultural onslaught – primarily from the United States – is going to be radical for us. It will be a strong process to go through. But Cubans are survivors. We are a country of survivors, of strugglers, of warriors. We have survived a total economic war [against] the world's largest economic empire, the United States. The experience of the Revolution has given us Cubans a great deal of confidence. That is what makes us who we are, culturally, socially, spiritually, and politically."

Actor and social commentator Alden Knight made this observation: "If we let the makers of tourist music take grasp of our music, it can happen that we'll lose our rumba. It could be dressed in tourism. Tourism everywhere means the simplification of culture. Everything is made simpler for tourists."

The musicians with whom I spoke were confident that they could withstand the pressures of commercialization. We will not compromise our music for the lure of the dollar, they assured me. But the popularity of salsa, which plays to the tourist market, is a red flag. Musicians have left other forms of music to cash in on the salsa craze.

Before I left for Varadero, I spoke with Pedro Monzón, the Director of International Relations, in his office at the Ministry of Culture. "Tourism is a challenge to any country in the world," he said. "It is good in that it brings an interchange between people, but it brings also many bad things. I worked in tourism in the 1970s and was a member of a special commission to study this issue. We addressed how to face the bad things of tourism, such as the popularization of culture due to the influence of tourism. It's a challenge, and it can cause harm. We have to face the damage. We cannot isolate ourselves, and we don't want to isolate ourselves. Here at the Ministry of Culture, we are trying daily to fight against the situation.

"We are trying [to ensure] that the musicians will not work only for commerce. In the case of Cuba, this phenomenon is more negative because, before the Special Period, artists lived on their government salary. They performed because they liked to. They painted because they liked to. There was not a validation in the process between creation and commerce. When the marginal economy was introduced, some artists said, 'Well, this situation is so and we have to find ways to work over it'." One example is Buena Vista Social Club, [which] achieved great success due to international promotion.

"Because of that success, some groups are concentrating in this area of music. Luckily, we have a great variety of music in Cuba, so it will be difficult for the tourists to manipulate the music process. Culturally, we are the most prepared country to face this pressure.

We have many highly trained painters and musicians. Artists in Cuba have a great culture level and cultural consciousness. For example, last year, the Writers' Union held meetings to discuss commerce and culture. The participants deeply discussed how to prevent and stop the homogenization of our culture and the harm it causes. This not only included the arts but also the McDonald's-ization of our cityscape. At the time, there were kiosks going up on the streets using the yellow-and-red McDonald's color scheme in an attempt to capitalize on the McDonald's image. Why should we repeat what was happening? Why not cultivate the personality of Havana? Those yellow-and-red kiosks were repainted different colors."

Pedro Monzón's words had a Brave New World tone. As Cuba opens more to mass tourism and the inevitability of the inherent commercialism, Cuban musicians and artists will face greater commercial pressure to bend their culture to its will.

The bus stopped at the airport halfway between Matanzas and Varadero. On the arrival board, I saw direct flights from Paris, Madrid, and Frankfurt. In the year 2000, an estimated two million tourists came to Cuba, according to official figures. That's only ten per cent of the Caribbean tourist trade, but it's a growing percentage, with three per cent growth projected for 2001. When 50,000 visitors were booked into Cuban hotels on the same night, it made the national news as a good omen. In 1982, the Cuban government began to divert resources into the tourist industry – for example, cement for housing was used to build hotels. "We are not an oil-producing country," Castro reminded Cubans as he asked for their patience. "The sea, the climate, the sun, the moon, and the palm tree are the natural wealth of our country, and we have to take advantage of them." In 1994, foreign investment in Cuba's hotels and beach resorts was $500 million, with the main investors from Mexico, Canada, Italy, and Spain.

Twenty minutes after leaving the airport, we rolled into Varadero. The town itself and the 11.5 kilometers of beach with the same name are on the Punta Hicacos peninsula, which is technically an island connected to the mainland by a bridge over the Laguna de Paso Malo. The Taino Indians named the land after the hicacos tree, which still grows there. In 1587, the entrepreneur Don Pedro

Camacho developed a salt-pork business on the peninsula's salt flats to supply the Spanish fleets. The tourist industry began in the 1870s, when Spanish families built summer homes and boarding houses for vacationers. By the late 1880s, the beach was a business, with promoters staging the Cuban Cup and other rowing regattas to attract visitors. The first hotel opened in 1915.

Rich Americans discovered Varadero in the mid 1920s. The DuPonts and Firestones built large estates there. By the 1930s and 1940s, the peninsula had become a private reserve for wealthy Cubans and Americans, and during the 1930s Batista invited the American mobster Meyer Lansky to oversee the casinos in Havana, fearing that dishonest casinos would discourage tourists. The mob had experience in running an efficient and, from their point of view, clean operation. From the 1930s to the 1950s, Havana and Varadero were American playgrounds.

Batista made the casinos and tourism in general a main engine for generating foreign investment income and revenue, the same policy that the Castro government is enacting, albeit without the casinos, which Castro closed down when he took power. But dependence on the tourist industry was also Batista's Achilles heel, which Castro exploited.

In 1957, Castro's increasingly successful Revolution was giving Cuba bad press. Bullets were flying and people were dying, and so tourists stayed away. Batista downplayed the danger and staged a Grand Prix Formula One race during the carnival season to attract American tourists, with the Argentinean Juan Manuel Fangio – then the world's top driver – as the main draw. On the eve of the race, two of Castro's men boldly kidnapped Fangio from his hotel lobby. The news hit the fan, but Batista didn't call off the race. After the race, Castro's men called the Argentinean Embassy, giving them instructions where to find Fangio, who was unharmed and unruffled. The stunt was a publicity coup for Castro. In less than a year, Batista fled Cuba for Florida and Castro's rebels triumphantly entered Havana. Many factors contributed to the downfall of Batista, but one was the perception that he didn't have control of the country and so couldn't guarantee the safety of tourists.

To a large degree, the tourist industry relies on perceptions. When the US government declared Castro to be a despot and an evil communist dictator in the early 1960s, Cuba's tourist industry took a nosedive. The overnight ferry service between Florida and Cuba was canceled. Things became so bad that the famed Tropicana Hotel closed its doors. Castro wanted tourism to continue as an important force in the Cuban economy, and to this end expanded Havana's airport (which needs serious attention today), while the government's Instituto Nacional de Industriales Turisticas (INIT) committed $200 million to a four-year development program. Still, the perception of Castro and Cuba under his regime discouraged tourism, at least for the Americans, although Canadians, Europeans, and South Americans rediscovered Cuba. Investment capital from Spain, France, Canada, Germany, Italy, Sweden, and Jamaica has built tourist hotels for what is seen as a growing market.

A surprising number of Americans are thoroughly convinced that Cuba is a dangerous place to visit, that travel to Cuba is forbidden by the United States government, that all religion is suppressed in Cuba, that Castro is a nasty dictator who rules with an iron fist and denies the people their freedom, and that Cuba lies in the ruins of poverty. All of the above are not true, which is something of an awakening when one visits Cuba. Americans are not forbidden to travel to Cuba. There are direct flights from Miami and Los Angeles. Churches and synagogues are open in Havana and Santeria is freely practiced. "We are all equally poor," one Cuban told me with a smile.

In 2000, over 100,000 Americans ventured to Cuba to see it for themselves. They were shocked to discover that none of the false impressions created by their government were true.

The Cuban government's effort to revive the tourist industry is bringing dividends, as evidenced by Mantanzas/Varadero Airport and the number of inclusive tourist-only hotels that line the Varadero beach. But what compromises are the Cuban government willing to make in order to create an image that the tourist industry can sell? Or, as a Cuban friend stated, "What are we willing to sacrifice on the altar of tourism? Are we willing to change our style of government? Are we willing to create an economic class system, like the one that existed before the Revolution? Are we willing to bastardize our culture to entertain the tourists? Is any of that necessary, and, if it is, should we just say no?"

When I got off the bus in Varadero, I looked left, looked right, and saw water in both directions. Only 1.2 kilometers of land separate the Cárenas Bay from the Florida Straits. Within two blocks of leaving the bus station, I stood on a stunning beach that stretched in both directions as far as I could see. Varadero is almost at the midpoint of the 18.6-kilometer-long peninsula and, as I discovered, is the dividing line separating "the tourist beach" from "the Cuban beach."

I arbitrarily started up the beach towards the end of the peninsula. Initially, the beach was almost deserted, with just a few local families enjoying Sunday picnics in the shade of the seagrape trees on the edge of the white sand. Within ten minutes, however, I came upon the tourist crowd and their entertainments: beach volleyball, Hobie Cat sailing, recreational kayaking, parasailing, and sunbathing. A mostly European crowd – primarily Germans and Italians – stay at the hotels set back from the beach. Cubans share the beach, but as the minority. Many European women sunbathe topless, but the Cuban women always cover themselves to some degree. On the streets, the Cuban women would dress provocatively, at least in the eyes of people not from a tropical country, but nudity is frowned on, perhaps for its lack of subtlety.

Until the Revolution, no local Cubans were seen on Varadero's beach – the elite hired an armed private security force to keep the riff-raff away, except as servants confined to the kitchen or maids' quarters – but Castro put an end to that. On March 17, 1957, he declared the beach public property and open to the people. Ordinary Cubans came to Varadero for a day or a weekend away from Havana. They reveled in their right, their entitlement, to this piece of Cuba, their country. But now, with the increased tourism, subtle shifts are occurring. In concept, Varadero's beach is not reserved for tourists, but in practice Cubans in general don't hang out at the tourist end, since they can't stay in the hotels built for tourists.

The beach itself impressed me. Hotels don't crowd the water's edge, as they do at Amberis Cay in Belize. Restaurants don't invade the beach space, as they do at Negril in Jamaica. A good 30 to 50 yards of open beach stand between the sea and the first buildings, giving a sense – or at least an illusion – of nature uncompromised. Vendors don't troll the beach, harassing people to buy their trinkets. (I saw only two vendors on the beach, middle-aged men pushing bikes through the sand with shell necklaces hanging from the handlebars.) There were a few stalls selling carvings and trinkets, but the sellers were not pushy and in your face, as is common on other tourist beaches in the Caribbean. It was a no-hustle, no-hassle beach.

By early afternoon, I had returned to the town in search of lunch. Varadero is a pleasant town that hasn't sold its soul for the tourist dollar – at least, not so far. It's a low-key place, considering that tourism is its major industry. There are no shops devoted to tacky souvenirs or gaudy advertisements of local tours, but make no mistake, tourism is the cash trade. Varadero is not a peso town or as inexpensive as Havana. To my dismay, I found no street food stands where I could get a 60¢ lunch, as I had become accustomed to in Havana. There were no three-peso ice-cream cones or ten-peso pizzas. A cup of coffee cost a dollar, instead of the nickel I paid at Havana's sidewalk stands. But I enjoyed a fine chicken lunch with salad, rice, and beans for $3.25.

After lunch, I went beach-exploring again, this time in the opposite direction. Every few blocks there was a mini-park that served as an inviting gateway to the sand and sea. I stepped out onto the beach and into a total Cuban beach party. There were Hobie Cat sailboats for rent, as at the tourist beach, but there were also raucous baseball games, large families spread out for picnics, music, laughter, and shouting, as people called to one another. I saw no foreign tourists.

Is the beach at Varadero a glimpse at the inevitable future of Cuba, Them and Us? Cubans are well aware that a tsunami of investment cash is poised to crash down on the island as soon as Cuba's economic system is adjusted to be more accommodating to capitalistic values. In 2000, 3,400 representatives from 2,500 US firms went to Cuba to assess the opportunities there and make contacts, according to John Kavulich, president of the US-Cuba Trade and Economics Council. Cuban-Americans are especially anxious to cash in on the homeland. Sergio Pino, a South Florida home-builder, has formed an investor group to raise $50 million to pump into Cuba for profit. He is quoted in *USA Today* as saying that he hopes to build apartments and townhouses for Cubans to ease their housing shortage. That begs the question of how those Cubans will be able to afford to buy the new housing. Does the housing become private property and subject to price speculation, which is contrary to existing Cuban government policies? Cubans make it clear that they want more economic opportunities to put cash in their pockets, but they are also wary of the injustices inherent in an aggressively capitalistic system.

On the bus ride back to Havana, I mentally returned to my conversation with Pedro Monzón at the Ministry of Culture regarding culture and commerce. He saw the possibility of the homogenization of Cuban culture as a clear danger, if globalization was allowed to invade the island unfettered. But he was confident that Cuban musicians and other cultural workers would not succumb. "The position of Cuban artists is to use their strengths to avoid the money imposed on their styles and criteria and to take care of their own style," he said. "We are not concerned, because we know how to face this homogenization via tourists' taste phenomenon. Our idea is that we have a well-educated people, a talented people, and a people that are ready to take the best of world culture. At the same time, it is in our interest to keep the diversity of our culture, as opposed to the homogenization process that is nowadays in the world. The homogenization process of culture is negative, because it gives up diversity. It's too closely related to commerce. It's a relation of offering culture to commercialization, and not all commercial is good. Many times, it's on the contrary – for example, the violence is commercial, the sex is commercial.

"Such commercialism is in those American films [that have] very bad scripts but are easily sold. They are a fool in the world. They don't have any cultural message. That is a concern of almost all the countries in the world. The French are very worried about that; the Canadians and British are very worried. Not only us but countries of the First World are worried because of this overflowing of this bad culture.

"Our policy is to give our people the best of the culture in films and the arts. The government – and especially our ministry – is making the best effort, although we have not the financial support.

The bad culture in movies and music that is prevalent is because it has the backing of many dollars. Our purpose is that the Cuban people know the best of the Cuban culture and the best of the world culture. In that sense, a culture is a means to create a more intelligent person, and that is what we are doing."

Back in Havana, I looked up Juan de Marcos, musical director of The Afro-Cuban All Stars and producer of Buena Vista Social Club, to hear his take on the future of Cuban music. "I've started a project mixing generations, using more young Cuban musicians to make a tribute to Cuban music. We are using elements of the contemporary Cuban music but keeping the roots. After that, I'm going to work a little bit with the Cuban hip-hop. Unfortunately, the rappers don't have resources to make their own music. Sometimes they have to use backgrounds from Tupac, or Ice Cube, or the top stars of American hip-hop. But the Cuban rappers' idea is to develop a Cuban hip-hop talking about our problems. Our language is different. We don't have the racism like there is in the United States. We don't have that kind of racist mind, but we have lots of problems in that area, mostly economical. But the hip-hop artists are talking about their problems using contemporary Cuban language. My idea is to make an album using different bands with their own styles. I'm very interested in the modern Cuban music to try to find a Cuban language for the international contemporary music."

"What do you see in the future for Cuban music?" I asked. "Are you concerned that the globalization of music will tone down Cuban music?"

"I think the next Cuban music will be a mix of the contemporary dance and traditional. Probably hip-hop as well. So it will mean big chords, big sequences of chords, hard harmony, excellent arrangements, but keeping the roots. This is the most important thing. You can play danzón but using contemporary elements. That's what's going to happen. That's what I'm fighting for."

Juan has his own personal war chest that he's willing to commit to the cause. He had three points of the album *Buena Vista Social Club*, which sold millions of copies. "That's a lot of money," he said without being specific. "I'm investing the money to promote the

Cuban music in my own projects. Of course, I cannot be in charge of the whole of Cuban music, but I will do what I think is proper. I've never been rich. I don't mind the money, because I grew up in a rough neighborhood in downtown Havana. I'm not a politician, but I've my own way to fight for my country, like to create Cuban music with quality and to invest money to promote this music properly. But I don't know what's going to happen. It all depends on the United States. When the United States opens the door for Cuban music, everything is going to be right. It's quite difficult to promote Cuban music in the world without the United States. It owns all the big companies. It owns the promotion in the world. With that kind of power, you can create an artist in three weeks, like Christina Aguilera.

"We cannot wait for the United States. We are going to fight. There are many people fighting for Cuban music. We are in alliance with musicians around the world, including the United States, fighting for Cuban music and doing things really positive for our music. That's why I'm not too concerned about commercial influences on Cuban music. In the end, Cuba is going to open the doors to the world, and the world is going to open the doors to Cuba."

On my last night in Cuba, I went to the park to see John. I brought him up to date on my travels and talks with musicians. "What do you think, John?" I asked him.

Numinous silence.

"Come on, John. What am I supposed to do? Hold a séance?"

The custodian was watching me talk to a statue.

"Any message for Paul?"

The custodian approached the bench.

"Any advice for him about song credits?"

The custodian sat down on the other end of the bench. He was wearing Groucho Marx glasses with an attached mustache. I did a double-take and we both burst out laughing. He took two cigars from his pocket. "One for Lennon. One for Marx. *Cuba va!*"

Visit Cuba as a good neighbor at www.ifconews.org and www.globablexchange.org

Bibliography

AMINA, JOHN and CORNELIUS, STEVEN: *The Music Of Santeria, Traditional Rhythms Of The Bata Drums* (White Cliffs Media, US, 1999)

CASTRO, FIDEL (edited by DAVID DEUTSCHMANN): *Capitalism In Crisis, Globalization, And World Politics Today* (Ocean Press, Melbourne and New York, 2000)

DANIEL, YVONNE: *Rumba, Dance And Social Change In Contemporary Cuba* (Indiana University Press, US, 1995)

DORSCHNER, JOHN and FABRICIO, ROBERTO: *The Winds Of December* (Coward, McCann & Geoghegan, New York, 1980)

GERARD, CHARLEY with SHELLER, MARTY: *Salsa! The Rhythm Of Latin Music* (White Cliffs Media, US, 1989 [1998])

GONZÁLEZ-WIPPLER, MIGENE: *Santeria: The Religion* (Llwellyn Publications, US, 1999)

MANUEL, PETER (editor): *Essays On Cuban Music, North American And Cuban Perspectives* (University Press of America, US/UK, 1991)

MILES, BARRY: *Ginsberg, A Biography* (HarperPerennial, US, 1989)

MILLER, IVOR: *A Secret Society Goes Public: The Relationship Between Abakuá and Cuban Popular Culture* (African Studies Review, volume 43, number one, April 2000)

MORALES, BEATRIZ: *Afro-Cuban Religious Transformation: A Comparative Study Of Lucumi Religion And The Tradition of Spirit Belief* (doctoral dissertation, City University of New York, 1990)

RIPLEY, C PETER: *Conversations With Cuba* (The University of Georgia Press, US/UK, 1999)

ROBERTS, JOHN STORM: *The Latin Tinge, The Impact of Latin American Music On The United States* (Oxford University Press, US/UK, 1999)

SARDUY, PEDRO PÉREZ and STUBBS, JEAN (editor): *Afro-Cuban Voices, On Race And Identity In Contemporary Cuba* (University Press of Florida, US, 2000)

SCHWARTZ, ROSALIE: *Pleasure Island, Tourism And Temptation In Cuba* (University of Nebraska Press, US/UK, 1999)

SCHWEAB, PETER: *Cuba, Confronting The US Embargo* (St. Martin's Press, US, 1999)

THOMPSON, ROBERT FARRIS: *Flash Of The Spirit: African And Afro-American Art And Philosophy* (Vintage Books, US, 1983)

Index

THE BAHAMAS

North Atlantic Ocean

Nuevitas
Camaguey
Holguin
Manzanillo   Bayamo
Santiago de Cuba   Guantánamo

Sensual, sexual, soulful and rhythmic, Cuban music – from its ethnic roots to the international successes of Gloria Estefan and the Grammy Award-winning *Buena Vista Social Club* – has been the Cuban people's means of expression under one of the world's last communist regimes.

By talking to dozens of ordinary Cubans and famous musicians about their daily lives, **Waking Up In Cuba** paints an extraordinary picture of a society and its cultural history that has flourished, through music, despite communist repression and western intransigence. The result is an honest, entertaining and informative account of what anyone travelling to the island can expect to find.

UK £12.99   US $18.

ISBN 1-86074-346

Travel/Music
Sanctuary Publishing

9 781860 743467